# Pets and the Elderly

## The Therapeutic Bond

**Odean Cusack** is a freelance journalist whose areas of specialty include animals and the environment. She has a B.A. in Psychology from The University of the State of New York and studied graduate Zoology at Temple University and Rutgers University.

Cusack's serious writing began in 1980 when she founded *Signature,* the Mensa special interest group concerned with animal rights and the environment, and functioned as editor and publisher of the group's newsletter "Signature News" which was widely distributed throughout the animal rights and welfare community. Currently, she is a contributing editor to *Agenda,* the newsmagazine of the Animal Rights Network. Her articles have appeared in such publications as *Omni, Orion Nature Quarterly, Pure-Bred Dogs American Kennel Gazette, Dog Fancy, Today's Animal Health, Woman's Day, Lady's Circle,* and *Guideposts* magazines, as well as Philadelphia-area and national newspapers.

A lifelong animal lover and pet owner, Cusack's current menagerie includes 5 dogs, 4 cats and 9 birds.


**Elaine Smith,** of Therapy Dogs International in New Jersey, has trained at St. Elizabeth's Hospital in New Jersey and the Royal College of Nursing in England. She owns, trains, and rehabilitates animals.

# Pets and the Elderly
## *The Therapeutic Bond*

**Odean Cusack**
**Elaine Smith**

The Haworth Press
New York

*Pets and the Elderly: The Therapeutic Bond* has also been published as *Activities, Adaptation & Aging,* Volume 4, Numbers 2/3, January 1984.

The Haworth Press, Inc., 28 East 22 Street, New York, New York 10010

**Library of Congress Cataloging in Publication Data**

Cusack, Odean.
    Pets and the elderly.

    "Has also been published as Activities, adaptation & aging, volume 4, numbers 2/3, January 1984"—T.p. verso.
    Bibliography: p.
    Includes index.
    1. Pets—Therapeutic use. 2. Aged—Rehabilitation.
I. Smith, Elaine. II. Title.
RM931.A65C88  1984          615.8'515        83-26409
ISBN 0-86656-259-1

# Pets and the Elderly
## *The Therapeutic Bond*

Activities, Adaptation & Aging
Volume 4, Numbers 2/3

## CONTENTS

# Pets and the Elderly
## *The Therapeutic Bond*

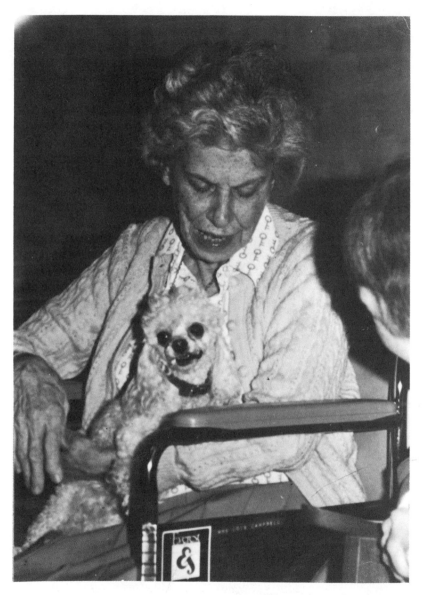

Photo by Bob Barber.

Chapter 1

# A Brief Introduction
# to Animal-Facilitated Therapy

Man and animals have interacted for as long as the two have co-existed on this planet. In fact, Dr. Leo Bustad, Dean of the College of Veterinary Medicine at Washington State University, says:

> Plants and animals in our environment are like parts of our body. If we eliminate them, we destroy part of ourselves. People must remain in contact with and relate to the environment throughout their lifetime to remain healthy. A strong people-animal-plant bond is critical to a healthy community.[1]

Certainly, our ancestors attributed healing, even magical, powers to the animals who shared the earth with them. In ancient Greece, for example, dogs licked the wounds of the sick because their tongues were believed to possess medicinal value.[2] More often, however, a part of the animal was presumed to offer the miraculous cure, and the living creature was often sacrificed for it. Even today the horn of the critically endangered rhino is pulverized to a fine powder and sold throughout the Orient as an aphrodisiac.

But until relatively recently, few in the medical community recognized the therapeutic value of association with the whole living animal. This is truly ironic, since most of us at some time in our lives have experienced the benefits of such a relationship.

Most of us can recall a time, probably as children, when the devoted companionship of a loyal dog or the contented purring of an affectionate cat gave us more comfort than the most modern tonics. In times of stress, the animal companion was the anchor whose unswerving attachment to us made all of life's burdens easier to bear. The animal fulfilled our needs in a way that no human could. As we matured, we thought our devotion to the pet was childish, doting, anthropomorphic, even silly; and we thought we alone had

*1*

such excessive attachment to our pets. Little did we realize at the time that association with our animals was actually healing our psychic and emotional wounds, revitalizing our strength to once again meet the harsher human-oriented world head-on. ✔

Just as our pets helped us through our crises, so have the pets of millions of our forefathers. And therein is the true paradox: animal-facilitated therapy is the most modern of medicines, as new as the latest issue of a medical journal; yet it is as ancient as the art of healing itself dating back to that twilight time in prehistory when humans found that animals were not simply sources of food or competitors for prey, but friends and companions.

Although we do not know when the association first came about, we have some clues. In 1976, Simon Davis, of Hebrew University, uncovered a tomb of a human skeleton in northern Israel. The hand of the skeleton was clutching the remains of a puppy, indicating, according to Davis, that the relationship between the two was affectionate, rather than gastronomic. This poignant archaeological find is estimated to be some 12,000 years old.[3] As the first animal domesticated, the dog was not only man's earliest friend, but also his first therapist.

The origin of animal-facilitated therapy can be traced to the 18th century. The earliest cited use of animals as adjuncts to treatment was the York Retreat founded in 1792 by a Quaker merchant, William Tuke. In contrast to the asylums of the day which often employed brutal and harsh forms of treatment for the insane, the York Retreat emphasized positive, instead of punitive, means to control behavior. Animals were part of the living environment, and patients were encouraged to learn to care for them.[4] The York Retreat was the forerunner of positive reinforcement programs and is to this day considered a model in this form of treatment.[5]

Bethel, a wide-based treatment facility in Bielefield, West Germany, is appropriately called "an institution without walls." Founded in 1867, Bethel was established for epileptics, but later initiated treatment for other disorders as well. Currently, Bethel has over 5,000 employees and 5,000 patients, and, like the York Retreat, animals are an important part of the living environment. In addition to traditional pet animals, Bethel includes farm animals and a wild game park. Bethel has an equestrian program that is especially helpful to epileptics. Leo Bustad visited the institution in 1977 and attributes much of its success to its warm, home-like atmosphere. Bethel is in the fullest sense a community.[6,7]

The earliest formal use of animals as aids to therapy in the U.S. was in 1942 at the Pawling Army Air Force Convalescent Hospital in Pawling, New York. The patients, victims of fatigue as well as physical injury, primarily needed rest and relaxation, and the program encouraged them to work with various farm animals as well as engage in academic studies. The patients also interacted with reptiles and amphibians that resided in the forests nearby. Some of the patients organized frog jumping contests and turtle races which inspired a competitive spirit and provided an educational experience.[8]

In the 1960s however, the work of psychiatrist Boris Levinson suggested that the use of animals as adjuncts to traditional therapy was only beginning to be explored. As with many great discoveries, Levinson's pioneering work began quite by accident in 1953 with a shaggy dog named Jingles. The dog was with Levinson in the office when a mother and child arrived unexpectedly for an appointment that was not scheduled till many hours later. The young patient's interaction with the dog eventually aided in his recovery.[9]

The work of Sam and Elizabeth O'Leary Corson in the 1970s also came about serendipitously when the team was researching dog behavior at Ohio State University. The kennels were in earshot of the adolescent ward, and the patients there, hearing the dogs bark, broke their self-imposed silence and asked if they might be allowed to play with the animals. Corson selected the patients that were the most withdrawn and the least communicative and studied the effects of interacting with the dogs on them. Forty-seven of 50 participants showed improvement; many eventually left the hospital.[10]

The Corsons extended their work at the Castle Nursing Home in Millersburg, Ohio, and obtained similar results. Interaction with the animals promoted self-reliance and increased responsibility among the patients, many of whom had previously been almost entirely unmotivated in those areas. The animals also facilitated social interaction between the residents themselves and residents and the staff.[11]

In 1970, Philadelphia psychologist Ethel Wolff prepared a survey for the American Humane Association and reported that 48% of the institutions she surveyed used animals in some capacity.[12] In 1972 Boris Levinson surveyed New York state psychologists and found that half of those questioned were engaged in some manner of pet-facilitated therapy.[13] Journalist Phil Arkow, whose overview volume of pet therapy is now in its 3rd edition, remarked that in 1977 he knew of only 15 humane societies utilizing animal therapy programs and eight U.S. university research projects investigating them. In his revised edition, he references 75 humane society programs, 44 academic projects, and numerous miscellaneous programs.[14] The actual number is probably much higher. Correspondence from members of Therapy Dogs International, a worldwide volunteer organization of trained dogs and their owners, indicates many dog clubs and similar organizations are involved in these projects also.

Most significant is the growing recognition of the human/animal bond in the scientific and academic community. Although the formal research in the field is just beginning, it has already generated a growing body of evidence that suggests that animals make people happier, healthier, and more sociable. Pets facilitate our recovery from illness and may even promote longevity. They enrich our lives in numerous ways just by being their own furry, feathered, or finned selves. In short, animals make us better people. The benefits of companion animal association are available to everyone; for the elderly, however, they have special value.

## REFERENCES

1. Bustad, Leo, K. *Animals, Aging and the Aged.* University of Minnesota Press, Minneapolis, 1980.

2. Ibid.

3. Miller, Harry. "Cro-Magnon's Best Friend." *Dog World,* April 1979, 24.

4. Bustad, Leo K. op. cit.

5. McCulloch, Michael J. "Pet Facilitated Psychotherapy," address delivered at the International Conference on the Human/Companion Animal Bond, October 5-7, 1981, Philadelphia, PA.

6. Bustad, Leo K. "Bethel—An Institution Without Walls." *The Latham Letter,* Winter 1981-82.

7. Film: "Bethel—An Institution Without Walls." Available from the Latham Foundation.

8. Bustad, Leo K. *Animals, Aging and the Aged.*

9. Editorial. "Dogs, Other Pets, Used to Treat Emotionally Ailing." *The Times Herald,* November 8, 1979.

10. Ibid.

11. Ibid.

12. Wolff, Ethel. "A Survey of the Use of Animals in Psychotherapy in the United States." *American Humane Association Report,* 1970.

13. Editorial. op. cit.

14. Arkow, Phil. *"Pet Therapy": A Study of the Use of Companion Animals in Selected Therapies.* The Humane Society of the Pikes Peak Region, 3rd edition, August 1982.

Chapter 2

# The Therapists' Casebook

To date research studies conducted specifically to determine the value of animals to the elderly fall into three categories: out-patient/ in-residence pets, pet visitation programs in institutions, and pets as in-residence mascots in geriatric facilities. This chapter will review several representative studies.

## OUT-PATIENT IN-RESIDENCE PETS

### Mugford and M'Comisky: Elderly Pensioners[1]

An early and now classic study which evaluated the therapeutic effects of pet animals on an out-patient population was conducted in Hull, East Yorkshire, England in 1975 by R. A. Mugford and J. G. M'Comisky. The researchers selected 30 elderly pensioners ranging in age from 75 to 81. Two groups were given budgerigars (parakeets) which were selected as the therapeutic animal because of their ease of care and adaptability to most home environments, and two groups were given begonias. A final control group received neither flora nor fauna. An additional factor, television, was considered as the researchers theorized that a pet may be less important to television owners since this does provide interaction with society as a whole and thus could affect the patient's evaluation of his/her loneliness. At the onset of the study, a 30-item questionnaire which measured attitudes towards self and others as well as the physical and psychological environment was administered to all the participants.

Throughout the course of the five-month study, the pensioners were visited by social workers, and at the conclusion of the time frame, the questionnaire was again administered.

Overall evaluation showed budgie ownership had a positive effect: the twelve individuals who had received the birds showed

5

marked improvement, especially in areas that concerned attitudes towards other people and their own psychological health. The presence or absence of television made no statistical difference. The birds became an important subject of the pensioners' conversations and enhanced their social lives with friends and neighbors. All the recipients immediately gave their colorful new friends endearing names and insisted on taking full responsibility for the care of their charges. Many bought toys for the birds and one recipient built an elaborate playground. Many trained the birds to leave the cages. One elderly woman taught her clever pet to recite the names of neighborhood children; as a result she had frequent young and enthusiastic visitors. A follow-up a year and half later revealed that the recipients still had the pets and were taking good care of them.

### Susanne Robb: Elderly Veterans[2]

Between 1980 and 1982, Susanne Robb, Associate Chief, Nursing Service for Research at the Veterans Administration Medical Center in Pittsburgh, Pennsylvania, surveyed a randomly selected sample of veteran clients receiving home health care through the Center. Total sample size was 56 including 26 pet owners and 30 non-pet owners. "This study was undertaken," she says, "to extend systematic efforts to explore the possibility that association with companion animals enhances human coping ability as manifested in selected indices of physical and psychosocial health." The measured variables were morale, social interaction, mental status, psychological symptoms, ability to perform physical and instrumental activities of daily living, number of diseases, number of medications, and control. These particular variables were selected, she explains, because they had (1) been mentioned in the anecdotal accounts as benefits associated with companion animal association, (2) had not been studied previously in this context, and (3) could be measured using previously developed criteria.

Upon analysis of the data, Robb found that there was no significant difference in the health-related variables between the pet and non-pet group. She conjectured that the strength of the pet-owner bond might be an important factor and re-assessed the data after dividing the sample into high-bond and low-bond clients. High-bond pet owners were those who selected pets when asked: "Do you prefer pets or people?" and high-bond non-pet owners were those who answered yes to the question: "Do you wish you owned a pet?'' Once again, she found no significant differences between the groups.

Robb suggests several reasons why this study did not corroborate earlier findings: a virtually all-male sample, difficulty of definition of variables, oversimplification of the alleged relationship between association with companion animals and human health benefits, etc., and indicates some direction for future research. She also suggests:

> Perhaps in living with companion animals on a day-to-day basis, in the absence of crises, no measurable impact exists. When events threaten or result in loss of contact between people and their animals or serve to restore contact after a period of separation or loss, however, this may be the time when measurable impacts occur.

### Ory and Goldberg: Pet Possession and Well-Being in Elderly Women[3,4]

Marcia G. Ory, medical sociologist at the National Institute on Aging, Bethesda, Maryland, and epidemiologist Evelyn L. Goldberg, of the Johns Hopkins University, Baltimore, Maryland, are currently exploring the role of pets in the life of the elderly as part of a larger five-year study of social factors affecting the health of older women.

''The purpose of the study,'' explain Ory and Goldberg, ''is to examine the role of pet ownership as an independent predictor of perceived happiness in the elderly.'' Interviews were conducted with 1,073 white married women aged 65-75 living in Maryland of whom 388 were pet owners. The women in the study were predominantly non-urban and lived in a household of at least two persons. Although health status and mobility varied among the sample, the criteria for the study excluded the very sick or the institutionalized. Pet owners were also asked to indicate their degree of attachment on a five-point scale (from ''very attached'' to ''not at all attached''). To measure the subject's subjective evaluation of her psychological well-being, these investigators chose ''perceived happiness'' as assessed by Gurin's measure of overall happiness, a single item that asks: ''Taken all together, . . . would you say you are very happy, pretty happy, or not too happy.''

Upon analysis of the data, Ory and Goldberg found that:

Controlling for sociodemographic, health status, and social interaction factors, the simple presence of pets in the household was not related to happiness. However, further analyses revealed that the relationship between pet ownership and happiness was complex, dependent upon the nature of the animal-human interaction as well as the social context in which the women lived.

"While attached pet owners were not very different from non-pet owners, women who reported being unattached to their pets were the most likely to be unhappy," explain the researchers.

There is partial support for the hypothesis that persons who are unattached to their pets are also less likely to be involved in close relationships with their spouses. These findings can lead to the speculation that certain women are less likely to have attachments, either with humans or with pets.

Ory and Goldberg also found that pet ownership among women from higher socioeconomic backgrounds was associated with greater happiness; in women from lower socioeconomic backgrounds, pet ownership was associated with unhappiness, suggesting that " . . . the meaning of pet ownership is different for different segments of the population."

Some other interesting findings concerning pet ownership emerged from this study. Elderly people, on the whole, are less likely to own pets than the general population; but the majority of those who do are very attached to the animal(s). Most (73%) of the pet-owners interviewed described themselves as very attached to their pets.

## PET VISITATION STUDIES

### A Wine Bottle, Plant, and Puppy[5]

Prior to her survey of elderly veterans, Susanne Robb, along with Michele Boyd and Carole Lee Pristach, registered nurses at the Veterans Administration Medical Center in Pittsburgh, Pennsylvania, conducted a study at that facility to determine the effectiveness of certain objects as catalysts for social behavior.

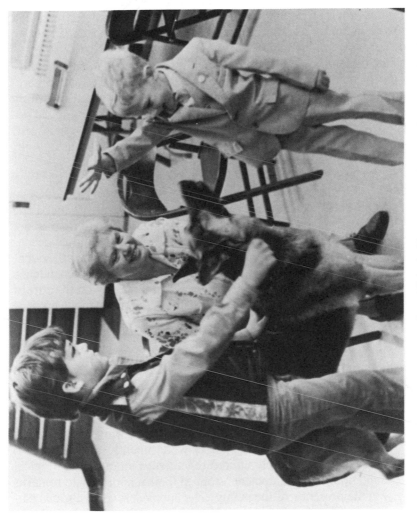

Elaine Smith and Therapy Dog Phila and Friends. Photo courtesy of Therapy Dogs International.

Robb hypothesized that the degree of animation, that is, faculty for life or motion, of an object would have a direct correlation to that object's ability to impact social change. She selected a wine bottle, an inanimate object that could however be an interesting visual stimulus for her population of elderly male alcoholic patients; a flowering plant, alive but not capable of motion; and a caged puppy to represent full animation.

The three objects were introduced into the environment, the dayroom of one unit of the hospital, one at a time, each for a ninety-minute period on two separate days. Subjects (who varied according to who entered the room) were observed for the following social behaviors: verbalization, smile, look (toward the object), eyes open, and leans-toward-stimulus. The subjects were all chronically ill, predominantly aged residents in a long-term care facility.

Robb reports:

> Of the three stimulus items, the caged puppy produced the most dramatic increase in social behavior. This effect is not surprising since a puppy offers love and unconditional acceptance in addition to stimulating multiple senses—smell, touch, vision, hearing. The perpetual, infantile, innocent dependence of a friendly dog may inspire a natural tendency on the part of humans to offer support and protection, even when the humans appear to have withdrawn from reality.

Although the purpose of the study was only to ascertain the effect of the stimuli on social behavior, several points of interest arose during the puppy phase of the project. "Verbalization became more conversational in nature," reports Robb.

> The one word remarks and inappropriate comments that characterized the other study phases were much less evident. Two clients who routinely uttered repetitive, monotonous, illogical and undirected statements stopped their inappropriate remarks in the presence of the puppy. The puppy served as a social catalyst. Clients talked about kinds of dogs they had owned previously. Many wanted to know if they could pet the puppy (they were allowed to do so after the project ended); some clients offered suggestions as to how to quiet the puppy when it barked. None of the hostile behaviors observed during other phases of the study were evident when the puppy was present.

Invasion of personal space had frequently triggered verbal arguments and physical violence between clients. When the puppy was present, invasion of personal space increased as clients moved to get closer to the puppy, but no hostility resulted.

## Robb's Pilot Study of Pet-Dog Therapy[6]

In 1981 Susanne Robb began a feasibility study

to identify effects of close contact with companion dogs on oriented, male residents receiving long-term care in a Veterans Administration facility. Effects considered were psychosocial symptoms, depression, hopelessness, morale, cathectic investment, loneliness, psychosocial functioning, activity, medication usage, physical injuries (caused by the dog) and zoonoses (transmitted from dogs to patients).

Additionally, Robb's study was designed to examine the cost/benefit of pet-dog therapy and to ascertain the perceptions of nurses on dogs in a facility.

The design involved seven four-week observation periods and three study groups (control, experimental/no-pet, and experimental/pet, based on subjects' interactions with the dogs). The treatment consisted of 12 companion dogs and 22 volunteer dog handlers. Subjects were residents who lived on two study floors who agreed to participate in the study and who met the criteria (oriented, not confused; aged 50 or older; male; no known allergy to dogs).

Robb's results found no significant difference between the three groups which she attributes to the baseline mental state of the subjects. "Opportunity for the companion dog program to effect changes was somewhat restricted by the fact that initial scores were favorable (indicating only mild to moderate levels of depression, hopelessness, and other problems) and remained stable throughout the study."

Nursing personnel, however, reported that disoriented and confused individuals appeared to benefit from the dogs' visits. "The nature of the benefit was usually some overt action or behavioral expression that had seldom, if ever, been seen before the dogs came," explained Robb.

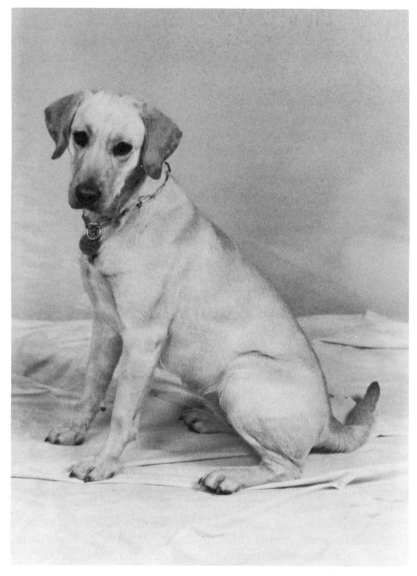

Therapy Dog Nessie. Photo by Bob Barber.

Examples included the engagement of residents in appropriate rather than inappropriate conversations, residents reaching out to hold or pet the dogs (when they had not reached out for other people or objects), smiling, and attentiveness to the dogs' movements for comparatively long periods of time.

Additionally, the nurses' perception of dogs in health facilities changed from "generally neutral" to "generally favorable." They continued, however, to doubt that use of pet-dog therapy would result in a reduced workload.

Perhaps most importantly, no zoonoic diseases or dog-related injuries occurred among residents or staff. Also, no negative effects on the dogs were reported.

Some of the implications from the study, concluded Robb, are:

1. Therapeutic benefits are probably not as obvious or common to large numbers of residents as proponents of companion dog programs believe.
2. Risks of adverse/untoward reactions to the presence of dogs on the part of residents and others are probably much lower than opponents of this intervention believe.
3. Precautionary measures taken for this program to ensure safety were probably more stringent than necessary.
4. Models chosen for companion dog programs need to match the kinds of residents who are expected to benefit.
5. Caution needs to be exercised in assigning work for companion dog programs to nursing personnel.
6. Companion dog programs that are evaluated need to take place for longer than six weeks.

## Domestic Animal Visitation as Therapy for Adult Home Residents[7]

Gloria M. Francis, Professor of Psychiatric Mental Health Nursing at Virginia Commonwealth University, along with Jean Turner, an instructor in psychiatric mental health nursing, and doctoral student Suzanne Johnson, conducted a study to determine the value of domestic animal visitation to semi-institutionalized elderly living in group homes.

The settings were two adult homes in which the residents were chronic mentally ill persons who had been discharged from psychiatric facilities. "The sample profile for the experimental home was a 72-year-old, white female who had been at the home 39 months. The control group profile was a 76-year-old, white female who had been in residence for 47 months. There were, however, blacks and men in both samples,'' explained the researchers.

The treatment consisted of eight puppies or kittens and four handlers who spent three hours at the experimental home once a week for eight weeks. The residents gathered in the large foyer. Puppies were handed to those who asked for them or reached out for them, or they were placed on the floor to play with each other and balls. The control group had weekly human visitors only. Each group was pre-and post-tested for eight variables: health self-concept, life satisfaction, psychologic well-being, social competence and interest, personal neatness, psychosocial and mental function, and depression.

The results indicated a dramatic difference between the two groups. The residents who had interacted with the puppies improved in six out of eight areas measured. The only two areas that were not impacted were personal neatness and health self-concept. Nothing happened to the control group. Although they had human visitors, it appeared to cause little interest. One resident remarked matter-of-factly: ''People come and go.''

The researchers are not surprised by their findings.

> It has been fairly well documented that animals are therapeutically effective with various populations. What then is the point? The point is perhaps the simplicity and the inexpensiveness of an apparent successful therapeutic mode. This program could be instituted entirely by volunteers from outside an institution, or possibly by lesser-paid, non-professionals from within. The effected, measured variables . . . could be said to be indications of quality of life. If one accepts this, the study has shown that a simplistic, inexpensive ''treatment modality,'' something long-term institutions could implement almost immediately, can significantly improve psychosocial function, hence ''quality of life.''

### Mary Thompson and Therapy Dog Misty[8,9]

Mary Thompson, a registered nurse and therapist, is also the owner of a therapy dog, a Golden Retriever named Misty. Thompson and colleagues conducted a study at the Coatesville Veterans

Administration Medical Center to examine the parameters of behavior change that may occur in psychiatric patients and to establish guidelines for implementation and operation of pet-facilitated therapy in institutions.

After careful screening, 20 subjects were selected ranging in age from 40 to 60 years of age; the group was randomly subdivided into a control group who would not interact with the animals and an experimental group who were assigned to a 6-week, 18-session pet-facilitated therapy program. The 45-minute sessions included instruction on animal care and handling, petting and playing with the pets, as well as group discussion involving animals. In addition to Thompson's therapy dog, other dogs and cats, puppies, kittens, parakeets, and guinea pigs were used. Overall results indicated that subjects with moderate functional impairment improved significantly over both the control subjects and pet therapy subjects on extremes of the range (low impairment and high impairment), suggesting to the researchers that subject selection for pet therapy programs is extremely important.

However, as in many of the studies described, there was dramatic improvement in one patient. Thompson describes her experience:

> During my three years of working as a gerontological clinical nurse specialist at a large Veterans Administration Medical Center, one of my major goals was to help to improve the quality of the lives of the geriatric patients. Unfortunately, there never were, nor will there ever be, enough humans available for this purpose, especially in large institutions. However, I have always had a deep interest in and love of animals and therefore, I decided to enlist the assistance of my furred friends in striving to achieve my goal.
>
> Author Gladys Taber summarizes well the difference pets can make in her following statement: "When everything goes wrong with human relationships, which happens at times, there is comfort and restorative power in the soft muzzle laid gently on your lap, an ecstatic tail wagging, or a small head rubbing against your neck while a purr-song says, "How absolutely wonderful you are."[10]
>
> This has been borne out so often in the patient population (many with long-term psychiatric problems) with whom I was associated. During the pet therapy research project upon which another nurse, a psychologist, and I embarked prior to

establishing regular pet therapy groups and ward mascots, we found one elderly patient, Mr. S, who had been extremely regressed on a locked ward, and who had shown no interest in anyone or anything, suddenly taking an active interest in the animals which were introduced to him in a group setting. After several group sessions, Mr. S asked if he could assist more directly with the pets and was given the task of taking care of the pets prior to and after the group sessions. During this same time, Mr. S. began to show improvement in other areas such as communication skills and personal hygiene. By the time the six week research project had terminated, Mr. S had shown so much improvement that he was transferred to an open ward and even became a messenger for the ward. In this instance, Mr. S's involvement with the dogs and the other animals had served as a catalyst for transforming him from an uncommunicative, regressed patient to a responsible, alert human being.

This was the most dramatic change that was seen in any given patient; however, there were many other instances where my dog, a trained Therapy Dog (and member of Therapy Dogs International), and the other pets that were employed helped to brighten a patient's day and bring a smile to many faces. One patient in particular was extremely uncommunicative—uttering only a yes or no response—unless he saw my Golden Retriever Misty. He would then become very congenial and, at times, tearful as he would talk about the hunting dog that had been so dear to him in the past. Another patient, a blind man, seemed to receive his sole gratification from food—until he met Misty. He actually got down on the floor with her, put his arms around her, and buried his face in her neck as she gently washed his face and ears. Many "normal" people are repelled by my dog's desire to express her affection by licking; however, the geriatric patients to whom she has been introduced have all appeared to crave affection and have been quite pleased by her manner of expressing it.

It is true that pet therapy is not effective with everyone, just as other forms of therapy are not effective with everyone, but how sad if we don't at least give it a try; it we don't discover all the Mr. S's out there who can become a new person, or at least a happier person, with the aid of a devoted four-legged friend.

## ANIMALS IN RESIDENCE STUDIES

### Corson's Nursing Home Studies[11]

Samuel and Elizabeth O'Leary Corson's pioneering work in animal-facilitated therapy began during the 1970s with disturbed adolescents at the Ohio State University hospital and was later extended to geriatric populations at the Castle Nursing Homes in Millersburg, Ohio.

Corson used several breeds of dogs in his studies and attributes much of the success of the program to his ability to match particular temperament and behavioral motifs to the various patients' needs. Corson found, among other things, that for bedridden and wheelchair-bound residents, small playful breeds such as wirehaired fox terriers and miniature and toy poodles were especially successful. These breeds also appealed to patients who were depressed and withdrawn, and these friendly and sociable dogs often were extremely effective as social lubricants, enhancing social interaction among the patients.

Corson observed that, good intentions to the contrary, hale and hearty adults, including those in the health-care professions, have a tendency to send negative nonverbal signals to the elderly, the ailing, and the mentally and physically debilitated. This, he says, can lead to a self-perpetuating cycle that reinforces the very difficulties that first caused the patient's incarceration. Pet animals, however, particularly well-trained, carefully selected dogs, offered an effective means to break the cycle thus creating a more congenial and sociable atmosphere in the institution.

### Cats as Nursing Home Mascots[12]

In a 1979 study, Clark Brickel interviewed nursing home staff personnel where patients had access to cat ward mascots for two years to ascertain the therapeutic value of these animals on a hospital ward.

In Brickel's study, approximately 20-25 patients, ranging in age from 50 to 70 years of age, had access to the cats. From his interviews, Brickel learned that most of the patients enjoyed the company of the cats if they happened to be nearby, and three to seven of the patients had an "intense" interest in the animals. For those few patients who were not particularly fond of the cats, however, no

Jenny of Therapy Dogs International. Photo by Bob Barber.

problem was reported as the cats appeared to instinctively know when they weren't wanted.

Interaction was both passive and active. Cats sat on the patients' laps and were petted and stroked. Others played and talked to the cats, and some just watched them from a distance. Time spent with the animals ranged from 1-10 hours with the average being about 3 hours. Brickel reported that little jealousy arose over possession of the animals, but on the few occasions that there was some argument, some staff members felt that this too was positive behavior since the patients were, for the most part, largely unresponsive.

Many staff reported that the presence of the cat promoted conversations and interactions between patients and patients and between patients and staff. Conversations began over the cat's current activities and previous cats owned by individuals in the past. New patients on the ward were told of the cats by the other patients.

In summary, the presence of the cats, while not attributing to any therapeutic breakthroughs, was viewed as beneficial to the patients in several areas. Patient responsiveness was described as being the foremost benefit and several individuals were reported to "open up dramatically" to interactions with the animals. Other benefits included the physical pleasure of stroking the animal, the enhancement of the ward environment (making it appear less like an institution and more like a home), and reality therapy. Often patients were aware of and reported to staff the cats' health condition. Patients saved food for the cats. Brickel suggested this particular example indicated that the animal had been integrated into the patient's reality. They established an emotional link with the animal, were aware of its needs, and incorporated these needs into their daily reality.

Most of the staff interviewed could not pinpoint a specific diagnostic condition in the patients that may have been benefitted more than others, but the few who did suggested that the most withdrawn of the patients appeared to have the most benefits from the cats. In this study, the staff interviewed selected cats as the ward mascot of choice because they require a minimum of care and attention.

## A Dog In Residence—The JACOPIS Study[13]

In July 1981, the research team of I. M. and P. W. Salmon, R. S. Hogarth-Scott, and R. B. Lavelle, along with the Caulfield Geriatric Hospital in Melbourne, Australia, with the guidance of JACOPIS (the Joint Advisory Committee on Pets in Society) embarked on the first formal patient-pet interaction program in that country.

In this study an ex-guide dog named Honey, a Golden Retriever trained at the Royal Guide Dogs' Association, was introduced into the hospital to interact with 60 patients in two long-term care wards. The patients selected were frail, with an average age of 80. Many suffered from cardiovascular complaints and arthritis. In general they were withdrawn, uncommunicative, non-ambulatory, and showed little interest in their surroundings. Preliminary questionnaires were administered to both the staff and the patients which measured the expected reactions to the dog. During the six-month study, patients were closely monitored both in responses to the dog and in general social, psychological and physical behaviors. A post-study questionnaire was also administered.

The evaluation of the data obtained confirmed what the researchers' colleagues on the other side of the globe had previously established: the dog had a positive effect on emotional well-being and physical activity of a significant number of patients. The dog promoted a greater joy in living which the researchers remarked was an extremely important aspect of institutionalized living. The dog's presence prompted increased happiness, sense of humor, laughter, alertness, responsiveness, an easygoing attitude, enjoyment of life, and an increased incentive to live for the patients. In addition, the dog promoted a greater interest in others and improved relationships between the patients themselves and the patients and staff. Honey's presence was something that the staff could share and talk about with the patients; the two factions now had a significant interest in common.

A particularly interesting aspect of the JACOPIS project is the pre- and post-test questionnaires which measured the patients' and staffs' anticipated benefits and problems with the dog. Expectation, both positive and negative, can be a self-fulfilling prophecy; however, although the positive benefits of the dog were anticipated and realized, the negative aspects were not. Additionally, the beneficial effect of Honey was even greater than expected.

At least 78% of the patients expected some benefits from the presence of the dog in the areas of companionship and friendship, love and affection, enjoyment and fun, an interest, a topic of conversation, making the ward seem more like home, and making the ward happier. (See Table 1.) A post-test questionnaire revealed that at least 89% of the patients had, in fact, experienced these benefits.

Honey, "a dog in residence." Photo courtesy of JACOPIS.

TABLE 1

Percent of Patients who Anticipated
and Experienced Benefits with the Dog

| Benefit | Pre-test (N = 49) % | Post-test (N = 45) % |
|---|---|---|
| Companionship/friendship | 82 | 89 |
| Love/affection | 82 | 91 |
| Enjoyment/fun | 84 | 89 |
| An interest | 86 | 89 |
| Something to talk about | 82 | 91 |
| Make the ward like home | 78 | 91 |
| Make the ward happier | 78 | 89 |

In all categories, the benefits experienced were greater than those anticipated with the largest increase in the category "making the ward more like home" (from 78% to 91%).

Staff anticipation of Honey's benefits was generally lower than that of the patients in all categories, but experienced benefits were again greater on all scores with the highest increase in the category of making the institution seem more like home. An additional category in the staff questionnaire proved surprising. In the pre-test survey 4% of the staff thought the presence of the dog might decrease their workload; the post-test questionnaire revealed that 24% had actually experienced such a decrease. (See Table 2.)

A number of patients expected problems with the dog in the areas of accommodation, discipline and training, barking, smell, mess, fear, damage to property, cruelty to dog, tripping over dog, and dog getting in the way. (See Table 3.) The patients' greatest concern was the dog's barking. Although 26% of the patients anticipated problems with this behavior, as the post-test questionnaire revealed, only 2% actually experienced problems in this area. In fact, the patients experienced virtually no other problems with the dog except that 3% had noted some problem with the dog getting in the way.

Staff expected more problems than patients with the dog which the researchers say was most likely "a realistic appraisal of fears associated with a novel experience and technique.''[14] Again, most problems anticipated were not realized. (See Table 4.) Twenty-four percent had expected an increased workload because of the dog; only 2% experienced such a workload. Staff reported no problems in the categories of barking, smell, damage to property, and cruelty to the dog even though a quarter to a third of the staff had expected such problems to occur.

Some additional interesting points of the study: male patients expected more problems with the dog than women patients, but realized greater benefits. Pre-test questions revealed that male patients would be less unhappy if the ward had a dog, yet post-test questions indicated that the men would be unhappier than the women if the dog were taken away.

During the 5th week, Honey got away and was missing for a short time. Patients who had previously been unenthusiastic about the dog expressed concern for her safety. Some were very upset and worried and one staff member commented that the incident was "like a

TABLE 2

Percent of Staff Members who Anticipated
and Experienced Benefits with the Dog

| Benefit | Pre-test (N = 50) % | Post-test (N = 42) % |
|---|---|---|
| Companionship/friendship | 52 | 55 |
| Love/affection | 52 | 55 |
| Enjoyment/fun | 66 | 79 |
| An interest | 62 | 71 |
| Something to share with patients | 84 | 86 |
| A talking point with patients | 84 | 93 |
| Make the ward like home | 64 | 88 |
| Make the ward happier | 66 | 86 |
| Decreased workload | 4 | 24 |

TABLE 3

Percent of Patients Who Anticipated
and Experienced Problems with the Dog

| Problem | Pre-test (N = 58) % | Post-test (N = 45) % |
|---|---|---|
| Accommodation | 7 | 0 |
| Discipline/training | 16 | 0 |
| Barking | 26 | 2 |
| Smell | 12 | 0 |
| Mess | 14 | 0 |
| Fear of dog | 12 | 0 |
| Damage to property | 5 | 0 |
| Cruelty to dog | 5 | 0 |
| Tripping over dog | 14 | 0 |
| Dog getting in the way | 19 | 3 |

death in the family.'' This finding suggests that patient involvement with the therapy animal occurs, even if it is not readily observable. The researchers reported:

> By the end of the programme, patients were reported to be significantly happier—they laughed and smiled more often, and, most importantly, their desire to live increased. They were more responsive and interested in others, and their relationships with other patients and with staff seemed to improve. Consistent with this apparent increase in socialization was the reduction of the number of hours that patients spent alone—11 hours at the end of the programme compared to 16 hours previously. These changes were more apparent in the men, suggesting once again that they benefitted from the dog more than the women.

Patients' comments included: ''She's lovely.'' ''It's one of the best things about the place." "I like Honey being around." "I love to watch her." A staff member commented: "The few times I see patients alert and active is when Honey is there." An elderly deaf women took up painting, specifically pictures of dogs, after Honey's arrival. Bob, the patient in charge of walking and feeding Honey, became more outgoing and participated in more activities. Honey went on bus trips and was taken to the park by patients in wheelchairs. She was encouraged to go on beds. An occupational therapist commented: "She is a wonderful participant in my movement to music group!"

TABLE 4

Percent of Staff Members Who Anticipated
and Experienced Problems with the Dog

| Problem | Pre-test (N = 50) % | Post-test (N = 42) % |
|---|---|---|
| Accommodation | 10 | 2 |
| Feeding | 8 | 10 |
| Bathing/grooming | 20 | 2 |
| Exercise | 20 | 12 |
| Discipline/training | 22 | 21 |
| Barking | 34 | 0 |
| Smell | 26 | 0 |
| Mess | 38 | 0 |
| Frightening people | 24 | 5 |
| Damage to property | 10 | 0 |
| Cruelty to dog | 24 | 0 |
| Complaints | 24 | 2 |
| Gets in the way | 40 | 21 |
| Increased workload | 24 | 2 |

"Various types of patient-pet interactions occurred," report the researchers. "Honey was watched, stroked and patted, talked to, walked and fed tidbits. All of these illustrate the important role that a pet animal can play for elderly patients especially—namely, that communication with the pet does not have to be on a verbal level."

At the end of the study, staff rated Honey 8.2 on a 10 point scale. When asked if they were pleased or sorry to have her on the ward, they gave her another high 8.4. Staff also reported more unhappiness if Honey were taken away than they had before the study. Two staff members commented:

> The ward has an atmosphere now with the dog being there—everyone knows her and those who can communicate make it very obvious that she is needed. She has made life interesting for the staff and has made some of us very happy.
>
> The ward is more like a home now. Most of the ladies just like to see her around—don't even want to touch her—seeing is all they want. The response from visitors has been very positive.

To summarize about the effect of Honey on the patients, all staff reported improvements. No detrimental effects were reported at all.

The final aspect of the study considered Honey and the effect of hospital living on her. About 30% of the staff anticipated problems because the dog would have so many masters; only 2% thought overfeeding could be a problem.

"As subsequent events showed," explain the researchers,

> the first fear proved to be unfounded while the second appears to be underestimated. At the end of the six months, 39% of the staff commented that although Honey seemed to be happy and content, she was definitely over-weight. One cannot help but wonder whether this is an inevitable price for contentment! On a serious note, steps were in fact taken to overcome Honey's weight problem and the consulting veterinary surgeon was advised.

Honey was gradually accepted as the "hospital dog," and benefitted patients not only on the previous experimental wards, but throughout the facility. "The success of this programme," say the researchers,

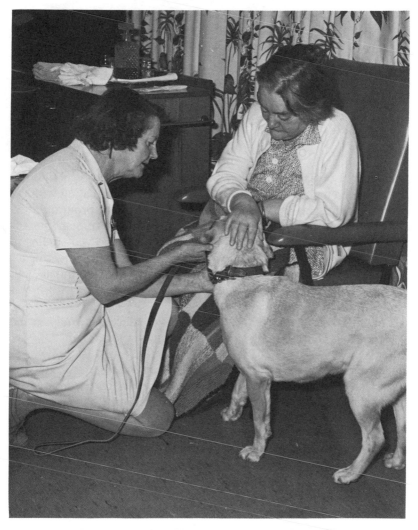

Honey, "a dog in residence." Photo courtesy of JACOPIS.

would seem to be due to two factors—staff support and careful planning. It was constantly apparent that the staff's desire to have a dog in the wards and their commitment to making the programme work, were vital to its success. Equally important, perhaps, was the initial planning that took place prior to the introduction of the dog.

## Pet-Facilitated Therapy in an Ohio Retirement-Nursing Community[15,16]

A student of Samuel Corson, Robert M. Andrysco, was the first graduate of a unique Ohio State University program dealing with the effects humans and animals have on one another. The program titled "The Ethologic and Therapeutic Basis of Human-Animal Interactions" is the first of its kind in the country and involved studies in the disciplines of psychology, psychiatry, and veterinary medicine. Andrysco is not only the program's premiere PhD candidate, but was instrumental in the design and selection of coursework for this innovative new program.

For his dissertation project, Andrysco conducted a study at the Westminster Thurber Retirement Community. He explains:

Pet-therapy, utilizing a well-trained dog, was introduced to the residents and staff of a retirement-nursing care community. Residents were examined prior to, during, and following introduction of the pet to the facility, and thus served as their own controls. In addition, they were compared to a similar group of residents who did not interact with the dog, but were otherwise treated identically.

The 23 control and 23 experimental residents were observed by both nurses and activity therapists and rated on a scale for psychosocial function in the areas of activity involvement, interactions with other residents and staff, self-care, and opinions and conversations concerning pet animals. Ten residents were studied by videotape, and all responded favorably to the dog as reflected in changes in eye-contact, smile, tactile contact, verbal response time, number of words in response, number of questions asked, verbalization of violence, and delusions.

According to Andrysco's study, "significant improvement was noted in fifteen of the patients who interacted with pets in the areas of activity involvement, verbal communication, conversations about animals, socialization with non-nursing personnel, socialization with other residents and socialization at mealtime." Other results indicated that socialization improved significantly when the pet was present.

Verbal and non-verbal communication also improved in that 10 of the patients, after examination of their sessions with the aid of videotape, showed improvement in both the quantity (number of words and statements) and quality (more positive response) of communication. Response time also improved as did eye contact with the investigator. In summing this study, Andrysco noted:

> Many of the residents involved in this study had perceptual problems concerning their existence. Many believed they were somewhere else, usually somewhere they had been in the past. These misconceptions made it extremely difficult to communicate with the residents. In individual situations the pet proved extremely valuable in breaking through these misconceptions, although adequate statistical data for analysis was not obtained.

For one patient however the interaction with the dog Obie changed her life. The patient, in her late 80s, had no physical problems but found it impossible to interact with the staff. She was physically and verbally violent and would often throw things at staff members. She was convinced the staff were trying to hurt her and would wake up in the middle of the night and "see" staff members digging her grave. When Andrysco first introduced her to Obie, she was convinced that the dog was brought to kill her. But eventually she reached out and petted the dog and her face broke into a wide smile. The initial contact proved the impetus that would spark her eventual recovery. She began to talk about her own experiences with dogs and over a process of 6-8 months, a drastic change took place in the woman. Presently, she is so well-integrated into the facility that she works to help newcomers adjust to their unfamiliar (and possibly undesirable) situation.

Andrysco explains: "She trusted the dog; then she transferred that trust to me, and eventually to the staff of the home. She was our miracle," he says.

Additionally, Andrysco found that the presence of the dog enhanced and facilitated his relationships with the institution's staff.

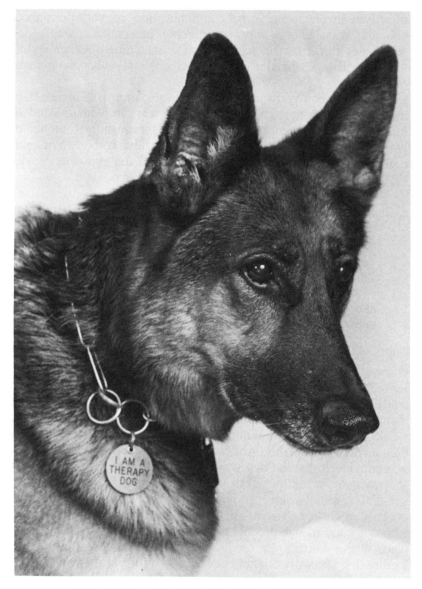

Phila of Therapy Dogs International. Photo by Bob Barber.

He chose an elevator setting since he could there isolate out many other factors. For ten weeks he rode the elevator alone; then for the next ten weeks, he rode it with Obie. "No one talked to me until I brought the dog," he says, "but eventually, the conversation began about the dog." Andrysco then rode the elevator alone for an additional ten weeks to determine the longevity of the effect. The social ties prompted by the dog remained. Thus, Obie proved to be a most effective social catalyst, though after the initial breakthroughs, his presence was no longer required and the social interaction remained.[17]

As we will review in the next chapter, companion animals offer distinct physical, psychological and social benefits to their owners regardless of age, sex, or other criteria. But for the elderly, the companionship of an animal friend may be especially valuable. Veterinarian Leo Bustad, founder of the People-Pet-Partnership Program in Pullman, Washington, and a pioneer in pet therapy for geriatric as well as other populations, says:

> Many older people have discovered that animal companions satisfy some of their greatest needs. Pets restore order to their lives; provide a more secure grasp of reality; and link their owners to a community of caring, concern, sacrifice and intense emotional relationships. When older people withdraw from active participation in daily human affairs, the non-human environment in general, and animals in particular, can become increasingly important. Animals have boundless capacity for acceptance, adoration, attention, forgiveness and unconditional love. Although the potential for significant benefits to a great variety of people exists through association with companion animals, the potential seems greatest in the elderly, for whom the bond with animal companions is perhaps stronger and more profound than at any other age.[18]

## REFERENCES

1. Mugford, R.A. and M'Comisky, J.G. "Some Recent Work on the Psychotherapeutic Value of Caged Birds with Old People." *Pet Animals and Society*, Anderson, R.S., editor. London: Bailliere Tindall, 1975.

2. Robb, Susanne S. and Stegman, Charles E. "Companion Animals and Elderly People: A Challenge for Evaluators of Social Support." *The Gerontologist*, June 1983.

3. Ory, Marcia G. and Goldberg, Evelyn L. "Pet Possession and Well-Being in Elderly Women." Unpublished report.

4. Ibid. "Pet Ownership and Attachment: An Analysis of Demographic, Health and Social Interaction Correlates in the Elderly." Unpublished report.

5. Robb, Susanne S.; Boyd Michele; and Pristash, Carole Lee. "A Wine Bottle, Plant, and Puppy: Catalysts for Social Behavior." *Journal of Gerontological Nursing, 6*(12) December 1980.

6. Robb, Susanne S. "Pilot Study of Pet-Dog Therapy for Elderly People in Long-Term Care." Unpublished report.

7. Francis, Gloria M.; Turner, Jean T.; and Johnson, Suzanne B. "Domestic Animal Visitation as Therapy With Adult Home Residents." Unpublished report.

8. Thompson, M.; Kennedy, R.; and Igou, S. "Pets as Socializing Agents with Chronic Psychiatric Patients." Research presentation at the International Conference on the Human/Companion Animal Bond, October 5-7, 1981, Philadelphia, PA.

9. Thompson, Mary. Personal Communication.

10. Taber, Gladys. *Country Chronicle.* Philadelphia: J.B. Lippincott Co., 1974.

11. Corson, S.A. and E.O. "Pet Animals as Nonverbal Communication Mediators in Psychotherapy in Institutional Settings." In *Ethology and Nonverbal Communication in Mental Health.* Oxford: Pergamon Press, 1979.

12. Brickel, Clark M. "Therapeutic Roles of Cat Mascots with a Hospital-based Geriatric Population: A Staff Survey." *The Gerontologist,* 19, 4, 1979.

13. Salmon, I.M.; Salmon, R.S.; Hogarth-Scott, R.S.; and Lavelle, R.B. "A Dog in Residence." A Companion-Animal Study commissioned by JACOPIS Australia, the Joint Advisory Committee on Pets in Society. (A summary of the study appears in *The Latham Letter,* Spring 1982.)

14. Ibid. Personal Communication.

15. Andrysco, Robert M. "Pet Facilitated Therapy in a Retirement Nursing Care Community." Presentation at the 1981 International Conference on the Human/Companion Animal Bond. October 5-7, 1981, Philadelphia, PA.

16. Ibid. "PFT in an Ohio Retirement-Nursing Community." *The Latham Letter,* Spring 1982.

17. Ibid. Personal Communication.

18. Bustad, Leo K. and Hines, Linda M. "Placements of Animals With the Elderly: Benefits and Strategies." In *Guidelines Animals in Nursing Homes. California Veterinarian Supplement,* 3/1983.

# Chapter 3

# The Human/Animal Bond

Although the bond between people and their animal friends dates back to prehistory, only recently has this relationship become the subject of serious scientific inquiry. In the past few years, researchers from disciplines as diverse as anthropology, ethology, gerontology, psychology, and veterinary medicine have begun to explore this human/animal bond, which is rapidly becoming a scientific discipline in itself. The findings, to date, are extraordinary. Not only do animals enrich our lives in the obvious ways, but they provide us with distinct physiological, psychological, and social benefits that help keep us healthy and happy.

## PHYSIOLOGICAL BENEFITS

### Pet Ownership Contributes to Recovery from Illness

Owning a pet appears to stimulate recovery from illness according to research findings at the University of Pennsylvania. In a much-cited study by Erica Friedmann and colleagues, the researchers found that post-coronary survival improved significantly if the patient was a pet owner. Fifty out of 53 pet owners were alive one year after hospitalization compared to only 17 out of 39 non-pet owners. This finding was independent of the health status of the subject.

The researchers considered that the health benefits associated with walking a dog could be the definitive factor in the difference in the samples, so they eliminated dog owners from the sample. The results were the same, suggesting that the intrinsic factor of owning a pet, aside from any related benefits, appears to contribute to the recovery of the patients.[1]

In a follow-up study, Friedmann conducted a survey of 100 pet-owning hospital patients to ascertain the effects of pet ownership on hospitalization. She found that a majority of the patients expressed concern for the welfare of the pet in their absence and maintained daily telephone contact with either the caretaker of the pet or the pet itself. She concluded that: "owners require frequent reassurance about their pet's welfare during hospitalization, but pets continue to provide a sense of being needed and an impetus for quick recovery for the hospitalized owner."[2]

## Interaction with Pets Lowers Blood Pressure

As early as 1929, laboratory experiments showed that canine heartbeat slowed and blood pressure lowered in response to human petting. Additionally, in situations where the dog was subjected to stress or physical discomfort, human contact was able to alleviate the stress factors and promote relaxation in the animal.

Now, researchers have confirmed that this effect is not one-way, but a symbiotic relationship between pets and people. As we benefit the dog, so it benefits us. Children entering a neighbor's home experience reduced blood pressure when the neighbor's dog is present. Subjects asked to complete the Manifest Anxiety Scale with the experimenter's dog present have lower anxiety scores than those completing the test without the presence of the dog. Persons in the waiting room of a veterinary clinic have lower blood pressure when touching or talking to their pet than when talking to the experimenter alone.[3]

Whereas talking to people raises blood pressure, talking to animals lowers it, according to Aaron Katcher, professor of psychiatry at the University of Pennsylvania. The research of Katcher and his colleagues also demonstrates that this beneficial effect is not exclusive to the canine contingent. Just looking at tropical fish can result in blood pressure reductions comparable to those obtained from lengthy and tedious biofeedback instruction. Katcher found the largest reductions in those subjects who had a normally elevated blood pressure.[4]

For the elderly, who are often reticent and withdrawn, these factors are of enormous importance. James Lynch, author of *The Broken Heart* which investigates the physiological devastation of loneliness, suggests that one reason the elderly withdraw is that their already high blood pressure is further elevated by communication with other people. Conversations with a pet, however, cause no such discomfort.[5]

## Caring for Pets Increases Self-Care

In his study at the Westminster Thurber Retirement Community, Robert Andrysco noted that five of his patients improved significantly in the area of self-care after interaction with the therapy dog.[6] Retarded adults at the San Francisco Recreation Center for the Handicapped learned about their own needs through caring for the pet rabbit Bubba.[7] (See Chapter 11.) The basic needs of both humans and animals are not so very different: proper nutrition; a secure and safe environment; adequate shelter; proper hygienic and health conditions; and an atmosphere that provides some degree of affection, companionship, and interaction. By providing the conditions necessary for the health and happiness of their pets, seniors and other special groups can learn or be motivated to provide these conditions for themselves.

Hypothermia, the abnormal lowering of the body temperature, for example, is a condition that is particularly dangerous to the elderly. Gradual and insidious, it can be caused by prolonged exposure to a too cold environment. Scottish education expert Dorothy Walster tells a story of an elderly woman in Perthshire, Scotland, who adamantly refused to maintain her quarters at the warmth level suggested by the health council. Then she was given a pet canary. Although she was reluctant to keep her thermostat up solely for her own comfort, she quickly acquiesced when she learned it was vital for the health of her feathered companion.[8]

Walster also suggests that obese patients might be motivated to decrease their food intake by saving a portion of their meals for the pet animal. Additionally, the pet may be a distraction and diversion that will take the patient's mind from the obsession of excess eating.[9] However, an incentive program of this sort should be carefully watched as it could have the effect of simply transferring the excess weight problem—from the patient to the pet!

## PSYCHOLOGICAL BENEFITS

### Companionship

In a study conducted by Lyle Vogel and colleagues at the School of Public Health at the University of Michigan, companionship was recognized by pet owners and non-pet owners alike as the major advantage of having the animal. The ranking was (1) companionship - 70.5%; (2) love and affection - 52.2%; (3) pleasure - 39.3%; and (4) protection - 36%.[10]

The aspect of companionship is particularly important to the elderly who may be isolated from contact except for an animal companion. But companionship does more than fill a psychological need in the life of the senior; it may actually increase his life span. In an interview with *U.S. News and World Report,* psychologist James Lynch contended that isolation and lack of companionship are the greatest unrecognized contributors to premature death in the U.S. today. Statistics indicate that premature death is two to ten times greater for those who live alone. Although Lynch stresses that a pet is not meant to take the place of human contact, he does believe that in many ways, the presence of the animal can greatly ease the pangs of loneliness and forestall the physiological consequences that might otherwise be experienced.[11]

## Love and Affection

Pets provide unconditional and non-judgmental love and affection to the human recipient. In the human society, a person's worth is too often judged by superficial characteristics: the ideal of beauty, youth, perceived status, or possessions. For those who do not fit the ideal mold, love can be automatically withheld.

The love an animal gives to its human companion, however, is dictated by no such notions. A dog doesn't care if its master is beautiful, rich, young, or healthy; it will accept a tender stroke from an aged trembling hand as enthusiastically as from that of a young and able athlete. Also, a dog puts no conditions on its affection. Love is not withheld or denied if the owner does not perform in a satisfactory manner. The love that an animal gives comes free of strings and conditions; it is open, honest, straightforward, uncomplicated, and not subject to change.

We communicate our feelings to others in a variety of ways: both verbally and non-verbally. And, as Samuel Corson has observed, the healthy often inadvertently send negative non-verbal signals to the sick or institutionalized. Pets, however, he noted, provide a means of positive non-verbal communication that is reassuring and comforting to the lonely and withdrawn elder.[12]

In addition to giving love and affection, the therapy dog also is a willing recipient of these feelings and thus a valuable, often the only suitable, emotional outlet. Boris Levinson notes:

> The elderly adult feels that it is inappropriate for him either to receive or to dispense kisses or hugs. He is too embarrassed to bestow such emotional behavior upon another human being. He finds it acceptable, however, to demonstrate love for a pet. (Even adults are uninhibited in bestowing hugs and kisses upon their pets.) A pet can serve as a new love object to whom one can give all the love he wishes without fear that the pet will not reciprocate or will desert him.[13]

### Safety, Security, and Protection

Safety, according to psychiatrist Aaron Katcher, is one of the factors in our association with animals that promote mental and physical equilibrium. "There is no doubt," he says, "that companion animals make people feel safer in situations characterized by a high degree of novelty."[14]

Randall Lockwood of the State University of New York asked two groups of subjects to interpret ambiguous line drawings of social interactions. One group of drawings included an animal; the other did not. Results indicated that the presence of the animal leads to the interpretation of social scenes as less threatening and improves the perceived character of the people associated with them.[15]

"Unless the animal is labeled as vicious or dangerous," says Katcher, "a person or face coupled with a dog is perceived as safer, more benign, more approachable, and less dangerous."[16]

For the senior living alone except for an animal friend, for the hearing impaired who rely upon the ears of hearing or signal dogs, for the physically disabled or handicapped who depend on assistance that the trained service or therapy dog can provide, the feeling of safety provided by the animal friend is even more than a psychological feeling of security. It can mean the difference between living alone without fear and anxiety and relinquishing one's freedom for the physically more secure harbor of an institution.

A loss of sensory acuity is an unfortunate but inevitable consequence of aging. Even an elder who does not suffer from a significant dysfunction is faced with the growing and annoying recognition that his own functioning is less acute than in younger years. Would he hear an intruder making his stealthy way in the night? Should a fire break out, would he be aroused in time? Animals, however, are valuable sentries. Their senses, in many cases, are much more acute than our own, and they are in tune to changes in their environment that we may not detect. The excited and incessant barking of a small dog would probably dissuade a burglar who in many cases is looking for the most vulnerable and accessible victim. Cats, as well as dogs, have been credited with alerting their families to the outbreak of a fire. Probably, your life will never depend upon an animal, but it's comforting to think that should the situation arise your pet may well risk or lose its life to save yours.

## Incentive to Keep Busy

Pets give elders something to care about and an incentive to keep busy and active. In the Mugford and M'Comisky study, all the recipients of the parakeets insisted upon making their own arrangements for the food and care of their little friends.[17] An elder who has an animal that depends upon him feels useful and needed. It's very easy to give in to depression and feelings of isolation when one is alone, very easy to simply drift farther and farther away from the world of reality and effort. But a dog still needs to be walked, a pet cat or bird needs to be fed. Knowing that at least one other entity depends upon you for its needs and survival can make the difference between apathy and surrender and participation in life.

Leo Bustad tells a poignant story of Jack, an old man who was never seen except in the company of his dog, Rags. But one particularly chilling winter evening, Jack, feeling the weather too bitter for his little companion, left the dog home. Feeling tired, Jack stopped to rest and froze to death. Bustad feels he would be alive today if Rags had been with him.[18]

The pet's role as something to care for probably accounts for some of the successful use of dogs at alcoholic rehabilitation centers. The Abbey, a treatment center in Winfield, Illinois, adopted a stray mixed breed and named him Tramp. The dog was raised in a tavern and the patrons fed him liquor among other foods. One day, the dog was hit by a truck in the tavern parking lot. A recovering alcoholic who lived at the Abbey found the dog and brought him back to the treatment center. There he was cared for and went through withdrawal like any other alcoholic. He is now a very important part of the program there acting as an inspiration and friend to the patients.

The Guenster House, a halfway house for alcoholics in Bridge-port, Connecticut, has several mascot dogs and assigns each new guest a puppy as part of the treatment program. Many of the dogs eventually return home with the patients, thus providing an ongoing impetus for recovery.

In Colorado Springs, a nursing home adopted a dog from the local shelter specifically for an elderly alcoholic patient. The dog, named Buffy, gave the patient "a new interest in life, arrested his drinking problem, and caused the patient to display more interest in group activities."[19]

## Reality Orientation

Caring for an animal's needs can provide seniors with a daily routine that contributes to reality orientation. In his study of cats as nursing home mascots, Clark Brickel found that the staff agreed that the presence of the animals contributed to the patients' keeping in touch with the real world. The patients would inform staff if a cat were, in their estimation, not feeling well and saved food from their own meals for the pets. According to Brickel, the food gathering illustrated that the animals who were a part of reality had been incorporated into the patients' own sense of reality. The patients were aware of the animals' needs and modified their own behavior to accommodate the cats' needs.[20]

In Andrysco's study, an elderly woman, prone to delusions and verbal violence, effectively ceased these behaviors through interaction with the therapy dog. "Prior to meeting the dog," says Andrysco, "she would not accept the reality of her life in the home. After interacting with the dog who was real, she began to accept her own reality in the present which was in the home. This factor led to her eventual recovery."[21]

## Humor, Morale and Ego Strength

Psychiatrist Michael McCulloch, vice president of the Delta Society, the international organization that promotes research into the human/animal bond, says that the presence of a pet can improve morale and prompt a sense of humor in an otherwise depressed patient. McCulloch tells of one of his patients, a victim of kidney failure, who was depressed and confined to his home. When medication didn't help, McCulloch had an innovative prescription: a dog. The entire family got involved in the acquisition of the pet and when the doctor called for a follow-up, the man's wife told him that the family had laughed together for the first time in years.[22]

Researcher Judy Harris, who grew up with a dog, conjectured that being raised with a canine friend would contribute to the development of trust and self-esteem, factors which on the Minnesota Multiphasic Personality Inventory comprise what is denoted Ego Strength. She theorized that subjects who owned dogs as children would score higher on this test than subject who had not owned dogs. Results confirmed the hypothesis: childhood pet owners scored significantly higher than non-pet owners.

Harris attributes the higher Ego Strength scores, indicative of a more adaptive personality, to the unconditional acceptance dogs give to their owners. "Dogs permit their owners to be themselves so that they can risk self-disclosure and form attachments. It becomes less frightening to trust yourself when another living creature views you as trustworthy," she says.

Harris cautions that since her study subjects were graduate students and future therapists who volunteered for the project, her results should not be generalized to other populations. But she adds:

> For a family systems theorist to ignore the importance of the functions and roles of a pet is to miss a significant aspect of the human experience.
>
> As a child growing up with a dog, I never doubted that he was a valued member of the family. Yet, it never occurred to me that our interactions had any significance beyond that of owner to pet. Of course, I was aware of the warmth, fun, acceptance, and love that Prince provided, but I felt this existed apart from the real world. In fact, I derided myself for my devotion.[23]

### *Fun and Entertainment*

Before we conclude our section on the psychological benefits of pets, there is one more important factor that can be overlooked with all the serious material we have considered. Pet animals are fun; they are entertaining. Their antics are amusing, their behavior often a comical satire of our own. They enjoy living and pleasing their owners and companions, and if we do not take advantage of this facet of animal interaction, we are missing a very valuable pleasure.

Institutional living, by its very nature, is mundane and prosaic. Routine may vary little from day to day; in fact, it could be argued that a well-run facility, catering to the needs of numerous and varied patients, must adhere to a well-set schedule. Unfortunately, this very routine, which is necessary to order and stability, is boring. A patient who has nothing to look forward to in the future will lose incentive to participate and get involved in the present.

A pet, however, provides a diversion. No matter how routine one's life is, an animal companion is guaranteed to interject unexpected moments—just ask any pet owner. These moments of spontaneity add seasoning and zest to a well-nourished life, and transform a mechanized and impersonal institution into a place that is very much like home.

And, as Dorothy Walster says:

> Even outwardly, well-adjusted, retired people will find pets provide them with an outlet to express their wishes, whims, and fancies. Great sums of money may be spent on pets and the commercial world has not been slow to provide the means to do so. One can even buy recipe books, insurance policies, burial ground, and birthday cards expressly for your pet.[24]

We have no objection to anyone who can afford to do so spending money on their pets, but we find that many of the elderly, institutionalized or living in the community, are on fixed and limited funds. We suggest that seniors instead use their latent creative abilities to fulfill their whims and fancies, and Chapter 7 gives some specific suggestions for doing so.

## THE ANIMAL AS SOCIAL LUBRICANT

### Social Benefits to Patients

We have already discussed numerous ways in which the presence of an animal facilitates social contact with others. In the Robert Andrysco study, the elderly woman first established contact with the therapy dog and eventually was able to interact with the therapist and subsequently the institution's staff.[25] In the Mugford and M'Comisky study, one of the elderly ladies who received the parakeet found she had frequent visits from the neighborhood children after she taught the little bird to recite their names.[26]

Some critics have cautioned that by establishing a bond with the animal the already withdrawn patient may even further withdraw from human contact. The relationship with the animal becomes exclusive of human interaction. Research, however, indicates that this is not the case. In his early work with disturbed adolescents, Corson noticed that this exclusive bonding between patient and dog did occur, but later subsided.[27] Studies to date indicate that the animal acts as a catalyst to social interaction; the preliminary bonding may be exclusively with the pet, but it later expands to include the therapist, other patients and staff within the environment.

The pet is not only something to talk to but something to talk about. The out-patients in the Mugford and M'Comisky study were preoccupied with their state of health, aches and pains, and the like, a preoccupation that affects many of the elderly. With a career finished and a family often far away or out-of-touch, there is little to talk about but oneself and one's complaints. The pet, however, is a topic of conversation that is of interest to everyone.

Clark Brickel noticed that caring for the cat mascots promoted a sense of camaraderie among the patients. Additionally, the affection and tenderness the patients expressed towards the cats generalized to other patients and staff also. By interacting with the cats, the elders learned how to better interact with each other.[28]

### Social Benefits to Everyone

An animal not only promotes conversation and a common bond among a populace in a given environment, but it also facilitates social interaction with strangers, and thus can encourage new friendships and associations for the pet owner.

This effect of an animal as social lubricant was observed by Peter Messent of the Animal Study Center, United Kingdom. Messent's study was prompted by a comment from his colleague, behaviorist Roger Mugford, who remarked that when his "good-looking self was accompanied by a good-looking dog, it facilitated a lot more social interactions during his walks in the park." Messent solicited eight walkers and observed them walking with and without their dogs in Hyde Park, an area outside of their usual route. He found that when the dogs were present, walkers experienced some sort of reaction from passersby on 22% of the walks, compared to only 2%

when the walkers were alone. On three occasions, there was a conversation betwen the walker with his dog and a stranger. Messent then conducted a follow-up study observing walkers with their dogs on their normal route and time of day. On the average his subjects had three spoken interactions per dog walk. One-third of these interactions involved extended conversation, and the tendency for lengthy conversation increased if the passerby also had a dog. Messent concluded that the pet dog increased the potential for social interaction with other people.[29]

Finally, a pet can encourage new friendships and associations via organizations about the animal. No matter what the species, there is at least one, and usually many more, associations concerned with the care of and interest in the pet. Mobile seniors can attend cat shows, bird shows, and dog shows or even get involved in a local conservation group. But even residents confined to an institution need not be excluded. Dog clubs, many of which have slides and programs about their breed or activities, could be encouraged to visit the home. An institution that acquires an animal mascot and would like to encourage outside contact among its patients, even if it is limited to letter-writing, should subscribe to a special interest publication about the animal. Often these publications list pen pals and correspondents who want to exchange information and experiences about their pets.

### Owning a Pet Is Good for Your Health

Intrigued by the studies conducted with infirm populations, Rosanne Wille, PhD, RN, Assistant Professor, College of Nursing, Rutgers University, designed a research project to investigate the effects of pet ownership on a self-defined "healthy" population.

Describing health as " . . . a feeling of wellness that relates to the interaction of the individual with the environment, community, society, family, and friends," she remarks that:

> Health behavior involves action, but it also involves attitude. Health and a feeling of wellness imply that one has a purpose in life. The healthy person is able to set appropriate short, intermediate and longterm goals and to move toward achieving these established goals. This results in a feeling of productivity and usefulness.

There is no question that a pet offers its owner the opportunity for constancy and challenges. The pet-human bond involves unconditional affection, warmth, and loyalty that may serve to reduce the possibility of achieving a state of "existential vacuum." The attachment that one has with a pet may create a purpose that stems from the sense of responsibility that one feels for a loyal pet. Furthermore, a pet allows the owner the opportunity to play and in many ways regress to earlier times. It is socially acceptable for adults to engage in certain forms of playful activity with a pet that would be unacceptable in the absence of that pet. These characteristics of pet-human relationships may significantly influence one's sense of purpose in life as well as one's health behaviors.

To examine her premise, Wille employed the Purpose in Life Test, an attitude scale geared to detect the feeling of emptiness or lack of purpose in life; the Health Opinion Survey which examines the relationship between social factors and neurotic behavior; and the Personal Data Questionnaire designed to obtain the normal data. Wille further included two brief questions; "Please write a short description of the pet and what the pet means to you" and "Do you think that owning a pet has an effect on your health status?"

Two selected populations were used: a mailing to members of a local dog club and distribution to clients in a veterinary practice. The subjects were 47 female and 13 males ranging in age from 20 to 80, with the majority between 21 and 40 years of age. None had any disabling mental or physical disorders, and all participants owned at least one pet.

All but one subject responded to the open-ended question of what the pet means to the person: 45 of the 60 subjects mentioned the word companion; 25 regarded the pet as a child surrogate; 32 mentioned affection; 46 said the pet was a family member; and 54 indicated that the pet gave them pleasure.

An analysis of the study revealed that pet owners scored significantly higher on the Purpose in Life Test and the Health Opinion Survey than a randomly selected sample of subjects. Additionally, the pet owners who described their pets as family members scored significantly higher on both tests than those who did not. Pet owners who described the animals as companions scored significantly higher on the Health Opinion Survey than those who did not.

Analysis by sex revealed that women were more likely to describe the pet as a family member or a child and men were more likely to look upon the pet as a companion.

In conclusion, Wille notes:

> The results of this study show that pet ownership does affect one's attitude toward health and toward purpose in life. In addition to this, people who consider pets as family members and companions score higher on tools that assess purpose in life and health opinion than those who do not.
>
> For centuries, pets have been a part of family life. Empirically, pets have been shown to be of significance in terms of leisure activity and diversion. The fact that, under scientific scrutiny, pet ownership has been shown to affect health opinion and sense of purpose in life is of major importance. This implies that pet ownership is not solely a diversion or hobby but may make a major contribution to the health and well-being of an individual, particularly if the pet is considered to be a companion or a family member.[30]

## SPECIAL SERVICES

The physical, psychological, and social benefits provided by an animal companion are available to anyone who is willing to accept them. They are exclusive of age, sex, health, condition, or living environment; and they are rich and varied indeed. But for those who have special needs, physical impairments, for example, the animal companion assumes an even more significant role.

### Guide Dogs for the Blind

Guide dogs do far more than enhance the blind's mobility, according to a study by Alysia Zee of the University of Pennsylvania who found that these dogs have a threefold physical, psychological, and social impact on their owners.

Social scientist Zee hypothesized that people who owned guide dogs for at least one year would report an increased capacity to cope with the stress of visual impairment. To validate her theory, she sent two sets of questionnaires to a population of 44 guide dog owners. The first questionnaire was designed to describe the relationship between the blind owners and their dogs. The second questionnaire was designed to describe more concretely the problems associated with blindness in a vision-oriented society. The subjects were also asked to explain how the dog helped them cope or not cope with these problems.

The first questionnaire revealed that the relationship between the owner and dog centered on the owner's knowledge of his canine companion's special needs and capabilities. Owners reported that the dogs had to be cared for personally and consistently to reinforce the bond between them; at work, the animal had to be regulated, systematically rewarded, and corrected in clear concise terms. The dog required respect, affection and attention and, at times, had to be calmed and protected when the work was extremely stressful. "The needs and capabilities of blind individuals and guide dogs are blended together in a facilitative way," says Zee, "if certain behaviors are maintained and exchanged."

In the second questionnaire, the owners identified problems particularly relevant to blindness. These included frustration, overprotection by others, isolation, dependency, depression, sedentariness, fear of movement, rigidity of activities, self-consciousness, tension, environmental discrimination, and goal achievement.

"In many reported instances," says Zee, "the dog seems to be an impetus, a catalyst for growth and change." The positive aspects of guide dog ownership included: acceptance of life and risk-taking, expression of feelings, assertiveness, personal achievement, orientation to the present, relaxation, improved body image, faster walking pace, freedom of movement, security, self-control, self-awareness, separation from home, tolerance for various weather conditions, and opportunities for social contact. Some of the negative aspects of owning the dog included worry about health of dog, anxiety, embarrassment, threat of loss, accounting for dog with others, and conflicts in home or public.[31]

### Signal and Service Dogs

The California-based Canine Companions for Independence trains dogs in three categories. The Social dog is trained to become a member of an institution, to interact with patients there, and in general to enhance the environment of the facility. Service and Signal dogs, however, are trained to be the companions of people who live outside of an institution in their own homes. A Signal dog is placed with the hearing-impaired; a Service dog will become the companion of someone who is physically disabled. Like guide dogs, they provide a wealth of benefits to their owners.

"While the physical assistance provided by both the Service and Signal dog is not directly related to the traditional concept of pet therapy, the added confidence and ability to function once again in the mainstream of society has a definite psychological effect,'' says Kerrill Knaus, placement coordinator for the organization.

> In the case of a person who has received a substantial physical disability as the result of a stroke or other ailment, the assistance of a Service dog can make the difference between spending the remainder of the individual's lifetime in an institution or being able to function again at home and sometimes even at work. As hearing loss is often a common problem among the elderly, Signal dogs can greatly reduce the sense of isolation and the vulnerability among this population. Again, the indirect benefits are that these individuals are therefore able to maintain a better self-image as well as to stay in touch with reality in the surrounding world.[32]

At the San Francisco SPCA, unwanted shelter animals get a new chance for a rich, purposeful life as companions for the deaf. Dogs selected are trained by the society and, although the cost of training is estimated to be about $2,500, placed free of charge with their hearing-impaired owners. Simba and Casper are two such placements.

"One of the reasons for getting a Hearing Dog," says Cyrus Colburn, the happy owner of Simba, a spunky Airedale mix who was the first Hearing Dog placed with a resident of the Monterey Peninsula, "is that the amount of dependency upon hearing people decreases. It means that I can now live by myself instead of depending upon my family or friends to let me know when the phone rings or someone is at the door."

Ambitious and determined, Colburn had the honor of receiving the first BA granted to a deaf person by the University of California at San Diego. "I have always taken a great pioneering step for deaf persons," he says, "being the first deaf graduate from UCSD and taking many posts not filled by deaf persons, and so I find I have a great deal of educating to do. If my life's work is to produce an independency for the deaf, then Simba has played a major role."[33]

For Robert Schaufele of Chula Vista, California, Hearing Dog Casper, a spaniel mix, meant freedom from anxiety and worry during business trips. Both Schaufele and his wife Margarita suffer profound hearing impairment, and have been victimized by burglars since they cannot hear a burglar alarm. Before Casper arrived, the

Schaufeles lost a $10,000 recreational vehicle because their neighbor, although hearing the alarm, did not realize it was theirs.

In addition to the original sounds he learned, Casper also responds to a special signal in the house connected to the Schaufeles' new vehicle, so they will not suffer another loss. And when the microwave oven beeps, Casper tells his owners that dinner is served. But most importantly, Robert's fear and anxiety for his wife's safety is gone. "I felt a Hearing Dog would be good company for Margarita and protection for her," he says. "Casper has lived up to those expectations and has become much more than a trained, working dog. He has become a part of the family, a devoted, faithful companion."[34]

The dogs perform a valuable service as ears to the deaf, but all the elements of the human/animal bond are there also. An elderly woman who received a Hearing Dog through the People-Pet-Partnership Program, told Leo Bustad: "I needed a hearing dog, yes, but most of all I needed a companion."[35]

Boris Levinson perhaps summarizes the value of pets most succinctly: "A pet is an island of sanity in what appears to be an 'insane' world," he says. "Friendship retains its traditional values and securities in one's relationship with one's pet. Whether a dog, cat, bird, fish, turtle, or what have you, one can rely upon the fact that one's pet will always remain a faithful, intimate, non-competitive friend—regardless of the good or ill fortune life brings upon us."[36]

## REFERENCES

1. Friedmann, E.; Katcher, A.H.; Lynch, J.J.; and Thomas, S.A. "Animal Companions and One-year Survival of Patients After Discharge from a Coronary Care Unit." *Public Health Reports* 95(4): 307-312.

2. Friedmann, E.; Katcher, A.H.; and Meislich, D. "When Pet Owners Are Hospitalized: Significance of Companion Animals During Hospitalization." Research presentation at the International Conference on the Human/Companion Animal Bond; October 5-7, 1981, Philadelphia, PA.

3. Katcher, Aaron H. "Health and the Living Environment." Address at the International Conference on the Human/Companion Animal Bond, October 5-7, 1981, Philadelphia, PA.

4. Katcher, A.H.; Friedmann, E.; Beck, A.; and Lynch, J. "Talking, Looking and Blood Pressure: Physiological Consequences of Interaction with the Living Environment." Research presentation at the International Conference on the Human/Companion Animal Bond, October 5-7, 1981, Philadelphia, PA.

5. Lynch, James. Comment to "Companion Animals and the Aged." Address at the International Conference on the Human/Companion Animal Bond, October 5-7, 1981, Philadelphia, PA.

6. Andrysco, Robert M. "Pet Facilitated Therapy in a Retirement Nursing Care Com-

munity." Research presentation at the International Conference on the Human/Companion Animal Bond, October 5-7, 1981, Philadelphia, PA.

7. "The Therapist with a Floppy Ear." *Our Animals.* Quarterly journal of the San Francisco Society for the Prevention of Cruelty to Animals, Spring 1982.

8. Walster, Dorothy. "Pets and the Elderly." *The Latham Letter,* Summer 1982.

9. Ibid.

10. Vogel, L.E.; Quigley, J.S.; and Anderson, R.K. "A Study of Perceptions and Attitudes Towards Pet Ownership." Research presentation at the International Conference on the Human/Companion Animal Bond, October 5-7, 1981, Philadelphia, PA.

11. Lynch, James J. "Warning: Living Alone Is Dangerous to Your Health." *U.S. News and World Report,* June 20, 1980.

12. Corson, S.A. and E.O. "Pet Animals as Nonverbal Communication Mediators in Psychotherapy in Institutional Settings." In *Ethology and Nonverbal Communication in Mental Health: An Interdisciplinary Biopsychosocial Exploration.* Oxford: Pergamon Press. 1979.

13. Levinson, Boris M. "Nursing Home Pets: A Psychological Adventure for the Patient." *The National Humane Review,* July-August 1970.

14. Katcher, A.H. "Health and the Living Environment."

15. Lockwood, Randall. "The Influence of Animals on Social Perception." Research presentation at the International Conference on the Human/Companion Animal Bond, October 5-7, 1981, Philadelphia, PA.

16. Katcher, A.H. op. cit.

17. Mugford, R.A., and M'Comisky, J.G. "Some Recent Work on the Psychotherapeutic Value of Cage Birds With Old People." In *Pet Animals and Society,* Anderson, R.S., ed. London: Balliere Tindall, 1975.

18. Bustad, Leo K. "Companion Animals and the Aged." Address presented at the International Conference on the Human/Companion Animal Bond, October 5-7, 1981, Philadelphia, PA.

19. Arkow, Phil. *"Pet Therapy": A Study of the Use of Companion Animals in Selected Therapies.* Colorado Springs: The Humane Society of the Pikes Peak Region, 1982.

20. Brickel, Clark M. "The Therapeutic Roles of Cat Mascots with a Hospital-based Geriatric Population: A Staff Survey." *The Gerontologist, 19*(4): 368-72.

21. Andrysco, R.M. Personal Communication.

22. McCulloch, Michael J. "Talking with . . . " *Redbook Magazine,* February 1982.

23. Harris, Judy. "Dogs Contribute to Ego Strength: Highlights from an MA Thesis." *The Latham Letter,* Winter 1981-82.

24. Walster, Dorothy. "The Role of Pets in the Mental Health of the Elderly." Paper available from the Latham Foundation, March 1979.

25. Andrysco, R.M. Personal Communication.

26. Mugford and M'Comisky. op. cit.

27. Arkow, Phil. op. cit.

28. Brickel, C.M. op. cit.

29. Messent, Peter R. "Facilitation of Social Interaction by Companion Animals." Research presentation at the International Conference on the Human/Companion Animal Bond, October 5-7, 1981, Philadelphia, PA.

30. Wille, Roseanne. "Rutgers Report on Pet Ownership and Health Stresses Value of H/CAB for Healthy Populations." *The Latham Letter,* Spring 1982, pp. 10-11.

31. Zee, Alysia. "Guide Dogs and Their Owners: Assistance and Friendship." Research presentation at the International Conference on the Human/Companion Animal Bond, October 5-7, 1981, Philadelphia, PA.

32. Knaus, Kerrill. Personal Communication.

33. San Francisco SPCA. "Meet Cyrus Colburn and Simba." Leaflet from The San Francisco SPCA Hearing Dog Program.

34. Ibid. "Meet Robert and Margarita Schaufele and Casper."

35. Bustad, L.K. op. cit.

36. Levinson, B.M. op. cit.

Photo by Bob Barber.

# Chapter 4

# Training a Therapy Dog

The foundation of successful dog therapy is a well-trained dog, and the value of such animals has been noted in the previously cited research studies by Corson, Andrysco, JACOPIS, and Thompson. Although it is beyond the scope of this book to discuss techniques and procedures in-depth, this chapter is presented to introduce the reader to the concepts involved and, most importantly, to stress the importance of such training.

Proper training is observed more in its omission than its presence. Consider the obedient, well-trained dog: it greets a friend or stranger pleasantly and calmly. It will not engage in incessant barking. While its owner is chatting or engaged in other activity, the dog waits quietly for its handler's next demand. Walking the dog is no problem; further, the animal is not destructive in the home or residence and causes the owner no undue worry. The obedient dog is a pleasant family member whose good manners and polite behavior seem natural.

But consider for a moment the opposite: a dog who greets a visitor with an exuberant lunge so boisterous it almost knocks one down or in the case of a small animal, paws incessantly at the legs. On a leash, the dog moves or doesn't move at its own pace, often dragging the owner along. And the owner dares not for a moment let go of the leash for fear the animal will take off through city traffic, country lanes, or an institution's corridors.

In the first example, anyone meeting the dog may likely take its calm and obedient behavior for granted. It is simply a nice dog and doesn't appear to have any distinguishing characteristics. In the second case, however, the ill-mannered pup will surely be remembered as that dog that barks all the time or knocks you over; if not a totally negative experience, certainly not a positive one.

Although there are immense individual personality differences between dogs, the primary difference between the two examples is not temperament, but a simple matter of training. The first dog has been properly trained to obey its owner's wishes, whereas the second has not. Obviously the first dog is a happier pet with a happier owner than the second. Unfortunately, the vast majority of pet dogs in the U.S. today fall into the latter category, a factor that no doubt contributes to the staggering number of animals abandoned or turned in to shelters yearly. This is especially tragic because virtually any dog can be trained relatively simply and most pet owners with proper instruction and practice can learn how to do so.

## *THE SOCIAL NATURE OF THE DOG*

Canines train easily because of their social nature. Dogs are the domestic cousins and ancestors of the wolf, social carnivores who in the wild live in an elaborate and complex social structure. In the wolf pack, which is an extended family group, the individual members cooperate for the good of the group as a whole. The leadership of the pack is handled by an alpha male and female who govern the activities of the others. Young animals are reared by all pack members, and the young wolf not only learns the skills necessary for survival, but also the social mechanisms that enable the pack to live together.

Anyone who has had several dogs at one time has probably noticed that the animals form a natural hierarchy; that is, one of them assumes a more aggressive, bossy, or dominant role over the others. This is a necessary survival mechanism for wild-living canines that their domestic descendants retain. The canine willingness to accept a pack leader facilitates training. The primary difference is that with the pet dog, the human handler/owner assumes the role of alpha wolf.

Many problems with later aggression in dogs can no doubt be linked to lack of dominance over the animal. Dominance, incidentally, is not established by cruel or painful means, but simply by control and discipline. By early obedience training, the dog learns to accept its master as the "boss," the "alpha personage," and once this is established, the dog will do anything he can to please you. In wolf society, young and low-ranked animals pay homage to the higher ranked individuals by a series of soliciting and submissive behaviors. If they do not, they are disciplined by older members of the pack. The same principles apply to dog training.

## THE VALUE OF PROPER TRAINING

From our brief examples at the beginning of this chapter, it should be obvious that the obedient, well-trained dog is a happier, more welcome member of the human family, community, or institution. And it should be obvious that a controlled animal is far less likely to cause property damage, run away, or otherwise distress its owner. But an even more pressing reason exists to stress the value of dog training.

In studies in both the U.S. and the United Kingdom, aggression in dogs is reported to be the number one problem that owners have with their pets. It accounts for more than half the cases in which the pet owner seeks outside counseling.

Veterinarian Victoria Voith of the Animal Behavior Clinic of the University of Pennsylvania found that of 100 cases interviewed, 99% reported their pet's problem as serious or very serious. Most of the problems involved intact (non-castrated) males.[1]

In a similar survey from the United Kingdom, British behaviorist Roger Mugford found, in a sample of 300 owners who needed counseling, 70% of the cases involved aggression problems. Through counseling and training, Mugford has had a success rate of seven out of 10, and reports that 40% of the dogs improve immediately.[2]

Veterinarian Katherine Houpt, associate professor of physiology at the New York State College of Veterinary Medicine at Cornell University, cites abnormal or inappropriate behaviors of dogs as the cause of most disruptions of the pet/owner bond, and the most frequent and potentially damaging behavior problem mentioned is aggression.

In a review of dog owners seeking counseling, Houpt reports:

> A detailed history was taken which often revealed that an apparently sudden onset of aggression had been preceded by instances of dominance or aggressive behavior. Frequently, the owners had inadvertently rewarded aggression.
>
> The owners were instructed to promptly punish any form of aggression, growling, snapping, barking but then to give the dog a command such as down or sit and to praise the animal for performing correctly. This simple exercise in teaching the dog the difference between acceptable and unacceptable behavior was combined with regular obedience sessions by all members of the family.[3]

Houpt reports a 70% success rate based on those who replied to her follow-up letter. Unfortunately, 50% of her survey did not respond and could not be reached by telephone. "If I count those as failures, my success rate is 30%," she notes, considerably less that her British colleague.

But as Houpt points out:

> I think that British dogs are fewer, better behaved, and rarely allowed to run free. This is in part due to the lack of violent crime that in this country leads to acquisition of dogs for protection as well as companionship. The dogs are encouraged to be aggressive, and the owners are surprised when the aggression may be directed toward their family or neighbors.

Houpt reports that her success rate is getting even better since, following the example of Mugford and Voith, she is concentrating on rewarding non-aggression rather than relying upon punishment of aggression.

"Early obedience training can help to prevent possible behavior problems, but only if obedience work is practiced in the home by all involved with the dog," she comments.[4]

## TRAINING OF THE CANINE CO-THERAPIST

We strongly recommend a minimum of a novice obedience course or its equivalent for any canine used in a therapeutic situation, either as visitor or in-residence pet. That is, the dog should walk mannerly on leash, sit down, lie down, stay, and come when it is instructed to do so. Additional training is highly recommended. A well-trained obedient dog is not only entertaining and useful, but the dog's exemplary behavior can obviate many potential objections to placing the animal in the institution.

## WHAT IS OBEDIENCE TRAINING?

Obedience training involves teaching a dog to perform certain behaviors at a given signal from the handler. These behaviors may be as simple as sitting at the owner's side or as complex as retrieving a selected object after dealing with a series of obstacles or barriers. The signals may be verbal or non-verbal or a combination of the two. Novice obedience instruction involves teaching the dog to respond to a verbal command and an accompanying hand signal. Later, as the dog learns, the spoken word can be eliminated. Some handlers have so expertly trained their animals that the dog responds to the slightest non-verbal signal, a roll of the eye or the slight flex of a finger. These signals may be imperceptible to the human audience, but are easily picked up by the trained dog whose full attention is focused on his owner. Even someone completely unacquainted with the sport of dog obedience has only to turn on the television and watch a program featuring a canine actor. What appears amazing on the screen is simply an extension of the principles involved in basic obedience training.

When training begins, the dog is conditioned to associate a given behavior with a given command. To solidify this association, the behavior is reinforced; that is, if the dog performs correctly, it is rewarded for doing so. Just a simple example will demonstrate.

## A Sample Training Procedure

We will demonstrate the command of sit, a simple and very useful behavior that most dogs learn easily.

Begin by making sure that you have the dog's attention; that he is involved with you and watching you. The dog should be standing at your left side with the leash held loosely in your right hand. Say the command "Sit," loud and distinct, and at the same time press lightly on the dog's hindquarters until he takes a sitting position. The first time he can only be expected to hold this for a few seconds, but if he does it correctly, praise him lavishly, both verbally ("Good dog!") and physically with warm hugs. You may also wish to give your obedient pet a biscuit or favored food treat as a reward for his obedience. Practice the command a few more times, and each time as the dog successfully completes the exercise, reinforce him with praise, affection, and, if you wish, food. The dog is learning that the word "Sit" means reclining on his haunches. The reward reinforces or strengthens the association. Basically, that's all there is to the principles behind obedience training. The most important elements of successful training are consistency, practice, and reinforcement. The dog will learn quickly what you want him to do and retain that knowledge, but he will easily become confused if, for example, you instruct him to sit and then jerk the leash which propels him to move.

## OBEDIENCE TITLES: WHAT THEY MEAN

The American Kennel Club recognizes distinct levels of obedience training, and honors dogs who have achieved such training with a letter designation behind their name. To achieve these titles, the dogs must perform a designated series of behaviors in competition with other dogs. The exercises each have a point value (totaling 200 points in each class); and to qualify for the title, the dog must have a score of at least 170, and be certified by three different judges. That is, the dog must have attained this score at three different competitions. Additionally, the dog must have earned 50% of the possible points in any given exercise. Points are awarded on how proficiently the dog performs each exercise, and points are lost by behaviors such as whining, sniffing, etc. The titles that can be earned are:

*CD (Companion Dog).* The CD title is the first title that an obedience-trained dog will attain. A dog must learn several easy and useful exercises and perform them on leash and by voice command from its handler. We strongly recommend a CD title or equivalent training as the absolute minimum training required before a dog is considered for a therapeutic situation.

To earn the CD title, the dog must heel on leash and off leash; it must stand for examination; perform the long sit, the long down; and the recall (come to its owner when called). The recall is in three parts: the dog must sit at a distance from its owner, come to the owner when called and sit in front of him, and upon another command, take the heeling position at the owner's left side. The value of any dog knowing these basic lessons should be readily apparent.

*CDX (Companion Dog Excellent).* The CDX title is the second level of training in an obedience course. The dog performs all the above tasks, but must do so off-leash and at a distance from its handler. In the long down for the CDX title, for example, the dog must lie down for five minutes and the handlers must be out of sight of the dog. Additionally, the CDX dog is required to leap a high jump one and one-half times its height (certain allowances are made for certain breeds) and perform a broad jump. The CDX dog will retrieve a dumbbell both on a flat surface and over a hurdle. The dog must also respond to the drop (lie down) during recall. If the usefulness of this command does not seem readily apparent, consider the following: suppose your dog is paying a friendly and welcome visit to a neighbor who lives across the street. You call the dog to return home and realize too late that a car is rapidly speeding down the road. You promptly give a ''drop'' command and the dog immediately falls to the ground. Because your dog is trained, you were able to avert its deadly encounter with the speeding automobile.

The retrieving and jumping exercises are the precursors to a wide range of activities that are entertaining as well as useful. A CDX trained dog can be easily taught to bring a slipper, for example, to a patient when asked.

*UD (Utility Dog) or UDT (Utility Dog Tracking).* A UD or UDT trained dog is a model of canine prowess. The UD dog performs all the tasks of a CDX dog, but does them by hand signal command only. During novice training, most instructors recommend that the handler train the dog with a combination of voice and hand signals. Later, as the dog becomes familiar with the exercises, the voice commands become unnecessary and the dog will respond to a simple hand movement. Those who train dogs for stage and screen and for entertainment purposes can make a fine art out of this instruction. The dog can be trained to respond to the most minute flex of a finger or elevation of the hand. Often the actual command is imperceptible to the human audience who assume the gifted performer is an exceptionally smart pup. Actually, the dog is simply responding to signals from its trainer. Unlike a human audience who are easily distracted, the dog's attention is focused entirely on its master. While the audience ''oos'' and ''ahs,'' the obedient dog is watching his handler intently waiting for the next signal.

Additionally, the UD dog will jump over a selected hurdle (the handler's choice) and retrieve a wooden or metal object. Dogs naturally resist picking up metal objects, so this training actually overcomes the animal's instinctual aversion to the substance. UD dogs are also trained to discriminate their owner's scent, thus being able to select their handler's glove, for example, from a medley of identical-appearing items.

The T or tracking title is obtained solely on the basis of tracking ability. The dog must follow a pre-set trail by scent (their owner's or a stranger's). Although this is often the last title sought, many dogs display a natural ability for this work and training in this exercise can begin very early in addition to novice obedience work.

## Schutzhund Training

Popular for years in Germany where the methods originated, Schutzhund training has only recently emerged in the U.S. Like the American Kennel Club titles, CD, CDX, and UD, the Schutzhund training also involves three levels of expertise, with the Schutzhund III being the most advanced title. The primary difference between the training procedures however, is that all three levels of Schutzhund require some tracking prowess, which is a separate title in the American Kennel Club. Additionally, all levels of Schutzhund training require some protection training. Therapy dog Sam is a fine example of a dog trained in all levels of American Kennel Club and Schutzhund obedience.

### A Protection and Tracking Dog Named Sam

Sam, a German Shepherd dog, and his owner Ursula Kempe of Chester, New Jersey, are founding members of Therapy Dogs International and participated in the organization's first demonstration.

At the age of eight, Sam has completed all levels of American Kennel Club obedience training and Schutzhund training. Additionally, because of his tracking prowess, Sam served a brief stint as a certified Search and Rescue Dog. Groups of these dogs and their handlers are called in to locate missing persons, particularly victims of natural disasters, such as avalanches.

Sam was trained to all his titles by Kempe, who began training dogs by reading obedience manuals. Later, she attended classes and seminars, but does not want to take much credit for Sam's accomplishments. "He has a natural retriever instinct," she says. "He has always loved to work and to find things." Additionally, she describes him as "sweet as pie" with a delightful sense of humor. "Sam is a huge dog and will often run up to you and push you with his nose. You must pretend to be startled or he's disappointed."

Sam's bedside manner comes naturally. Since he is so large, just a mammoth paw on a frail lap might be too heavy. "I tell him, be gentle, Sam, but I really don't have to," says Kempe. "He instinctively understands and some of the little old ladies are a bit afraid of him at first. Then when they begin to pet his big head, they quickly lose their fear."

"I think it is important for people to understand that a dog who is properly trained as a protection dog is not vicious or mean," she says. "The protection work is simply one aspect of their training, a job they can do when they are called upon to do it."

Sam, a gentle, affectionate therapist, is a splendid example of the many roles a well-trained dog can fulfill.

## HOW TO SELECT A TRAINING FACILITY

Obedience training is a multi-faceted sport and similar to other competitive endeavors, abounds with numerous different theories and methods in its practice. It is beyond the scope of this book to discuss in detail the various training methods and procedures; the interested reader is invited to pursue these subjects on his own. (See our bibliography for selected readings.) Instead, we will present guidelines for selecting a facility and/or instructor who will teach you to train your dog. Many individuals who have experience in this area can successfully train their dogs at home without outside instruction; however, for the novice who has no prior experience, we strongly recommend a formal training school and a qualified instructor. Often there are many such schools in a given geographic area, and costs are usually nominal (about $25 for 10 lessons), particularly if the owner is part of a large class of other pet owners. Below are some guidelines to help you choose such a facility.

### (1) Recommendations

Perhaps the best endorsement that a training instructor or facility can have is a multitude of successfully trained dogs. Do the trainer's dogs or those of his students have American Kennel Club titles? Is the trainer part of an obedience club in his area? Have the trainer's dogs achieved special commendations? (For example, Diane Bauman who operates an obedience school in Sparta, New Jersey, successfully trained her Golden Retriever Charo, who is also a therapy dog, to the renowned title of "Superdog" at the 1981 Gaines Obedience Classic.) Beware of any self-proclaimed instructor who has nothing to show for his/her alleged expertise.

### (2) What Is the Trainer's Philosophy—Is It Compatible with Yours?

Perhaps the two most controversial areas of dog training are reward and correction, but there are some generally accepted methods upon which most reputable trainers concur.

### Reward or Positive Reinforcement

Reward or positive reinforcement is the basis of dog training, and properly rewarding a dog for good and accepted behavior is even more important than correcting a dog for bad behavior. Food as a reward remains controversial; some trainers swear by it, others say it is totally unnecessary and insist it only creates future problems. Whether or not you decide to use a food treat or not, it should never replace praise; that is, verbal and physical praise for the dog's proper behavior.

The primary reward for a dog is praise from its owner. Not only is this pleasurable for both you and the animal, but it strengthens the pet/owner bond between you. Remember that you are the pack leader, and your pet wants to please you. If it knows it is doing something you want it to do, it will learn that behavior all the quicker.

We would not recommend any trainer who said that talking to and hugging the dog was unnecessary. As we mentioned, food may or may not be used. Generally, the use of a food treat as a bonus can facilitate training, particularly an exercise that may be difficult for the dog. It is also a valuable incentive for the older dog, for example, who has not had previous training and may even have some bad habits to unlearn. Never use food treats as a replacement for praise, and under no circumstances, withhold a meal as a form of correction. The dog's meals are part of its basic care requirements.

### Correction or Negative Reinforcement

Correction or negative reinforcement is an even more controversial subject, since some methods appear to cause discomfort to the animal even though they may not. The situation is further confounded since the term "punishment," which suggests painful or punitive measures, is often used as a synonym for correction. Punishment, however, can be as benign and innocuous as simply withholding attention from the dog. We much prefer the use of the term "correction"; however, should the reader come across references to punishment in the training literature, he/she should not automatically assume the term implies painful methods. Judge the method on its own merit. We do, however, urge the reader to avoid any trainer who uses harsh, cruel, or otherwise painful methods to produce the desired results.

How do we define harsh or cruel methods? After all, there are some very sensitive souls who do not even like to yell at an animal, let alone use physical means to discipline it. There are some generally accepted methods that, while they appear rough, are not painful to the dog, but only annoying or at worst humiliating.

Perhaps the most important thing to remember is that, dogs, like people, are individuals. There are those who will respond to the slightest inflection of their owner's tone of voice; others need far more to convince them who is the boss. Correction should always be administered depending upon the dog's personality, the temperamental proclivities of its breed, and, of course, its size.

A dog who refuses to heel on leash is often corrected by a sharp tug on the leash and the severity of the tug can depend upon how unruly, how big, and how unmanageable the dog is. This does not hurt the dog; it is annoying to him. A small dog will usually need only a light tug, a larger dog might require a lot more effort. But again there are exceptions. For example, an Irish Wolfhound is an incredibly large dog, standing over seven feet on its hind legs and weighing well over 100 pounds. Wolfhounds, however, are the gentlest of dogs and have an extraordinary desire to please their owners. Usually only the mildest correction is sufficient to teach these gentle giants what you wish them to do.

A good trainer will have had experience with many different breeds and should be sensitive to your dog as an individual. Beware of any trainer who uses excessive force on a dog, or uses anything other than his hand to correct the dog. For example, an accepted correction for undesirable behavior such as snapping is a firm slap under the chin, accompanied by a loud and decisive "No!". This does not hurt the dog; it startles him and informs him that you find his action unacceptable. You should not, however, kick the dog, hit the dog with a newspaper or any other object, nor correct the dog from behind. The dog should know that the same hand that cuddles, pets, and feeds him is also dissatisfied with him.

Finally, beware of any trainer who emphasizes correction over reward. And, if any trainer says that in order to have an obedient animal, you must instill "fear" in your dog, look elsewhere for instruction. A trained dog is loving, healthy and happy; he fulfills his owner's expectations because he knows what they are; he is only too willing to please once he knows what you want. Fear should never be a part of this relationship.

### (3) See a Class in Person Before You Enroll

When you have selected an instructor or facility, ask to sit in on a class or two and watch carefully. Are there enough instructors for the size of the class? Often a trainer has several apprentice instructors who help the owners train their dogs. Although group classes cannot offer as individualized instruction as a private class, some effort should be made to deal with the individual problems encountered by the owners.

Does the trainer encourage questions? Does he encourage the owners to speak up if they do not understand an exercise or if they have a special problem with it? Is the trainer's own dog a well-trained canine and a good example for the students?

Watch particularly how the trainer instructs the class to administer praise and correction. If a trainer uses any method that you question or feel may be excessive, ask about it. If you are still uncomfortable after his explanation, ask another source.

## SPECIALIZED TRAINING

Dogs can be trained to lead the blind, to act as ears for the hearing-impaired, and even function as arms and legs for the handicapped. This specialized training involves many months of instruction, and the final phase usually is geared to the dog's new owner and his special needs. But the cornerstone of this and any other training is basic obedience work. Hearing dogs, for example, are trained to alert their owners to the onset of a particular sound. Service dogs who aid the handicapped will pick up a variety of objects that the disabled owner may need. This is an extension of the dog's retrieving instinct. In Appendix II, we list various organizations that train dogs for special purposes, and we urge readers to contact these groups if they require a dog who has such special skills. For example, the previously mentioned California-based Canine Companions for Independence trains Social dogs who function as co-therapists in institutional settings, Signal dogs who assist the hearing-impaired, and Service dogs whose wide-based training and multi-faceted abilities allow the disabled to lead independent lives.

The story of Thunder, which follows, is a superb example of the limitless ability of a therapy dog and the extraordinary bond that develops between such a dog and his owner.

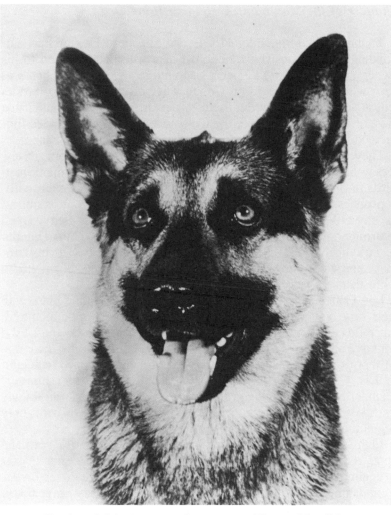

Thunder, a helping hand dog. Photo courtesy of Betty and Len Cohen.

## Thunder of the Mountain: A Helping Hand Dog

Thunder was a much-loved German Shepherd Dog and an outstanding companion who functioned as a true helping hand to his owners, Len and Betty Cohen of Montville, NJ. Betty Cohen was born without arms, and Len Cohen was born with one arm. With only a single hand between them to perform the myriad tasks that most of us take for granted, the Cohens, early in their married life, decided that a well-trained dog could make life easier for them.

They obtained Thunder, a four-month-old puppy, from a New Jersey State Trooper who trained bloodhounds and German Shepherds for the police department. Their first meeting, however, hardly prophesied things things to come. Unaccustomed to automobiles, the shy little pup became carsick and vomited all over Betty. Upon returning home, he got sick in the house. They named him Thunder because his heavy footsteps thudded throughout the house. In retrospect, these early misadventures were but a humorous beginning to a life that was rich in service and devotion.

Len Cohen's first impulse was to join a dog training class with their new family member. He was told he could not be admitted. Since dogs in America are taught to heel at the left side and he did not have a left arm, instructors felt he would only disrupt the class. At that time, there were few provisions for handicapped handlers; so Len Cohen got a book and started to train Thunder himself. Thunder responded well and by the age of seven months was already starting to do things for them. His full prowess, however, was only beginning to be realized.

Lights in the Cohen home are turned on and off with a cord and upon returning home one evening, Thunder noticed his master struggling to pull it. He proceeded to do it for him. Realizing his accomplishment, "he turned on every light in the house," says Betty. This, say the Cohens, was one of his earliest feats.

Thunder performed a variety of tasks around the home. He cleared the dinner table and placed dishes in the sink. He brought out the vacuum cleaner for Betty and followed her around with the needed attachments held in a basket he carried in his mouth. Thunder opened the door; and when the phone rang he answered it. A friendly growl informed the caller that they had indeed dialed the Cohen residence. Thunder liked to play Parchesi, but, say the Cohens, he cheated. He liked to roll the dice and often did so even when it was not his turn. His special sport was Frisbee, and he was

Thunder, a helping hand dog. Photo courtesy of Betty and Len Cohen.

always willing to make a game out of catching the flying disks in the air.

Thunder's helping hand extended beyond the home. He picked up mail for the Cohens at the local post office and delivered their bank deposit every Friday. "We would drive to the bank," says Len, "and Thunder would jump out of the window with the deposit in his mouth. He never waited in line but went right up to his favorite teller to make the deposit. No one ever complained." Except once, recalls Len, when he was cited for violation of New Jersey's leash law. At the court hearing, however, the judge ruled that since Thunder was a working dog and not a pet, the ruling did not apply. This valuable legal decision was a precedent for service dogs. Recently California passed legislation that legally grants service dogs the same privileges as guide dogs for the blind, and similar legislation has been introduced into other states. Thunder, however, enjoyed those privileges years before. "He carried a letter," says Len, "explaining that he was a helping hand dog for the handicapped. No one ever questioned it, and he was admitted everywhere."

As word of Thunder's abilities spread, he was dubbed the "wonder dog," a title he assuredly earned. The Cohens were invited throughout the U.S. and Canada to display the prowess of their incredible helpmate. Since Len and Betty have always been outspoken advocates of independent lives for the handicapped, they were more than willing to accept these invitations. Thunder traveled throughout North America and was invited to the White House where he met then president Richard Nixon. He also accompanied his owners to a special dinner held in the Senate dining room and was the first and last canine to be so honored.

In 1974 Thunder became the first dog accepted into the Raritan Valley German Shepherd Dog Club Hall of Fame. His placque reads: "To Thunder whose loyal devotion and faithful service to his master is a reminder that a dog is one of man's most precious gifts." In 1979 Thunder was elected Grand Marshall and led the Parade of Champions and Service Dogs at the German Shepherd Specialty show. In the last two years of his life, his hearing became impaired, and he was fitted with a special hearing aid collar designed by the Director of the National Rehabilitation Institute of Engineering in Butler, New Jersey.

Thunder died in 1981 at the ripe old (canine) age of 16½. Had he

Thunder, a helping hand dog. Photo courtesy of Betty and Len Cohen.

lived to be 100, his life would still have been too short for the Cohens.

Although Thunder was trained entirely by his master, Len Cohen denies he has any special abilities as a trainer. The credit, he says, should all go to Thunder.

"What he learned to do was less extraordinary than the fact that he did it so effortlessly. He was constantly in tune to us, looking for things to do for us; and in that sense, was a workaholic in every sense of the word. He instinctively knew our needs. As soon as he understood what we wanted him to do, he did it." says Len. "If I asked him to get my pen, he went to the bedroom and took it out of my jacket pocket. He could carry an open soft-drink can upstairs for Betty without spilling a drop. He would find and pick up a penny on the floor."

"Sometimes I think he could read my thoughts," says Betty. "Being with Thunder was like being with a person. He understood everything we said and thought. Even his facial expressions were human. He lived with us, went everywhere with us, did everything with us. It's been two years since he died, and I still can't believe he's gone."

"When he died," says Betty,

> some friends of ours suggested I get a monkey. They had heard of projects that train primates to assist paraplegics and quadriplegics. But I didn't want a monkey. Could you imagine me taking a monkey to a restaurant? A dog is different; you can take a dog anywhere. They are like "people." Besides, what could a monkey do that Thunder couldn't do.

Although the Cohens have a new puppy, Buck, who at one year of age is showing promise as a helping hand dog, neither Len nor Betty expect he will be another Thunder.

"Thunder was one of a kind," says Len.

> I never met another dog like him, and I don't expect to. He was special, and I guess that's only fitting. I understand there are now some 5,000 dogs trained to help the handicapped who are doing things for their owners similar to what Thunder did for us. Thunder paved the way for these dogs. He was the first.

Thunder, a helping hand dog. Photo courtesy of Betty and Len Cohen.

Thunder, a helping hand dog. Photo courtesy of Betty and Len Cohen.

## TRAINING AS THERAPY

In her columns in *Dog World* magazine, Edi Munneke, obedience editor for that publication, chronicled a moving story about her Golden Retrievers, Rusty and Rocky, and the courage and determination of her husband Al, who, although denied access to other sports because of a crippling illness, was a top competitor in the field of obedience competition until his death. Portions of these columns are reprinted with the author's permission.

Dogs have always meant therapy at my house. My husband is handicapped, but he has probably clocked up more miles in the obedience ring than any exhibitor still in the sport today. More than 40 years ago, he had polio and was told he would never walk again. By sheer grit and determination, he educated a new set of muscles which at long last are going bad— and there are no more in reserve.

Obedience trials opened up a competitive sport that Al could handle. His training methods had to be different, but no one can deny that they worked. He has shared his training skills with many handlers. His Golden Retriever, Am-Can Ch (American-Canadian Champion) Sun Dance's Rusticana, UDT (Utility Dog tracking), Can UD (Canadian Utility Dog), is the top scoring dog of all time in American Kennel Club (AKC) records. Rusty scored 36 scores of 200 in AKC records and three scores of 200 in Canada. (For those unfamiliar with AKC obedience competition, 200 is a perfect score.) Al and Rusty competed in most areas of the U.S. and Canada and he became an obedience judge, admired and respected for his kindness and consideration for exhibitors. There are thousands of people all over this country who have warmly expressed their appreciation for what they believe he has contributed to sportsmanship.

You will never know how difficult it was to persuade Al to take a cane into the ring when he worked his dog, but it became necessary as an aid in walking. Our present Golden, Rocky, is a great, great grandson of our first golden, Rusty. This dog is very responsive and all the more beautiful to us because he will be the last dog Al will ever be able to train. He is a remarkable dog, well aware of his share of responsibility and visibly devoted to his handler. I am sure no dog has ever tried harder to adapt his pace to that of his handicapped handler.

Through the years, Al has earned many titles, including Utility titles on seven of our dogs. He has worked in the ring hundreds and hundreds of times. Suddenly in the Open B ring last September in Indianapolis, calamity fell and Al collapsed in the ring. Rocky had been left in a sit-stay for the Drop on Recall. There he remained while the life squad carried his handler off to the hospital, protesting that he wanted to get up and finish the exercise.

I followed the ambulance, but not before the judge told me not to worry—someone else could handle the dog. When I left the building, Rocky was still sitting where Al had left him. I knew we had friends who would take care of him, just as we had those who would take care of us. The verdict at Indianapolis was hyperventilation, or incorrect breathing, which results in a blackout.

Al loves to show his dog, but fear of his growing physical handicap puts him under great pressure. We had a choice to make—he could give up and quit or we could try to learn to cope. We chose to cope. At his next two trials, Al had such a difficult time that the judges decided to have him sit away from the ring while I handled Rocky in the group exercises. Al did not ask for this consideration, but the judges took this right under the regulations.

Is it ever possible to be prepared for a sudden change in lifestyle? I knew that my husband's health was failing, but he preferred to go on showing his dog rather than give in to his growing weakness. Al's last activity came as he would have wanted it—in the open B ring with Rocky at his side. We were in Painesville, Ohio, almost three hundred miles from home when the heart attack struck on July 16. On August 23, the battle was over.

We are not complaining—we had far more than most; it would have been difficult to crowd more into one lifetime. During April and May, we traveled more than 10,000 miles in our motorhome while I judged 13 trials. We have no regrets, because we did not wait to live. Al enjoyed the life our dog activities made possible. Our circle of friends is wide and sincere. What Al accomplished is a credit to the obedience world. His example as a handicapped person will remain an inspiration to others. Al was the quiet one, seldom ruffling feathers. I am the one who often tilts with windmills.

Al worked hard in the sport of obedience, and devoted much of his time to teaching others to be good competitors. I can think of nothing more fitting than to dedicate his memory to the helping of other handicapped persons to find joy in a relationship with a faithful four-footed companion. Al and I had decided many years ago that at our passing, there would be no pomp or flowers, but I know that a memorial to other handicapped persons would please him.

Because Al was handicapped, he tried harder for perfection. His work with his dog was almost his only activity—it gave him a purpose in life. Obedience was the one sport within his capability, so it became his moving force for the last 25 years of his life. He died at age 75, his last effort devoted to his dog.[5]

A second example in which the art of training itself is a therapeutic activity comes from Columbia, Missouri, where the Boone County 4-H Dog Care Drill Team teach children at the Mid-Missouri Mental Health Center to train dogs. The results expressed in this letter by Joel S. Ray, a clinical psychologist at the Center to Milt Winn, the executive director of Therapy Dogs International, speak for themselves.

Dear Mr. Winn:

I am delighted to write this letter in support of the Boone County 4-H Dog Care Drill Team. They have made their presence felt here at the mental health center in many ways; and we are most grateful for their contributions to our treatment programs for our preadolescent youngsters.

Most of our in-patient children have not had many success experiences. All of them have problems with social encounters and generally have poor self-concepts. What has made the therapy dog project here so gratifying is the immediate success and positive reinforcement obtained from the initial, small encounters with the dogs and their young handlers. The 4-H kids have provided marvelous peer models for our children. In fact, a local photographer had trouble telling them apart. Even the most aggressive of our children has responded with patience and care when training a dog. We can easily note that positive changes have happened for most all of our children.

I must comment, too, about the expert guidance and leadership provided by Mrs. Ann Gafke. She has been able to maintain control and interest with a gentle but firm attitude. Seeing that many children and dogs working together and paying attention for that long is no small feat and is a testament to her patience and commitment.

We do look forward to our project continuing. In fact, we have just started a new group of our inpatient children in the last few weeks. Again, we are extremely pleased with our therapy dog project and encourage you to accept their application for membership in your organization. We think they can be a new model of treatment both here in Missouri and nationally.

Training is both an art and a craft. Some dogs learn more quickly and expertly than others, and some people have a natural talent for communicating their needs to their dogs. Some dogs appear to almost train themselves; others are so incorrigible that only an expert handler can make them obey. The vast majority of dogs, however, are in the middle. They learn relatively quickly and work willingly for their human handler once they understand his/her wants. In its highest expression, the bond between dog and trainer seems almost magical. However, like any craft, with patience and practice dog training can be learned. When you have learned to train your dog, you and your pet are on the same wavelength. You have learned to speak a common language; you can communicate with one another, and both of you will be the happier for it. The capabilities of a trained dog is limited only by his handler's imagination.

## REFERENCES

1. Voith, Victoria. "Animal Behavior Problems." Research presentation at the International Conference on the Human/Companion Animal Bond, October 5-7, 1981, Philadelphia, PA.

2. Mugford, Roger. "Management of Behavior Problems in Companion Animals." Address presented at the International Conference on the Human/Companion Animal Bond, October 5-7, 1981, Philadelphia, PA.

3. Houpt, Katherine A. "Disruption of the Human-Companion Animal Bond: Aggressive Behavior of Dogs." Research presentation at the International Conference on the Human/Companion Animal Bond, October 5-7, 1981, Philadelphia, PA.

4. Ibid. Personal Communication.

5. Munneke, Edi. "Obedience News." *Dog World,* July 1978 and November 1978.

Chapter 5

# Implementing Animal Therapy in the Institution

## WHY HAVE ANIMALS IN AN INSTITUTION?

In 1970, Boris Levinson, stressing the tremendous need among the elderly for unlimited affection, constant companionship, and opportunities to do for others, wrote:

> If the nursing home is to provide for even one of these needs, namely for constant companionship, it would require staffing on a one-to-one basis which would, obviously, not be feasible financially, even if it were possible to find the necessary number of employees. However, I do firmly believe there is a solution to the problem I have been outlining.
>
> Shocking as it may sound, what I am about to recommend is the introduction of pets into the nursing home as part of a carefully planned and structured method of therapy for the aged.[1]

Levinson's idea is not nearly so shocking today; but it is even more urgent. In 1977 more than 1.2 million persons were housed in geriatric institutions, and this number is expected to double by the end of the century. Lack of qualified staff continues to be a problem, and the patient/staff ratio has been reported as high as 30:1.[2]

"In order to cope with these increasing figures," says Robert Andrysco,

> nursing and retirement homes have begun to develop new means of care and new therapies, aimed at lessening the burden of the staff while maintaining a high quality of care for the residents. Traditional care is seen as detrimental in that residents are expected to be sick and fulfill a passive role. The lack of demands on the residents has been demonstrated to lead to physical and psychological deterioration and does not pro-

vide for the learning of new skills and activities. It has become apparent that the elements of the physical environment must be changed and utilized as therapeutic agents. Many geriatric facilities have reported changing their physical environments to encourage socialization between residents and self-management within residents.

Companion animals can be utilized in nursing-retirement communities to relieve residents' feelings of loneliness, depression and boredom. Individuals have also exhibited dramatic improvements in their ability to interact and communicate with other residents and staff. These beneficial effects have resulted in a decreased staff work-load, as well as an improved cost-benefit ratio.[3]

## WHY NOT HAVE AN ANIMAL IN RESIDENCE?

Like any innovative new treatment, animal-facilitated therapy has its share (perhaps more than its share) of critics. Before we discuss implementing an in-residence program, we are going to address the most frequently raised objections to animals in institutions.

### "Animals Are Not Legally Permitted in Institutions."

This is a common, but erroneous, comment. Author and former nursing home activity director, Cappy McLeod surveyed health departments state by state. She found that the majority of them had not considered the possibility of animals in residence, thus there are few laws that are concerned with this practice. In fact, there are only a few states which specifically prohibit animals from long-term care facilities.[4] Appendix III discusses the current legislation affecting the status of therapy animals, but with the growing recognition of the value of pets for elderly and other populations, even as we go to press, and certainly within the next few years, we can expect many changes, hopefully, for the better.

### "Animals Are a Health Hazard; They Can Transmit Diseases to Humans; They Scratch and Bite and Cause Injuries."

Some communicable diseases are common to animals and humans, and dogs and cats have been known to scratch or bite. Animal waste can be a health hazard and patients could be allergic to certain types of animals.

Photo by Odean Cusack.

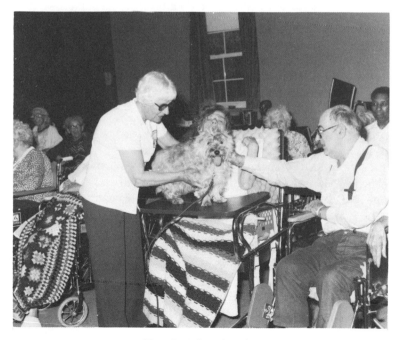

Photo by Odean Cusack.

These are certainly valid considerations, and they could pose a problem in an institutional setting. However, in the research studies, informal residence programs, and visitation projects to date, these fears have proven to be groundless. These are possible problems; they are not, however, probable problems.

In his survey of the research to date, Phil Arkow remarks that in over 67,000 hours of patient exposure to dogs, neither injuries nor diseases occurred.[5] In her long-term pilot dog study, researcher Susanne Robb found that risks were not nearly as common as opponents of pet therapy would suggest and that stringent precautions may not be necessary.[6] In the dog-in-residence study by JACOPIS, the problems anticipated with the coming of Honey simply did not materialize (see Chapter 2).

Careful selection of an animal and proper training for a dog can reduce injury risks. Continued veterinary supervision can eliminate health problems. Proper nutrition, required grooming, and care of the animal's cage or bedding can prevent most sanitation hazards. In short, responsible pet ownership and common sense will eliminate most problems before they begin.

In spite of the frail and susceptible population in an institution, the chances of injury or disease are probably less likely than they are in the average home for several reasons. Unlike the home where the housepet is everywhere, most institutions maintain strict sanitation procedures, and laws generally do prohibit animals from certain areas (the food preparation area, for example). Institution mascots are kept inside or in a fenced-in yard outside when they are not interacting with the patients. Thus, the chance of the animal contacting parasites from other animals is reduced. Care requirements for the animal become part of the institution's routine; for example, the cat litter box must be changed daily. A busy pet owner might "let things go" a day or so, but institutional life demands more rigor. Also patients known to have an allergy to animals can be kept away from the mascot; the institution has the benefit of foresight.

### "No Staff Have Time to Take Care of the Animal and No Patients Are Able To. The Animal Will Just Create More Work."

This is a valid consideration, particularly in institutions where the staff-to-patient ratio is extremely low. However, there are pets, for example, fish or a caged bird, that require relatively little maintenance and endless enjoyment. And interestingly, in the JACOPIS study, the researchers found that 24% of the staff actually reported a decreased workload after the therapy dog Honey arrived. Since the researchers had not expected such a finding, they were not sure exactly how it came about, but suggested that with the companionship of Honey the patients demanded less time from the staff. Even if there is initial reluctance, most reports indicate that once the pet is in-residence, staff reaction to it is usually quite favorable.

If an institution is interested in acquiring an in-residence animal, but fears resistance from the staff, an excellent suggestion comes from Jules Cass, the chief veterinary medical officer for the Veterans Administration Headquarters in Washington, D.C. Cass strongly recommends that the care of the animal mascot be written into the job description of an institution staff person. Traditionally, the activity director has been responsible for the care of the animal, but Cass suggests that the person delegated should be in a lower ranked position; for example, an aide whose duties would include washing bedpans.[7] We will discuss this in depth later: suffice for now, one example of a variation on this technique. A nursing home in New Jersey requires its guards to walk the therapy dog during their designated rounds. This is part of their job description, so there are no complaints.

And for institutions which positively, absolutely do not have the time for an in-residence pet, consider pet visitation programs. These activities are usually so well-received that an otherwise overworked or hassled staff has a much-needed opportunity to relax.

## *"Not Everyone Likes Animals—Those Patients Shouldn't Have to Be Bothered with Them."*

Patients who don't like animals do not have to associate with them. In fact, the studies indicate that the animals instinctively avoid people who do not encourage them and are not fond of them.

However, we do suggest that staff make no hasty decisions about who is adamantly opposed to pets and who isn't. We have seen numerous examples in which patients who were disinterested in the animal later revealed that they had formed an emotional attachment to it. In the JACOPIS study, for example, patients who previously seemed uninvolved with Honey were worried and anxious about her when she was lost.

We certainly do not recommend forcing an animal upon anyone, but if a dog appears to gravitate toward or initiate contact with a

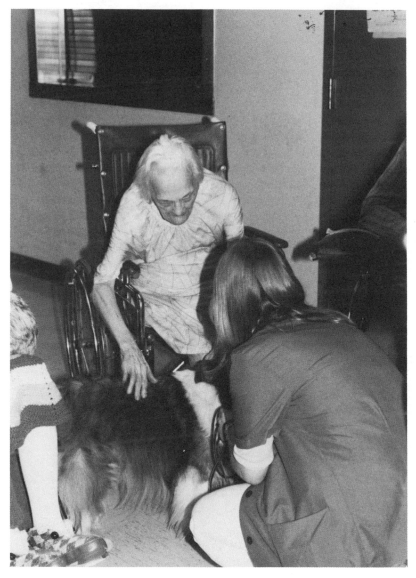

Photo by Odean Cusack.

seemingly disinterested patient, why not let nature take its course. The animal can always be removed if the patient expresses annoyance. Dogs respond to body signals that may be imperceptible to us, and possibly the patient really wants contact with the animal, even though only he and the dog know it. In this case, the therapy dog may know best!

## *"What If the Animal Dies?"*

Eventually pet death is a fact of life of pet ownership. Until relatively recently, the grief surrounding pet loss has not been accorded the support that normally accompanies human loss. Research, however, has established that for people who are very attached (which would be a good number of the institution's residents) to their pets, its loss can be a devastation and contain many of the elements that accompany human loss.[8] For this population who is already coming face-to-face with their own mortality, would not this unfortunate event produce considerable trauma?

If a relatively young, healthy, and hardy dog or cat is selected and if the animal's health is maintained through proper care and periodic veterinary treatment, it will likely outlive many of the residents. Should the situation arise, honesty is probably the best policy. When Cappy McLeod's cat was scheduled for euthanasia, she cried in the arms of one of her residents, Mabel. McLeod later apologized for losing control, but Mabel insisted no apology was necessary. She appreciated the opportunity to comfort and listen to someone else for a change.[9]

## *"An Institution Is No Place for an Animal; It Will Be Neglected, Abused by the Residents, and a Dog in Particular Will Be Stressed from Having Too Many Masters."*

In any animal therapy program, the welfare of the pet is a vital concern. The animal may well be a tool of the therapist, but it is first a living, sentient being with distinct psychological and physical needs that must be met. Fortunately, pet therapy is a symbiotic relationship between pets and people. The animals benefit as well as the patients. One staff member who takes the therapy dog home at night reports that the dog "can't wait to come to work in the morning." A friendly, outgoing dog (which is the ideal temperament for this sort of work) will enjoy meeting and interacting with a wide variety of people.

Neglect or abuse of the therapy animal, by staff or patients, should never be tolerated. Such action is not only inhumane, it is directly counterproductive to the purpose of animal therapy. Neglecting an animal's needs (grooming, exercise, for example) actually increases the probability of disease or injury.

Abuse, particularly by patients who may have a grudge against the institution, society, the family that placed them there, even other patients, might appear a potential problem. Research studies indicate, however, that although this could occur, it simply has not and there is some evidence to suggest that peer pressure (concern for the animal) can act as an effective deterrent if there is a potentially abusive patient in the ranks.

Perhaps the strongest indicator comes from the Lima State Hospital project. We will discuss this project in more detail in Chapter 11, but for now, suffice to say that the program includes 175 animals of various species, and the patients are criminally insane. It would appear that if any institutionalized population had a potential for animal abuse, it would be a population of this sort. In fact, the animals have acted as a calming factor on the prisoners, and no abuse has occurred.

David Lee who instigated the project says:

> The abuse of animals expected has not been a problem because we screen closely and monitor constantly. Because our pets are not used with acute short term cases or the assaultive cases, any likelihood of abuse is reduced. We use pets with depressed and suicidal patients only, and usually they are initially considered chronic cases.[10]

In the JACOPIS study, both patients and staff were concerned that the therapy dog Honey would suffer from having too many masters. This did not prove to be a problem. As that study expressed so well, individuals vary considerably in their interaction with the animal: some were happy just to look at Honey.

A problem that did arise in the JACOPIS study that does warrant comment is obesity. The dog was often bribed with treats and, as a result, gained an unhealthy amount of weight. To safeguard against this possibility, however, an institution can carefully monitor the quality and quantity of treats given to the pet. For example, a certain amount of biscuits can be set aside each day for the therapy dog and different patients can earn the privilege of feeding it.

A final consideration is canine burnout. Remember, these dogs are working therapists and just like human staff can experience stress if they do not have ample time to relax. Phil Arkow reports one such case: The dog, Pepper, was the resident pet at the Colorado State Hospital's geriatric ward and developed diarrhea and anxiety attacks from her non-stop duty. The solution was a relatively simple one: staff members took the dog home on weekends for a welcome change of pace.[11]

In summary, the potential problems of animal therapy are few in number if in fact they occur at all. The benefits, on the other hand, are numerous. So what are we waiting for? Let's get started!

## PLANNING THE PET THERAPY PROGRAM

### Legal Restrictions

The first step is to determine if there are any legal restrictions or requirements (housing, for example) that must be met before an animal can be introduced into a facility. As we mentioned earlier, most states do not prohibit animals: but even if you reside in a state that presently does have such a restriction, you may be able to obtain a waiver. We also recommend checking with municipal authorities for specific requirements (dogs will require a license, for example). An institution is also advised to check its insurance coverage to be certain there are not animal-prohibitive clauses in the policy.

### Which Animal Is Best?

Some animals have simply "walked in off the street," and become valuable and loved mascots. Some institutions elect to adopt an animal companion based upon a successful experience with a visitation program. Others follow a careful evaluation of staff and patient preferences before deciding upon which pet is right for them.

To date, there are no precise evaluators which determine which type of animal works best in a given situation. However, an extremely informative new publication offers detailed guidelines to aid an institution in its mascot (and visitation) selection. We strongly recommend *Guidelines: Animals in Nursing Homes,* co-authored by Ronnal L. Lee (gerontologist and behaviorist), Marie E. Zeglen (anthropologist and sociologist), Terry Ryan (obedience instructor and vice president of the National Association of Dog Obedience Instructors), and Linda M. Hines (director of the highly successful People Pet Partnership Program which will be discussed in detail in Chapter 10) for a more detailed description of some of the recommendations in this chapter. (See Bibliography for availability.)

Animal selection should be based on staff and patient preference, availability of space (both physical and social), type of population housed, care and cost considerations, type of program expected, and, of course, operative legal statutes. As a general rule of thumb, the types of animals that require the most care and planning also offer the most potential for personal bonding and therapeutic application.

Hines and company note that animals can be available in three ways: as occasional visitors, as the individual pets of residents, and as group mascots. We will discuss visitation programs in detail in Chapter 8, so for now we will look at individual pets and mascot pets, and an institution may consider a variety of both. An important consideration is the areas where patients spend most of their time. If the residents congregate in a large activity or recreation room for most of the day, group mascots might be a good choice; on the other hand, facilities in which individuals remain in apartments or single or double occupancy living quarters might investigate the possibility of individual pets.[12]

If individual pets are the choice, selection is much easier. Essentially, it depends upon (1) the patient's preference, (2) ability of patient to provide adquate care, and (3) possibility of accommodation in the living quarters available. If the patient has a roommate those needs and wishes must be honored also.

A group mascot, however, must be agreeable not only to patients, but to staff as well, and staff support for such a project cannot be overstated. Hines et al. stress:

> The full participation and co-operation of the entire staff (nurses, aides, and housekeeping and custodial personnel) will be necessary if any animal placement is to succeed. Without staff involvement, the chances of unsuccessful placement are high. The staff of an institution must possess the knowledge to plan a placement well, the energy and enthusiasm to make the placement work, and the commitment to care for an animal properly.[13]

## Types of Animals

Numerous species are successfully used in institutions, both as personal pets and group mascots. We will briefly describe some of these possible choices, indicate advantages, disadvantages, care, cost considerations, and potential for therapy. This section is in no way intended to be a complete and total guide to animal care and application, but simply to provide a quick summary and easy-to-use reference. More complete animal care requirements are outlined in the aforementioned *Guidelines;* however, we strongly recommend that before placement is finalized, the institution know *in advance* the total physical, environmental, and, if applicable, emotional needs of the animal. Usually the best place to obtain this information is the breeder, specialized pet shop, or humane society where the animal is obtained. Costs, where indicated, should be considered in the most general sense, as they will vary widely due to locale and particular animal selected. Although traditionally, humane shelters have housed only dogs and cats, lately they are admitting many more animals to their ranks. Rabbits, birds, and small rodents are often turned in to these facilities, and though selection may not be as varied as in a specialty store, the cost is minimal and most reputable shelters offer veterinary support and advice as well. A modern, progressive humane shelter (perhaps one that is already bringing visiting pets to your institution) is a good starting point to look for a pet of any species.

### Aquariums

*Advantages;* colorful, tranquil, low maintenance.

*Disadvantages:* lack of tactile interaction—some say as pets they're rather boring.

*Pet Potential:* limited—fish cannot be handled.

*Therapeutic Potential:* watching fish reduces stress and lowers elevated blood pressure; some therapists report that eye contact can be made by meeting a patient's eyes through the aquarium.

*May provide:* entertainment, diversion, creative stimulation, visual stimulation.

*Won't provide:* tactile stimulation, affection, companionship.

*You will need:* the largest size tank affordable (a ten gallon tank will hold 12-20 small fish), filter, thermostat and heater, gravel, plants, some decorative shells or ceramics, cover, fish net, siphon, and water conditioner.[14]

*Care:* minimal: daily feeding (caution: overfeeding is a common problem—if patients feed the fish, they *must* be supervised); general check on aquarium function; if system functions and feeding is supervised, you seldom, if ever, need to re-locate the fish and clean the tank.

*Cost:* depends mostly on size and species selected; a visually stimulating, relatively large set-up can be had for under $75.

*Availability:* pet shop that specializes in tropical fish.

*Location:* away from bright sunlight, protected from accidental damage from wheelchairs, preferably in a social area where patients congregate.[15]

*Comments:* The Little Sisters of the Poor, who have a network of nursing homes throughout the country, have aquariums in the waiting rooms for physicians' and other offices. Since gazing at tropical or gold fish has proven to reduce stress (see Chapter 3), a small tank might be suitable in any high-stress area (therapists' or doctors' offices) or even the waiting room for visitors.

### Vivarium

A vivarium is similar to an aquarium except that it houses land-lubbers, small reptiles (lizards or snakes), or amphibians (frogs, small tortoises, toads), instead of fish.

*Advantages:* unusual, educational, low maintenance.

*Disadvantages:* little tactile stimulation (if removed from habitat, animals require careful handling—patients must be supervised), some patients may have negative reaction to reptilian-type species.

*Pet Potential:* limited. Creatures remain in cage most of the time.

*Therapeutic Potential:* Pawlings Air Force Hospital found recuperating trauma patients responded well to similar species found in woods nearby (see Chapter 1); Chum, a turtle, provided support and entertainment in a tubercular ward even though the patient who received the pet had an initial aversion to it.[16]

*May provide:* entertainment, visual stimulation, educational enhancement, possible occupational therapy project if patients can construct habitat.

*Will not provide:* much companionship (there is a certain element of companionship present just in knowing another living creature shares space with you), love and affection, opportunity for interaction.

*You will need:* a large aquarium with sand, pieces of wood, rock, shells, perhaps a small pond. Needs vary considerably depending upon species selected, plants, cover.

*Care:* minimal. Many species do not require daily feeding, depends alot on species selected.

*Cost:* again, depending upon species selected, can be kept under $50.

*Availability:* a speciality pet store—look for one who provides a natural habitat for the tiny reptiles it sells; ask what is needed to recreate the habitat. Also, inquire about any local health statutes that may prohibit certain species.

*Location:* same as aquarium.

*Comments:* Since this is a low-cost and low-maintenance project, it might work very well for a resident who wanted an individual pet and had no aversion to reptiles.

### Small Caged Mammals (rats, mice, gerbils, hamsters)

*Advantages:* active, furry, offer some tactile interaction, entertaining, low maintenance and cost.

*Disadvantages:* generally do not afford the one-on-one interaction of dogs or cats, if they are not used to human handling, they may bite, some patients may have aversion to them.

*Pet Potential:* relatively low, with the exception, ironic considering their bad public image, of a rat. Rats become very attached and affectionate pets and will sit on an owner's shoulder for hours.

*Therapeutic Potential:* used in the Lima State Hospital environment (Chapter 11) and often are part of visiting zoos; rats, in particular, can be trained which could be a therapeutic activity in itself; if several are in residence, you might consider a Rodent Race in which the small animals are placed in containers and scurry across the floor (see Chapter 7), amusing to the patients, good exercise for the animals, and inspires some friendly competition.

*May provide:* entertainment, diversion, some tactile stimulation, some companionship, limited opportunity to express love and affection, offspring if you want them!

*Will not provide:* extensive opportunity for companionship, love, and affection (except for rat).

*You will need:* a 10 gallon aquarium (will house 4 mice, 1 hamster, or 2 gerbils) or a 20 gallon aquarium (will be comfortable quarters for one rat),[17] bedding materials, an exercise wheel, a plastic self-waterer (readily available in any pet shop), a cover that fits tightly (all these creatures can climb and jump). An alternative is a self-contained plastic cage that has a removable tray for cleaning and may have several compartments.

*Care:* daily food (commercial chow, supplemented with fresh vegetables), wild bird seed, dog biscuits and kibble provide treats and chewing material; bedding needs periodic changing (about once or twice a week), cage needs weekly scrubbing to prevent odor; animal must be removed if aquarium is used (keep a small carrying container handy to contain the pet while you clean its house).

*Cost:* pet and cage with a few toys (an exercise wheel, for example) under $25.00; maintenance cost minimal.

*Availability:* any pet store or commercial breeder.

*Location:* can work in social setting or in patient's room; for a patient who is able to care for them, these inexpensive and readily available animals can give hours of enjoyment and a sense of being needed.

*Comments:* for a patient who wishes a dog or cat, but is unable to care for or house them, a rat might be a nice companion, assuming that the patient has no negative perceptions of them.

### Rabbits and Guinea Pigs

*Advantages:* though still caged, these pets offer more opportunity for interaction than the smaller rodents, generally calm and can be handled (but with care); rabbits in particular can become companions just like cats and dogs.

*Disadvantages:* generally require more socialization if they are to be pets than cats and dogs, shorter life span, opportunity for interaction probably limited to one patient at a time (animal on lap).

*Pet Potential:* good.

*Therapeutic Potential:* both species used at Lima State Hospital, both species effectively used with children and in pet visitation programs, rabbit has proven to be enormously beneficial to mentally deficient adults (see "Bubba—the floppy-eared therapist" in Chapter 11).

*May provide:* companionship, opportunity to express love and affection, constructing rabbit hutch could offer residents occupational therapy (see Bubba).

*Will not provide:* much incentive for exercise, wide range of therapeutic possibilities of a dog or cat, excitement (both species tend to be calm and passive—they are less active than smaller rodents and do not learn tricks).

*You will need:* a 20 gallon tank will comfortably house one guinea pig; bedding material and a water bottle are needed. Guinea pigs do not use exercise wheels, and since they do not jump, no lid is necessary. For rabbits; a hutch measuring two feet deep, two feet wide, and four feet long made of corrosion-resistant wire with a wood nesting box that is totally enclosed except for the top half of one side. This is comfortable for 2 females or 1 male. A removable tray underneath the wire makes cleaning easier.[18] Bedding material and a plastic water bottle are needed.

*Care:* daily feeding (laboratory chow and fresh vegetables), fresh water. Bedding must be changed every three days. An aquarium should be scrubbed every week, a wire cage about once every 3 weeks, the rabbit tray every week. (Rabbits, though, can be easily taught to use a cat litter box, and if the pet is out of its cage often, we heartily recommend this: take some of the droppings and place them in a low, easily accessible litter box. Acquaint the rabbit with the box. Repeat if necessary; they usually learn quickly.) A piece of unpainted hardwood is recommended for chewing. Rabbits require a salt or mineral block.[19] Long-haired varieties of both species require brushing.

*Cost:* Guinea pig and cage—under $25; rabbits slightly more; however, if the construction of the hutch is an occupational therapy project, costs can be reduced.

*Availability:* well-run pet shops and breeders.

*Comments.* Both species are relatively docile companions. Guinea pigs are very pretty and soft, and since they can be kept in a small aquarium make an excellent individual pet. Rabbits should be handled frequently, but gently.

### Caged Birds

There are two types of caged birds that make suitable institutional pets: the finch-type (which includes Zebra finches, Society finches, and many others, and canaries) and the psittacine (parrot-type) which include parakeets (also called budgerigars), cockatiels, lovebirds, and large parrots.

*Advantages:* colorful, vocal, entertaining, Psittacine types can be hand-tamed, trained to do tricks and trained to talk; many finch species breed readily if in good health and in an ample cage: this can provide additional stimulation for the residents.

*Disadvantages:* Smaller birds (parakeets), if handled, must be with extreme care, interaction somewhat limited, some species have short life spans, constant vocalization can annoy some residents, site of cage may be messy (seed on floor).

*Pet Potential:* for Psittacine species—high; finch species—moderate.

*Therapeutic Potential:* Lima State Hospital (Chapter 11) has a large number of birds of many varieties, budgies of proven therapeutic value (Mugford et al. - Chapter 2).

*You will need:* as large a cage as possible; a 24" x 20" x 14" cage houses 8 small finches comfortably; large birds require a cage that gives them enough room to fully spread their wings; perches, gravel, seed, occasional fresh greens, liquid vitamins, food and water containers, a small detachable bird bath (for small species), a small nest (if offspring desired); psittacine varieties enjoy toys: mirror, ladder, etc., cuttlebone (a calcium supplement) is also recommended.

*Care:* food and water checked daily, paper on cage bottom cleaned twice weekly and fresh gravel; occasional scrubbing of wire cage (although these types of birds are relatively clean).

*Location:* like others, cage must be away from a draft and out of direct sunlight. Temperature should be relatively constant. A cover over the cage at night will keep the birds quiet and guard against drafts.

*Cost:* small common finches (Zebra finches, for example) and cage; parakeet and cage: under $35; male canary (males sing): about $50; cockatiel and cage: under $100: lovebird and cage slightly more; large parrot: astronomical!

*Availability:* specialty pet shop or breeder. Most of these species (except the very large parrots) are easily bred in captivity and many breeders hand feed the newborn to insure a sociable and easily tamed pet.

*Comments:* excellent in-room pets since they require little care and take up little space. A singing finch or canary might provide companionship for a bed-bound patient. Patients allergic to cats and dogs might welcome a feathered friend. For someone capable of more care who desires interaction, the psittacine varieties offer enormous possibilities. Best bet: the cockatiel, they are larger than parakeets and tame more easily. They become affectionate and constant companions. Though never reaching the verbal fluency of the larger parrots, they do learn to talk. Cockatiels are very pretty birds and the albino variety looks like a miniature cockatoo. Veterinarian

Joan Schaeffler of the California Veterinary Medical Association reports that the group successfully placed one of these delightful birds in an area veterans hospital. The bird sits on shoulders and rides around on the nurses' carts.[20] A playpen for the pet could become an occupational therapy project.

### Cats and Dogs

Cats and dogs offer the maximum pet and therapeutic potential, but require the most care and supervision; in Chapter 6 we will discuss selection and placement criteria for these animals in detail. In general, a cat will probably require somewhat less care and supervision than a dog, and no special facility for housing is necessary (a dog kept outside will require an ample run and housing).

### Other Possibilities

Some final possibilities include wild bird feeders (placed at windows), an outside fish pond, and, especially if the facility has the space and is situated in an area where zoning does not restrict them, small farm animals.[21]

In the third category, we would like to suggest the African pygmy goat. This delightful miniature species has been a favorite at children's zoos for years. Newcomers to the pet therapy scene, these happy hoofers are already making marks. Scampy and Skippy, who belong to one of the authors, have an enthusiastic following everywhere they go. They are affectionate and friendly, paper-trained, and trained to ride in the car. Since they are small (about 24" high), a pair of them can be housed relatively easily.

They require a large dog house and a fenced-in area in a sheltered location. Though they are very hardy, damp conditions can be a problem for them. Fresh water, of course, and goat chow keep them healthy. Though somewhat expensive (about $100 each), the institution that acquires a pair of these charmers not only have good therapy pets, but an efficient lawn-mower service as well. They enjoy fresh grass in the spring and summer, but be sure the lawn has not been sprayed or treated with pesticide!

Which brings us to one final point before we conclude this section on pet selection and care. We recommend that you clean cages and aquariums with a mild detergent (Ivory Snow or liquid, for example). Species have different tolerances for chemicals, and since

Photo by Bob Barber.

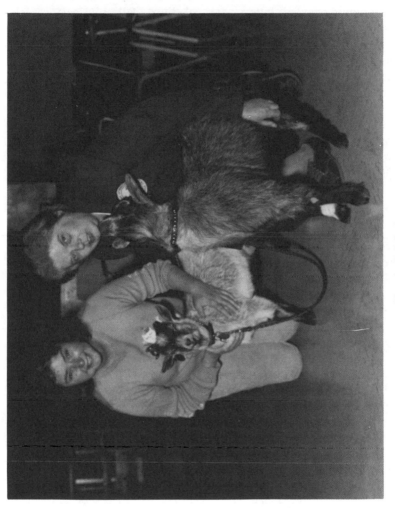

Photo by Bob Barber.

many institutions use commercial-strength cleaners, these sub-stances could be toxic to the pet. We recommend that you ask the breeder or dealer what they personally use to clean the habitat and follow his example. Also, some plants are poisonous to animals. These include azalea, bittersweet, caladium, calla lily, castor bean, crocus, daffodil, daphne, dieffenbachia, elephant's ear, English ivy, foxglove, holly, hydrangea, Japanese yew, Jerusalem cherry, lark-spur, lily-of-the-valley, milkweed, mistletoe, monkshood, night-shade, oleander, philodendron, poinsettia, and string-of-pearls. Since plants are abundant around holidays, it's a good idea to post a list of those that could potentially be a problem. Since reactions vary widely among species, consult your veterinarian or the breeder for a complete list of substances that may be toxic to your pet. You want to insure your therapy animal a happy, healthy, and as-long-as-pos-sible life.

## Techniques for Selection

Assuming that legal statutes, space limitations, and population mix would accommodate virtually any species, you might consider polling staff and residents to determine what pets they would prefer. Two excellent forms are reprinted here from *Guidelines: Animals in Nursing Homes*.[22]

## Pet Preferences

Your nursing home administration is interested in whether or not pets should be allowed in the facility. There are several ways in which pets can be available. Pets can be brought in for visits by family, friends, or staff, and leave after a short time. Pets may be-come full-time residents at the home. A resident may bring a pet to live in his/her room (or a pet given to a resident may be allowed to live in his/her room). The pet may be a group pet that is allowed to visit with many residents. The group pet would not be allowed in certain areas such as the dining room, kitchen, or linen room. Or the full-time pet may be confined to an aquarium or a cage in one loca-tion.

Please place a checkmark (X) indicating your feelings about each of the ways the following animals could be available in your nursing home.

| Animal | Not Allowed at all | Allowed to visit | Permanent Group Pet | Permanent Personal Pet |
|---|---|---|---|---|
| Dog | | | | |
| Cat | | | | |
| Bird | | | | |
| Fish | | | | |
| Guinea Pig | | | | |
| Hamster | | | | |
| Gerbil | | | | |
| Rat | | | | |
| Mouse | | | | |
| Rabbit | | | | |
| Small farm animals outside | | | | |
| Wild Bird Feeders (outside windows) | | | | |
| Other (Specify) | | | | |

A second form allows residents and staff to more precisely identify problems and benefits associated with the types of animals they would deem most welcome.[23]

We are interested in your comments about the three animals you would *most* like to have in your nursing home.

| | 1st animal | 2nd animal | 3rd animal |
|---|---|---|---|
| Benefits: | | | |
| Problems: | | | |
| Care of the animal: | | | |
| Comments: | | | |

The authors also recommend that key staff personnel in the institution be interviewed in depth since their cooperation is essential. Residents who are unable to fill out the form themselves could also be interviewed.

A nursing home in Florida used a variation of this technique to ascertain the feasibility of bringing a dog into the facility. Administrators decided a therapy dog was in order and simply polled staff, residents, *and* families of patients to see if there were any objections. Fortunately, there weren't.

## DELEGATING RESPONSIBILITY

You have now selected the proper pet(s), have located a breeder or humane shelter who will supply the animal, you have adhered to all legal and zoning requirements for the animal, and either have, or are constructing, a proper facility for it.

The next step is to decide who will be responsible for the pet's care. Patients eventually should be encouraged to help care for the animals; you may find that in time the residents can provide for almost all the animal's need themselves. However, patients should never be the ones given total responsibility for the pet. Even if the pet will be the personal companion of a resident, a staff should still supervise and oversee the care to assure (1) that the pet is not neglected or abused and (2) that the patient's condition is stable (that is, the patient has not suffered an illness or accident that might diminish his capacity to care for the animal).

Traditionally, the pet's caretaker has been the Activity Director (who is often the staff person most enthusiastic about implementing the program, and thus, is more than willing to take the responsibility for the animal). An enthusiastic and voluntary caretaker is fine and works out very well in most settings. Problems arise, however, if the person is absent, for whatever reason, and someone else is required to take on the duties.

Jules Cass of the Veterans Administration remarks that very often pet therapy arises through the vision and vigor of one individual in the institution. The program may work well, even extremely well, yet if the person leaves, the program ends. The animal often accompanies the departee, and no new therapy animal is sought. A better idea, he says, is to decide that (1) we will instigate a pet therapy program and (2) that the care of the animal will be written into the job description of a particular position in the institution. This should, preferably, he says, be a lower-ranking individual; perhaps an aide; and it really is not important if they particularly want to do it, if they like animals, or if they have had prior experience with them. "If they don't know anything about animals," he adds wryly, "they may have less bad habits to unlearn!" Thus, a position, rather than an individual, is responsibility for the pet. If the individual leaves, his replacement will resume the duties.[24]

We believe this is an excellent suggestion. (1) Susanne Robb has pointed out (Chapter 2 - pilot dog study) that the nursing staff may already believe the addition of a pet is a burden, and they should not be held responsible for its care. (2) The Activity Director has more pressing duties; for one, part of his/her role may be monitoring the patients' reaction to the pet and this person can always act as a final overseer for the lower-ranked individual. (3) Probably this idea has not been implemented before because those of us who care deeply for animals are reluctant to trust their care to someone who may not share our feelings. However, once again, we point out that this is required duty for a particular position, and the individual, if he/she wants the job, must carry it out. It is no longer a voluntary duty; it is obligatory and if it is not properly carried out, the individual runs the risk of reprimand, even dismissal. Additionally, as part of a formal job description, no one feels "put upon" or unduly burdened if they are asked to help with the pet. This could be the case if, for example, the Activity Director was absent for a few days and asked another staff member to "take care of the dog while I'm gone."

A staff position on each shift should have responsibility for the therapy animal. Additionally, a "back-up" position should also be written into the job description to cover sick days, absenteeism, vacation, etc. The animal's care needs should be in writing and a copy given to all staff members responsible for its care. If any special handling or procedure is required, the personnel involved should be trained. Usually, this would be a brief session with the breeder or dealer who will demonstrate anything needed. We emphasize that since this is now a formal position (part of it, we should say, because caring for pets is not all-consuming), personnel involved should not be expected to learn on their free time; the training period should be part of their working day, and allowances should be made for it. In addition to the personnel deemed responsible for the pet, we recommend that several other staff members become knowledgeable in the care and treatment of the pet. These could be the Activity Director, his/her assistant, a secretary, or any staff person that expresses an interest. In this manner, the institution can provide a wide range of support and back-up, which is important for any new program, but especially so for animal therapy.

## PET POLICY

The next step is to write a pet policy and incorporate it into your facility's formal regulations. The policy should be rigid enough to observe all existing statutes, sanitation measures, and patient phobias or allergies. It should be flexible enough to provide leeway for the inevitable new "situations" that arise when a new individual (the therapy animal is in every way an individual) enters the facility. An excellent model (because it covers a number of animals) is offered by Phil Arkow. It is an existent policy adopted in 1980 by the Garden of the Gods Nursing Home in Colorado Springs, Colorado.[25]

### Pet Policy in the Nursing Home

#### Purpose

An animal can reach an individual in many ways and does not expect anything in return except love. It can fill a void of loneliness and can give a sense of belonging to someone else. Not all residents can or desire an attachment to the dog, but as with all activities, they are based on individual needs.

#### Philosophy

*Companionship.* Friendships can be formed between resident and pet.

*Concern and motivation.* Caring for the pet, i.e., grooming, feeding, etc., gives the residents a feeling of usefulness. It provides for something else to think about besides themselves.

*Touch.* Petting and stroking the animal provide good sensory stimulation and physical exercise.

*Attention.* Watching the activities of the animal gives the resident something to observe and something to do, and is a soothing pasttime.

*Exercise.* The animal can provide healthy movement when going on a walk with residents.

*Social Influence.* Staff, administration, resident, and visitors can become involved with something in common.

*Homelike Atmosphere.* Having an animal within the facility can bring back memories of pet ownership in the past.

## Legal and Public Requirements

The dog must be currently licensed in Colorado Springs, be spayed, have all the necessary vaccinations, and be under the supervision of a veterinarian.

The cat must also meet all health vaccination requirements and be spayed. Because cat litter can be a potential health hazard, the cat has been trained to eliminate outdoors.

Certain species of birds are restricted by state health law due to psittacosis and other disease problems. Most small cage birds, such as parakeets, canaries, budgies, etc. may be considered safe. Birds must remain caged, and cage waste must be cleaned regularly.

## Housing

The fenced-in yard between the dining room and the north wing has been designated for the dog's living quarters. The gate is locked at all times to prevent the dog from wandering away from the property, and from coming inside the facility at the improper time. There is a dog house for sleeping, providing warmth and shelter during all types of inclement weather. The yard is large enough for exercise.

## Feeding

All food and water for the dog is provided within the fenced yard. Under no circumstances is she to be fed elsewhere. She is now considered an adult dog and needs to be fed once a day. She receives dry kibble. She is also given chew sticks and dog biscuits, and her water is changed daily.

The cat is fed and watered daily, and her food is provided for her in the housekeeper's utility room. The birds are fed and watered daily within their cages.

## Daily Time Schedule

The dog is to remain in the yard during the night, sleeping in her house. She may come into the facility between mealtimes for the residents (9:00 a.m. to 10:45 a.m., 1:30 p.m. to 3:45 p.m., and at 6:30 p.m. until bedtime, usually 7:30 to 8:00 p.m.) Under no circumstances is she allowed to come in at mealtime. She is to be put in the yard by the responsible staff member, not just let out the door. No animal is allowed in the kitchen at any time.

## Walking the Dog

If the residents wish to walk the dog, they may request the leash which is kept in the office. The staff member will unlock the gate (two keys are provided, one at the nurses' station and the other in the office). After the walk, the staff member is responsible for returning the dog to her yard.

## Visiting Area

Acceptable visiting areas for the dog are hallways, residents' rooms (except those not wishing her in their rooms), the office, and activity area. This applies to the cat as well. When the dog is outdoors outside of her yard she is to be on a leash and attended by a resident under the supervision of the staff member.

No animal is allowed in the kitchen area, nurses' station, utility room, or tub rooms. Animals are not allowed up on chairs or on other pieces of furniture.

## Responsible Person

The staff member responsible for the overall care and supervision of the pets and pet therapy is the Activities Director. She is to delegate responsibility to another employee on her days off from the facility.

## BUDGET

The cost of pet therapy is relatively small compared to the potential benefits. The Lima project uses over 175 animals and costs less than $600 a year.[26]

Although staff and patients are usually willing to contribute to the care of a pet, we recommend that it become a formal allotment in the institution's budget. It is, after all, a therapeutic activity. The initial investment, as we noted earlier, can be kept to a minimum. Upkeep will vary greatly, depending upon the circumstances, but here are some estimated costs, compiled by *Money* magazine. Costs include food, grooming, and veterinary costs.

—Large dog: $500–$700
—Large bird (parrot or cockatoo): $150–$400

—Cat: $150-$200
—Small fresh water fish: 25 cents to $2.50[27]

The costs can be offset tremendously for a dog, for example, if a veterinarian or humane shelter volunteers support service.

Additionally, within the pet therapy budget, we recommend an allotment for conferences, reference materials, and, if possible, training sessions. The International Conference on the Human/Companion Animal Bond, October 5-7, 1981 in Philadelphia, Pennsylvania, was not the first conference of its type, but possibly, it has been the most important to date. This conference inspired tremendous interest in pet therapy and since then, numerous regional conferences have been scheduled. We do urge an institution to keep informed on the current research in the field, and we strongly recommend that, if possible, the supervisory personnel (not the aide responsible for pet care) attend some of these gatherings. Information is available from the Delta Society, the international organization formed to investigate the human/animal bond. (See Appendix II for membership information.)

## ASSESSMENT—THERAPY DOG OR DOG THERAPY?

In the broadest context, the term therapy can apply to any activity that improves, slows, or eliminates a debilitating or undesirable condition in an individual. One person's therapy can be another person's problem. For example, a professional musician preparing for an important engagement could practice to the point of burnout; a few hours spent gardening might be a therapeutic diversion. Conversely, a professional landscaper could work to exhaustion trying to impress an influential client. A few hours relaxing at the piano could give this individual just the break he needed. These forms of therapeutic activity are common to all of us; we usually make no attempt to precisely measure the benefits we are receiving, yet, we know they have value. Each of us have our own special therapies that work for us when social or professional pressures become overwhelming.

In the strictest sense of the term, therapy is a treatment of a condition (or disease). The implication is that benefits can be measured, and given certain conditions, are applicable to other individuals who are plagued by the same disease.

Pet therapy programs, for the most part, fall into the first category. Some attempts have been made to measure the precise benefits within populations (Chapter 2), but most experts in the field agree that formal assessment of the programs is possibly the biggest challenge facing the discipline if, in fact, it is to be recognized as a formal, valid, and creditable treatment.

Perhaps the biggest obstacle to formally assessing pet therapy programs is the nature of the treatment: one unique entity interacting with another. Even holding certain factors constant—breed, size, temperament, traits (such as friendly, outgoing, obedient, calm)—strong personality differences exist. This is most apparent with dogs, cats, and large birds; however, be assured by anyone who has spent time interacting with a lot of different individuals of a given species, that this holds true even with the less complex species. Additionally, there will always be unknown factors that cannot be defined. For example, Mr. Jones can explain why he prefers the dog to the cat, but the dog cannot explain why he seeks out Mr. Jones more often than Mr. Smith.

A second problem is the interactive effect of an animal on a large, confined population. An almost universal comment about pet therapy is that it makes an institution seem more like home, in the sense that the atmosphere is more congenial, more relaxed, more interesting, less sterile. If a therapy animal has an impact on a single individual, be it staff or resident, the change in that individual will have a carry-over effect on the rest of the population. Let's assume that Mr. Jones and Mr. Smith spend long hours in front of the T.V.; they may exchange a few words, but they do not have what could be called an active friendship. The arrival of the therapy dog has a strong impact on Mr. Jones who assumes responsibility for walking it, feeding it, etc. Though Mr. Smith does not seem nearly as aware of the dog, there is a change in him too. Without his silent partner at the T.V. screen, he begins to engage in more activities; he begins to play card games with other individuals and volunteers to do some gardening.

Certainly both men's conditions have improved; one directly, the other indirectly as the result of the therapy dog, but can we precisely measure the effect of the dog on Mr. Smith? Probably not. The point is that apathy, lethargy, depression, and other symptoms that point to poor emotional health are contagious, particularly in an isolated and confined population. By improving these conditions for a few individuals, there is a good possibility of carry-over to the entire population.

Still another difficulty is improvement itself. What exactly are we measuring? Psychiatrist Michael McCulloch, for example, asks: "How do you measure the smile on an old woman's face when she picks up an animal?"[28] We can measure the number of smiles within a given period of time and compare it to a previously obtained baseline figure, but what value can be assigned to a behavior that occurs for the first time in many weeks, months, even years?

The fact remains that most formal scientific investigation culminates in a statistical analysis that measures the difference between a baseline condition and the same condition after treatment. The effectiveness of the treatment is based upon the deviation from chance (that is, the change that would have occurred at random with or without the treatment). Obviously a person who speaks after months of silence has improved more than an individual who simply speaks more than before. But this can be easily lost in data compilation.

There is a certain skepticism that accompanies the interpretation of anecdotal accounts of patient improvement, yet the full implication of the potential benefits of this treatment can, to date, most effectively be reported in this manner. Recall the very dramatic account by Robert Andrysco (Chapter 6). The woman in point was delusional, paranoid, violent; she made a virtual complete recovery. In his own words, "she was our miracle." Andrysco's study itself yielded impressive results, but the subjective account of this individual's reaction to the treatment more fully illustrates the incredible potential of this therapy.

A final point to consider and a most valid one is that potential long-range effects might be lost if the staff of an institution do not know what to look for. Andrysco says: "It's not enough to simply walk a dog through a patient population; you have to know what to expect and what to look for."[29] If you recall his dramatic recovery, when the woman was first introduced to the dog, she resisted and insisted it was brought to kill her. As an experienced therapist, Andrysco was able to proceed slowly and reinitiate the contact between woman and dog that eventually led to her recovery. An inexperienced staff member, following the rules about patients who don't like pets, would probably have taken considerable precautions to make sure the woman never had contact with Obie again (and rightly so). Unfortunately, there are few personnel currently who are skilled or trained in pet therapy. This is partially because the treatment is so new; it is also because researchers themselves are just beginning to define procedures. The new Companion Animal Services, founded by Robert Andrysco, and discussed in detail in Chapter 10, will eventually provide such a training ground. Chapter 12 reviews various evaluation techniques and Appendix IV contains a complete set of questionnaires that an institution can use to conduct a formal pet therapy project. Also, Chapter 7 offers numerous activities that can maximize the benefits of a pet therapy program.

For those institutions who are willing to embark on this exciting new program, yet lack the resources for a formal research study, Jules Cass offers some excellent advice:

> To my knowledge, no one formally evaluates, for example, occupational and art therapy. They are accepted methods that institutions take for granted will improve the lives of certain patients. In my opinion pet therapy should be instigated in the same way. I also suggest that if formal evaluation is to take place, the assessment begin after the program is well-established; this could take a few weeks to several months depending on the circumstances. The very novelty of the introduction of the animal is going to have an impact; I suggest that the pet, patients, and the staff all have a chance to settle in with one another.
>
> Sure, some of the dramatic effects may occur at the beginning, but if the physicians and therapists do their jobs, that is, follow-through on the patients' charts and case histories, there is no reason that this effect should be lost. All personnel in the health care professions have their own internal guidelines, the parameters that they themselves use to determine if a given individual is improving or not. Keep notes, mark your files, the patient's chart. Later, when all the excitement has died down, take a good look.[30]

## PET DAY

When all the arrangements have been made and you are ready to move the pet into the institution, schedule a staff meeting. At the staff meeting you might invite suggestions for activities. Chapter 7 discusses a number of potential programs, but we urge you to encourage your staff to think of others as well.

Determine a day and time and inform the patients as well as the staff. Arrange to have a brief introductory talk about the new pet, either by a staff member or a breeder. If any special activities have been ongoing in anticipation of the pet (a rabbit hutch, for example), applaud the residents involved and show off the work to the entire population. This should be a fun day for everyone. Usually, a caged animal, even a cat, can be introduced without prior visits. For a dog, we recommend a few short visits prior to the full-time residence to acquaint the patients with the pet and the dog with the facilities.

Expect some confusion at first, and don't be alarmed if you find you have not accounted for all eventualities. You are embarking on an exciting new project. You may have some difficulties at first, but the therapeutic potential is enormous, and problems, if you do have them, will probably be minimal.

Finally, don't expect miracles at the beginning. Individual animal and patient reaction may vary tremendously. Give the whole program a chance to acclimate, keeping in mind Jules Cass' suggestions. But, it you do see a miracle in the works, be sure to document it.

## REFERENCES

1. Levinson, Boris M. "Nursing Home Pets: A Psychological Adventure for the Patient." *The National Humane Review,* July-August 1970.

2. Andrysco, Robert M. "Companion Animal Service, Inc." Proposal prepared for the Columbus Foundation, December 1982.

3. Ibid.

4. Arkow, Phil. *"Pet Therapy": A Study of the Use of Companion Animals in Selected Therapies.* 3rd edition. Colorado Springs, Colorado: The Humane Society of the Pikes Peak Region, 1982.

5. Ibid.

6. Robb, Susanne S. "Pilot Study of Pet-Dog Therapy for Elderly People in Long-Term Care." Unpublished paper.

7. Cass, Jules. Personal Communication.

8. Stewart, Mary. "Loss of a Pet—Loss of a Person: A Comparative Study of Bereavement." Research presentation at the International Conference on the Human/Companion Animal Bond, October 5-7, 1981, Philadelphia, PA.

9. McLeod, Cappy. *Animals in the Nursing Home: A Guide For Activity Directors.* Colorado Springs, Colorado: McLeod, 1981.

10. Lee, David. Personal Communication.

11. Arkow, Phil. op. cit.

12. Lee, Ronnal L.; Zeglen, Marie E.; Ryan, Terry; and Hines, Linda M. *Guidelines: Animals in Nursing Homes. California Veterinarian* supplement, 1983.

13. Ibid.

14. Ibid.

15. Ibid.
16. Ross, Geraldine. "Chum—A Turtle With a Mission." *The National Humane Review*, July 1974.
17. Lee et al., op. cit.
18. Ibid.
19. Ibid.
20. Schaeffler, Joan. Personal Communication.
21. Lee, R.L. et al. op cit.
22. Ibid.
23. Ibid.
24. Cass, Jules. Personal Communication.
25. Arkow, Phil. op. cit.
26. Ibid.
27. Editorial. "*Money* Magazine Publishes Definitive Dicta on Pet Costs." *The Latham Letter*, Winter 1981-82.
28. McCulloch, Michael J. "Pet Facilitated Psychotherapy." Address presented at the International Conference on the Human/Companion Animal Bond, October 5-7, 1981, Philadelphia, PA.
29. Andrysco, Robert M. Personal Communication.
30. Cass, Jules. Personal Communication.

Chapter 6

# A Dog (or Cat) in Residence

## *SELECTING A DOG*

Since a dog in residence demands careful selection and more pre-planning than less mobile species, we will discuss this application of pet therapy in detail. Criteria, where so indicated, apply to cats also. We will also highlight some successful placements.

There are numerous considerations in selecting a dog. What size dog should you choose? Should it be long-haired or short-haired? Male or female? Pure-bred or mixed breed? Where will the dog come from? Where will it be housed? Inside, outside? Could the patients benefit from assisting in the dog's care or will this remain primarily a staff responsibility?

There is no single ideal breed, size, or type of dog that will work best in all environments, but there is probably an ideal dog for your needs. Here are some factors to consider:

### *Size*

Geriatric institution mascots cover the spectrum of size, and Therapy Dogs International canines include both toy and giant breeds. Generally, if an institution's population is composed primarily of infirm and bedridden subjects, the smaller dog that can sleep comfortably on a lap or in bed might be most suitable. A dog of this size generally requires somewhat less care also. However, in a mixed population that includes a number of well and mobile elderly, the medium or larger dog might provide more opportunity for play and exercise. Walking the dog could be a privilege and used as an incentive for patients to improve their own mobility and self-care.

## Coat Length

Just as dogs range widely in size, so coats vary from a short skin cover to lengthy and luxurious manes of hair. Obviously, a short or close-cropped, wiry-coated dog will require far less grooming than a pup whose mantle falls to the ground in silky filaments. Also, a dog who sheds can present both a health problem and housekeeping headache. Yet many people prefer the more fully endowed canine and enjoy keeping such an animal in immaculate perfection. Generally, if an institution's staff will be expected to provide most of the dog's care, the fewer the grooming requirements, the better. However, if the patients themselves will be expected to get involved in the animal's grooming, then the choices are less restrictive.

Brushing and combing of a long-haired dog or cat can provide many hours of tranquil relaxation for the patient and even needed exercise for partially crippled hands. Whatever the decision, the staff person initially responsible for obtaining the animal should know beforehand what the grooming requirements are. Many breeds whose curly, bushy coats look as if they require round-the-clock brushing are actually very simple to care for, requiring only a seasonal clipping and a few minutes of daily brushing.

## Pure-Bred or Mixed-Breed?

Advocates of pure-bred dogs cite numerous advantages including getting the exact type of dog you want, knowing the history and parents, and selecting certain desirable traits and characteristics. Mixed-breeds, however, also come in all sizes, shapes, and colors and may be less high-strung and more adaptable. They may be less susceptible to certain genetic defects. Also, with the tremendous problem of pet overpopulation, selecting a mixed breed dog from the local shelter is saving a life that would otherwise be destroyed. Although often these dogs do not have the early advantages of many of their pure-bred siblings, with proper care and training, there is no reason why such an animal cannot become a loving and suitable ward mascot.

Cost is an additional consideration. Pet therapy programs are, for the most part, relatively inexpensive, requiring only the food and veterinary care for the animal. Pure-bred dogs, however, are expensive, so unless there is a specific reason for selecting a specific breed, the institution hardly needs to take on an added expense. Unfortunately, there are a large number of pure-bred dogs turned over to shelters every year, but in this case, the advantage of knowing the dog's early upbringing is lost. Some breeders have been known to donate their dogs for worthy projects, but generally, the institution that wishes to adopt a dog mascot should first consider the local shelter. Therapy Dogs International incidentally has no restrictions on breeds; training and temperament are the criteria.

## Age

Puppies have been raised in institutions and the puppy's growth and progress have provided enjoyment and a learning experience for the residents. If a puppy is selected, however, the program must be very carefully supervised. A young animal is fragile and can unknowingly be hurt. It does not always have the sense to remove itself from a potentially negative situation. Additionally, if the puppy is not yet housebroken, its accidents can be a source of annoyance to both the staff and the patients. With these considerations in mind, the puppy's growth, training, and development can be a source of interest to the institution's entire population, and the maturation of the youngster can be an educational experience. Some homes have noticed an exceptional bonding between dogs first acquired as puppies and residents.

In most cases, the best choice is a mature dog who is housebroken and who has completed the rudiments of basic obedience training. After 9-10 months, the dog's personality is defined, its behavior patterns set, and the distinct personality that makes each dog unique has developed. Also, certain genetic diseases and disorders are not always obvious at birth and may heighten as the dog gets older. By selecting a mature animal, the institution will have a good idea of exactly what it's getting.

## Health

Obviously the dog should be healthy and free of external parasites. Fortunately, there are vaccines against the most common ailments that afflict dogs. Before a dog enters the institution, he should have a clean bill of health from the veterinarian and all current innoculations and/or boosters.

Selecting a good veterinarian is as important to your dog's health as a good general practitioner is to your own. If you do not have personal experience to draw upon, find those who do; for example, a local all-breed dog club. Since your program is contributing to research in pet therapy, you may find medical personnel willing to donate their services or charge you only a nominal fee. Ideally, your veterinarian should have some knowledge of behavior problems (or have an associate who does). Inquire about emergency service, and the possibility of a house call (to the facility) if necessary. If you have a progressive humane shelter, they will probably have a veterinarian(s) on staff who would be willing to lend support. Your veterinarian will help you set up a health card for your new pet (which should become part of the institution's records) and advise you of needed booster shots and periodic check-ups. If an unforeseen problem arises, he/she could be your best friend!

*Sex*

The dog or cat that becomes the ward mascot of an institution should be neutered. Ideally, this should be done before the animal is brought into the institution. Myths abound about the negative aspects of altering animals, but they are, in fact, myths. The animal will not become obese (unless it is overfed); its personality will not change (if it does, it will be ever so slightly for the better); nor does neutering rob the animal of anything. Many behavior problems and additional care requirements are associated with the onset of the breeding season in dogs and cats, and an institution with an intact male or female should be prepared to take precautions. Castration is often recommended to curb excess aggression in males, the animal will be less likely to roam (if it has access to the outside), and often females in season exhibit behavior that may be offensive or unpleasant to patients or staff. And, for humane reasons considering the current problem of pet overpopulation, there are overwhelming reasons in favor of neutering the animal. Operations to do so are relatively safe and inexpensive and can be performed when the animal is about six months old.

Perhaps the only reason for an institution to keep an intact dog or cat is if the animal is of the calibre that it will ultimately be bred. This might be the case if, for example, a breeder donates a dog and later wishes to use the animal in breeding. (A good therapy dog would have excellent characteristics to pass on to its offspring.)

## Temperament

Temperament is the single most important criterion for selecting an in-residence dog. To obtain the optimal benefit from the program, you will want a dog that will interact with as many different patients as possible. Additionally, patients will expect and desire different things from the dog. Some patients want an affectionate nuzzle and a spirited paw shake; others expect the dog to sit quietly by their side. An energetic elder may wish for a friendly walking companion; a wheelchair-bound patient might appreciate a gentle head on his/her lap. The therapy dog may be expected to be a model for an art class, an enthusiastic participant in a music movement class, a quiet confidante, a talented performer who can do tricks, an assistant for various services, and an impeccable, well-mannered resident. In short, the dog is expected to be all things to all people. Can a single animal possibly fulfill all these roles?

Incredible as it may seem, experience suggests that the dog can, and regularly does, meet the expectations of most institutions' residents and staff. Says Kerrill Knaus of Canine Companions for Independence whose Social dogs are specially trained for institutionalized living:

> One of the most remarkable traits of a well-established Social dog is the animal's ability to convey to each resident a quality of relationship often unobtainable by even the most skilled volunteer or visitor. Each resident sincerely believes that, according to the dog, he is the dog's favorite person in the whole facility, and often will not hesitate to tell you so. These dogs develop a remarkable sensitivity to the emotional needs of their charges and often radically modify their behavior according to the individual they are interacting with.[1]

You will want a dog that is friendly, outgoing, obedient, well-mannered, alert, and calm. The dog should readily acclimate to wheelchairs, walkers, and individuals with impaired motor coordination. The dog should not be aggressive, high-strung, boisterous, unruly, noisy, or fearful. If your institution has experienced successful dog visitation programs, consider consulting one of the participants when you make the decision to acquire a dog. Breeders have donated dogs, puppies, even already-accredited therapy dogs to institutions for their projects. Even if they do not, someone may be willing to accompany you to a humane shelter and help you select the most suitable dog.

## Environmental Considerations

### Outside Dog

If a dog is kept outside, it must have an ample kennel and a good-sized run or fenced-in area. The kennel should be weather-resistant and dry, and the inside should be fitted with warm and comfortable bedding that can be removed for cleaning. The ideal location is in a sheltered area that has trees and shrubbery to provide shade from the sun. It should be in an area that is observable to the patients, outside the window of an activity area for example, so even when the dog is not interacting with them, they can get pleasure from watching him. The larger the dog, the larger the area required; however, if the dog spends the majority of its day inside interacting with patients, this factor is not as critical. The dog still should be walked regularly, 2-3 times a day, as many animals will not get adequate exercise on their own. The dog's yard requires regular clean-up (about 2-3 times a week) of excrement.

### Inside Dog

Either a small or large dog can be housed inside an institution in various ways. The dog can be kept in an activity room, in an office, in a patient's room, and one home even provided their therapy dog with a room of his own!

A dog kept inside will be less susceptible to parasites (often transmitted by other dogs in the neighborhood), safer (dogs do manage to dig out of their pens or scale the fence), and will provide the added benefit of being a resident burglar alarm. Even if the dog sleeps under a patient's bed or a director's desk, it should be provided with a bed of its own. Though many commercial beds are available, you can easily make one yourself. A small dog will enjoy a basket with a blanket or soft bedding; for a large dog, an old mattress or cot with a removable, washable cover will work nicely. The bed should be located in a quiet spot easily accessible to the dog, preferably away from the bustle of activity. Dogs in institutions are working therapists and like their human counterparts, are subject to the stress of overwork. By providing a dog with a place of his own, you give the animal a place to rest and retreat if he feels he needs it.

## Nutrition

The nutritional requirements of dogs and cats have been carefully studied, and many commercial brands offer a menu that is satisfying, varied, and nutritionally complete. We recommend that you consult the breeder and veterinarian for advice. Adult dogs usually require a once-a-day feeding; however, for very large breeds or breeds that have a susceptibility to gastric torsion bloat, two smaller meals may be preferable to one large one. Fresh water must be accessible at all times.

## Other Requirements

Your dog will require a license, a collar and leash, a brush (possibly other grooming utensils), and his own food and water bowl (ceramic is preferable to plastic). Treats (dog biscuits) are a good idea, but their availability should be supervised. Patients fond of the dog may show their affection by hoarding food from their own meals or saving the special delicacies they receive as gifts for the dog. This is a fast road to canine obesity since most dogs will overeat if given the chance, particularly if the food is handfed. By allowing the patients to give the dog biscuits sparingly, this problem can be reduced.

A few toys are recommended, particularly for a young dog. You might want to get some obedience-type dumbbells to hone the dog's retrieving instinct. This activity is fun and provides the patient with moderate exercise. A young dog may have a tendency to chew and should be provided with some acceptable objects. Do *not* give the dog bones; they can splinter and cause injury or death. Some owners recommend the large knuckle or marrow bone since they do not sliver. However, a large dog can pulverize a bone like this in a matter of hours. Rawhide or beefhide chew toys are usually recommended, but check again with your veterinarian and a breeder with a successful past history of raising healthy dogs.

## Where to Get Your Dog

We recommend that you get your dog from a reputable breeder or a local animal shelter. We do not recommend getting a puppy from a pet store. Most of these animals come from puppy mills, and many are not properly supervised. Additionally, since licensing of these facilities varies widely from state-to-state (often it is non-existent), the conditions under which the parents live and the puppies are born are often less than exemplary. Puppy mills produce in quantity, not quality; their primary motivation is profit. Reputable breeders, on the other hand, place the welfare of the dogs and the breed first. The cost of a pure-bred dog is high; however, the puppies are the product of parents who have had extensive pre-natal care and who have been screened for genetic defects. You have the advantage of support from an individual who has a vast background in the particular breed offered.

A shelter offers the benefit of a large selection of dogs at a nominal cost. Many shelters have a considerable array of support services: veterinary, behavior and training counseling, etc. You will have the additional benefit of saving a life that might otherwise be destroyed simply because there are too few homes available. You will probably not have the advantage of knowing the dog's complete history and background, but many shelters screen the animals to a degree before they are offered for adoption. For example, trainer Diane Bauman regularly takes problem dogs from the local shelter, rehabilitates them, and returns them as potential candidates for adoption.

### Selection Procedure

(1) Selecting a puppy—beware of sentiment here. The puppy that makes a beeline for your waiting arms has not, as is commonly believed, selected you; it is probably the most aggressive of the litter. Similarly, although the woeful and shy pup who huddles in the background while its littermates play may tug at your heartstrings, excessively shy and fearful dogs can become fear biters. If you cannot resist this puppy, fine, take it home, that is, your home, not the institution. Look for a puppy that is friendly, that welcomes your handling, that is alert, playful, and in good health. If you have no experience with dogs, ask the breeder for help in making a selection.

(2) An adult dog requires more careful selection than a puppy; he's lived longer and has had more of an opportunity to learn bad habits. Again, keep your emotions in check. Health-care professionals, by nature, have a strong altruistic bent (or they probably wouldn't have selected the career), and may naturally extend this

compassion to animals as well. Do not select a dog primarily because (a) it has only 2 hours to live, (b) it is so pathetic you believe no one else would want it, or (c) or it is so pitiful, it needs your loving care. These are admirable motives, and people who adopt such animals often work wonders with them. However, you must remember that you are selecting an animal who will be therapist for a large number of patients. If the dog itself requires excessive medical care and/or extensive remedial training, it will cause more problems than benefits. If you absolutely, positively cannot resist such a dog, take it to your home, not to your workplace.

There is a notable exception to this rule, and we can only explain it in very unscientific terms. Sometimes as you walk through a shelter, you may experience instant rapport with an animal. Your eyes meet and something stirs. Something tells you this is the dog for you. This concept has been expressed by trainers of protection dogs, by those who select dogs for theatrical productions, and by ordinary pet-owners. The operative mechanism here may be less a mystical bond than a simple response to imperceptible body signals. A dog who is very people-oriented, which is the type of dog you want, will pick up signals from you that you are not even conscious of. If you have had experience with dogs and can trust your instincts, and all other factors are equal, go for it!

But let's do it more scientifically first. Avoid dogs who snap and growl or lunge at you through the cages. If the dog is supposed to be friendly, find out. Allow him to sniff your hands through the cage. Talk to him gently and see if he responds. If he gets too excited or vocal, he may be too high-strung. When you have chosen a few possibilities, ask an attendant to let you see the dogs at close range.

First, allow the dog to sniff your hand. If he nuzzles or licks it and does not retreat from contact, he is probably affectionate. Stroke the dog gently and talk to him reassuringly. Make eye contact. Begin at the head and slowly stroke the dog behind the ears, under the chin, along the shoulders and the back. Let the dog see your hand approach; if he acts fearful, he may be hand shy (that is, he may associate the human hand with punishment).

If all proceeds well so far, ask to walk the dog on the leash. If you have had some experience training a dog, try to get the dog to heel and sit. These are easy commands to learn and if the dog is not too unruly the first time out, you have a potentially excellent candidate for training. After your brief walk, praise the dog verbally and physically. Is he responsive but still controlled? (some very excitable dogs urinate when praised).

If this brief encounter has been pleasant and unproblematic, you may have found your therapy dog. Try to find out as much as possible about the dog. Why was he turned in to the shelter? You may not always get an honest answer (or the personnel simply may not know), but you can try. Ask about any specific phobias or aversions. There are perfectly good dogs abandoned at shelters for reasons as deplorable as the owner simply got tired of them. Often, however, persons who sell their homes (many elderly) and move into no-pet apartments must surrender their animals to a shelter.

The next step is to have the animal checked by a veterinarian. Be present at the examination and watch how the animal reacts. This is a stressful situation for most pets, so don't expect impeccable behavior. If the pet gets a clean bill of health and conducts itself fairly well during the examination, you've got your animal.

Before the dog is introduced to the institution and its residents, he should be trained at least to sit, stay, lie down, come when called, and walk mannerly on a leash (preferably off-leash). You can do this yourself by attending a training class or you can place the dog with a trainer who will do it for you and then instruct you how to maintain the learned behaviors.

This period of training is also an excellent time to determine if the dog has any problems not previously known. We recommend that you acquaint the dog to a variety of social situations. Walk him through a shopping center, an enclosed mall (if permitted), the neighborhood, anywhere large numbers of people congregate. Observe how the pet reacts to strange sounds, sights, and strangers. Some nervousness is fine, and an initially aloof demeanor toward strangers is not objectionable. As the dog gets acclimated, he will feel more comfortable. Try it a few times and watch how the dog reacts.

The final step before formal placement is to bring the dog to the institution as a visitor. Acquaint the dog with wheelchairs and walkers, and let the dog mingle with the patients. Keep the first visit short, and if the dog is nervous, reassure him with soft words and gentle petting. This is a novel situation for him; give him a chance to sense out the environment.

We recommend several visits prior to full-time residence and close supervision during the first week or two. When the residents, staff, and the dog get used to each other, everyone can relax a bit.

Also remember that these are guidelines, not hard and fast rules, as we will see in the section on successful placements.

## SELECTING A CAT

Many of the criteria for dog selection can be applied to cats as well, but there are some differences worth noting. In general, a cat requires less grooming than a dog. A long-haired cat will require daily brushing, but your average American short-hair type is a remarkably fastidious creature. A cat also has less tendency to overeat; dry kibble can be accessible at all times without fear of the animal eating to excess. Additionally, cats are less willing to accept "junk food" (candy, crackers, people snack-type items) than a dog, thus reducing the potential problem of patients overindulging the pet. Most cats provide their own exercise and do not need to be walked regularly like a dog. A cat, thus, usually requires less care than a dog.

We recommend a cat be kept indoors; it will be healthier, less susceptible to parasites, and safer from accidents. Contrary to popular belief, house cats are very content. The cat will appreciate access to a window and, if a comfortable berth is provided, will spend hours indulging its curiosity simply by looking outside. Cats can be trained to walk on a harness, and very sociable cats can be taken outdoors under supervision for a brief romp on the grass.

The cat should have its own bed, a basket with a blanket will do nicely, but an enclosed "kitty house" is even more welcome. Cats enjoy curling up in small places, and a hideaway can be easily constructed from a large cardboard box, with an open door, fitted with some bedding or blankets inside. The cat will require a litter box, and will learn to use one that is covered in this manner also.

You will need a brush (even short-haired cats enjoy brushing), other grooming utensils (special combs may be recommended for a Persian or other long-haired breed), ceramic water pan and food bowl (we recommend a self-feeder with a lid for kibble), and toys. Balls, catnip-filled toys, and yarn toys with bells are all readily available and inexpensive. They can also be made by residents (see Chapter 7).

Get your kitty from a breeder or the shelter. Although kittens in pet shops do not come from "cat mills," per se, you will usually pay just as much for an exotic variety as you would from a reputable breeder who can assure the quality.

A kitten may not be a bad choice. Although they must be handled carefully and sensitively, a small kitten is usually more self-sufficient than a puppy. And research has established that if a kitten is handled gently and often during its early months, it becomes as sociable, friendly, and affectionate as a dog.[2]

Current research suggests that there distinct personality types that prefer cats to dogs.[3] Additionally, according to a Yale University attitude survey, cats are not nearly as popular as dogs. According to this survey conducted by Stephen Kellert, dogs were the most liked animal, followed by horses. Cats, instead of being a close third, placed in the middle, which the researcher says is because most people are polarized in their attitudes towards them: they either adore them or hate them.[4] However, to their credit, even if your facility has a percentage of patients who strongly dislike cats, felines generally are less obtrusive than dogs, and have an innate sense of whom to avoid.

Guidelines for selecting a cat are similar to those for a dog; you want a friendly animal that does not bite, scratch, or hiss. Allow for most cats' natural aloof and independent demeanor. Look for a cat who purrs when you pet it and solicits further contact. In lieu of the leash test, assess the cat's willingness to play and socialize by bringing along a toy. (A ball of yarn with a bell attached will work fine.) Dangle the item in front of the cat and watch its reaction. A cat that will approach you and play with the toy is a good choice.

As a final consideration, cats, because they are very clean and self-sufficient, are a good choice for an individual who wants a pet in his room. They are naturally mannerly (in a feline way), are usually less vocal than dogs (thus less potentially annoying to another patient), and will lay contentedly purring at a patient's side or on his lap for hours.

These selection criteria are meant as guidelines only. For more extensive temperament tests for dogs and cats, we suggest you consult the previously cited *Guidelines: Animals in Nursing Homes.* But keep this in mind also. There are no hard and fast rules for selecting an animal. You may have done "none of the above," and still come up with a therapy pet you wouldn't trade for the most exquisitely trained and laudably cited animal in the world. In the next section, we will discuss a variety of placements; in each case, the animal differs by breed, size, housing, and place obtained; but they all have one element in common: they have proven themselves to be enormously successful therapists.

## SUCCESSFUL PLACEMENTS

*Chipper*

Chipper, a young Labrador Retriever and member of Therapy Dogs International, is the resident dog at St. Joseph's Home for the Aged in Towaco, New Jersey. Chipper first came to the facility 18 months ago when he was only a 10-week-old puppy, and the experience was the highlight of the patients' lives there.

"The patients all responded to the puppy," says Eileen Fattal, Activity Director. "They watched him mature, go through all the stages of puppyhood, and watched his training. It was like having a baby grow up in the home."

The facility is arranged so that relatively well and mobile residents live in congregate living quarters while those who require more extensive care are on separate floors. "When Chipper was a puppy, he was taken to these patients and placed on their laps or trays; they really enjoyed it," says Fattal. "Now, of course, he's too large to be a lapdog, but we still take him up for a visit. Everyone remembers what he was like when he was little."

Caring for a puppy, says Fattal, did not prove too burdensome. Chipper was housebroken in two weeks. When it was time for training, instructors came to the home to teach the staff how to train the dog. Many of the patients also got involved.

Chipper has an outside kennel and an ample 25 foot run, but he spends much of the day inside with the patients. His kennel is located outside the window of the activity room so patients can watch him. "When it rains," says Fattal, "they worry about him and complain to me that he shouldn't be outside in those conditions. Of course, he's warm and dry inside the dog house, but all they see is that it's raining and their Chipper is outside."

Several staff members share responsibility for the supervision of his care, and several patients feed and walk him. One patient accompanies Fattal to the veterinarian when Chipper requires his periodic check-ups. The security guards are required to walk Chipper during their shift. Most don't mind at all, reports Fattal, but the occasional grumbler has little to say about it: it's part of the job description.

Chipper has a fantastic temperament and, although he has many masters, is very well-behaved. He is quiet and barks only when he needs to go outside. "Everybody likes him," says Fattal. "It takes him 20 minutes to walk down the hall because everybody wants to pet him and talk to him. The staff work here and even the Sisters come and go, but with Chipper, it's different. He's 'theirs.' He belongs to them, and loves them without asking for anything in return. Patients who have no interest in any other activity are particularly drawn to Chipper."

Interestingly, the home decided to get a puppy when an adult dog, donated by a local family who moved from the area, didn't work out. The dog, a large and boisterous Irish Setter, refused to settle in; he jumped on the patients, and many of them were afraid of this somewhat large dog. After three weeks, another home was found for the Setter.

"Chipper is just as large now," says Fattal, "but no one is afraid of him, except maybe a potential intruder. Because he grew up in the home, he's accepted as a member of the family. Sure, he's more mannerly than the other dog, but patients still make allowances for him that they just wouldn't make for another dog."

The only problem Fattal has had is with patient possessiveness. One man became so attached to Chipper, he hid him away in his room. "Whenever Chipper was missing for long periods of time, that's where he'd be," she says.

The placement is ideal. Chipper is a hardy, low-maintenance dog who is liked by everyone and who generally makes life more pleasant in the facility.

### Skipper

Skipper, an Old English Sheepdog who after five years of service at the Little Sisters of the Poor Home for the Aged in Enfield, Connecticut, certainly qualifies as a veteran therapy dog, is another successful puppy placement. This breed is relatively large and requires extensive grooming. They resemble an animated shag rug that didn't know when to stop growing; and some breeders have said that "Keeping an Old English Sheepdog in immaculate condition is a fulltime occupation!" Sister Rose, however, explained that the extra care required has never been a problem. One patient feeds him and regularly bathes him. Many patients enjoy brushing him. Occasionally, he becomes a bit matted and is quickly taken to a professional grooming facility, but most of the time, the patients do very well on their own.

Skipper has the run of the facility, except for the dining room and the chapel. He knows all the patients and goes everywhere with them. If they wait in line to see a doctor, he waits in line too. "Once during a movie," says Sister Rose, "we had acquired a popcorn maker and had it in the back of the room. Someone called out 'Anyone for popcorn?' and Skipper was the only one who got up." This enchanting therapy dog also accompanies patients on outings, and he regularly escorts the patients in wheelchairs to the park.

Skipper lives inside the home; in fact, he has his own room. His bed, made by the patients, is a covered mattress and the housekeeping staff regularly launders the cover to insure that Skipper has "fresh linen." The walls of Skipper's room are decorated with pictures of dogs cut from magazines and books, another patient project. There are several chairs in the room, and residents often visit Skipper in his room, just like he visits them in theirs. "He's very much a part of the family," says Sister Rose.

The extent of patient involvement with Skipper can be illustrated by a particular incident. On one of his rare moments of mischief, Skipper indulged in the common canine misbehavior of car chasing. He had a run-in with a mail truck and wouldn't move. Fortunately, a veterinary examination revealed the big dog had not sustained serious injury, but was only stunned. The prescription was a few days of rest and relaxation. He didn't have to add tender loving care.

Skipper was tenderly placed in his room, and the patients were advised of his needs. They took turns visiting him being careful to speak gently and softly. They made sure he was covered with a soft blanket. They sent him get-well cards. Skipper still needed to go outside to relieve himself, but he was reluctant to move. So the patients got a pushcart, gently placed him on it, and wheeled him outside. Skipper jumped off the cart, did his business, and jumped right back on. The patients wheeled him back in and put him back to bed. "This went on for a few days," recalls Sister Rose, "then he was back to his old self, but it gave the patients a rare opportunity to do some nursing themselves. And they did it beautifully."

Skipper is obedience trained and has an engaging personality. "He learns very fast and knows all the residents," says Sister Rose. "He's always willing to get involved. One woman was a steadfast loner; she just didn't get on with anyone, except Skipper. Eventually, however, through her involvement with him, her outlook improved and she began to participate in other things.''

The Little Sisters of the Poor homes are located throughout the country and most of them have resident pets. ''We have aquariums in all the waiting rooms here,'' says Sister Rose, ''and we also have parakeets. We've found that most of our patients have had to give up everything when they come here: their homes, friends, their own pets. By providing companion animals, we can partially replace that loss, we can fulfill a need and make our facility more like home.''

Skipper, however, is someone extra special. ''He's a friend, a companion, a confidante, a sheer delight,'' she says.

### Roman

Roman is a Shetland Sheepdog in residence at the Orange Park Care Center in Orange Park, Florida. Although he has been at the facility only a few months, the placement is working out ''beautifully,'' describes Suzanne Lyda, the Activity Director there.

Previously, the Orange Park Dog Club visited the facility and put on a show. The presentation was so successful and the patients so responsive, the administrators decided that perhaps they could get their own dog. They became even more enthused when one of the dog club members volunteered to place an animal in the facility.

To determine how the placement would be received, Lyda polled the staff, residents, and families of the residents to see if there would be any objection to having a pet in residence. ''Fortunately,'' she says, ''the dog won.''

The dog donated, Roman, is two years old and a trained member of Therapy Dogs International. Shetland Sheepdogs are a small breed who look like miniature collies. Even though Roman is low to the ground, he has no problem with wheelchairs. He sits on coaches with the patients and is small enough to cuddle in a lap. He is kept inside, in the activity area, but spends most of his time with the patients. ''His favorite shift,'' says Lyda, ''is the 11 p.m. to 7 a.m. shift. He makes the rounds with the nurse on duty and nuzzles each person's hand to make sure they're okay.''

Both staff and patients are impressed with the friendly little dog, and Lyda reports many volunteers for baths and long walks. A local veterinarian is donating medical care. Incredibly, the facility has not received a single complaint from patients' families. ''We've been very fortunate,'' says Lyda.

Roman's presence had an immediate impact on some patients, reports Lyda.

> One lady would not respond to anything for months; she is responding to Roman. Another patient's main goal in life was to stay in bed. She would not get up for any reason. When she heard Roman was coming, however, she was the first one at the door that day. Another woman has difficulty remembering her own name, but she has no trouble remembering Roman's.

Lyda says that Roman does have a tendency to form attachments to one person, but also feels this may be part of the adjustment period. When Roman and the patients are more acclimated to one another, he will be involved in more activities. Already, he accompanies patients to Mass and is beginning to sense the individual needs of the residents.

"He did an odd thing the other day," says Lyda. "We have a patient who wanders around and goes in rooms where he's not supposed to. Roman followed him, and each time, he went in someone else's room, Roman circled around him till he left. Finally, he brought him back to his own room." Shetland Sheepdogs were originally bred to protect and care for sheep. Roman, apparently, has extended this natural inclination to a special flock very much in need of his services: the residents of Orange Park Care Center.

### Bashful

Bashful is a large, long-haired mixed breed dog who has been in residence for 18 months at the Hospitality Care Center of Jacksonville, Florida. This long-term care facility decided to get a dog because the local Humane Society's visitation program was so enthusiastically received. "The residents requested one," says Suzanne Smith who is a co-activity director and social service liaison.

Bashful lives inside, he sleeps under a patient's bed (a special one that he selects, says Smith) and when he needs some "time-off" retreats under Smith's desk. Both residents and staff care for the dog, and all departments, activity and housekeeping, share the task. "Everyone likes him, and all the staff, even the administration, pet him and talk to him; except the food department, they can't because of their job. The night shift feel more secure with him here; they are positive his presence has prevented break-ins."

A representative of the Humane Society selected Bashful, and Smith reports no problems with him. He was not formally trained, to her knowledge, but is obedient and well-mannered. When he's out, he stays on the property, and inside, he is quiet and gentle. He has a tendency to attach himself more to some than others, but during the day he makes the rounds and socializes with everyone. "At Christmas, he wears jingle bells, and on the 4th of July, he wore red, white and blue for our Parade," says Smith.

Touching and petting Bashful gives the patients an opportunity to express and receive love and affection, says Smith. Once during a reminiscence class, Bashful walked in and sat down. Smith, who intended to do the recollection on farms, switched to dogs instead, using Bashful as a model. The result was an outpouring of memories; most of the patients had owned dogs and the gentle canine's presence provided the impetus for recall. "It was an extremely successful session," says Smith.

Since the Center's goal is to eventually discharge patients, Bashful's role is especially vital. One patient in particular, Joe L., benefitted enough from interaction with the dog that he moved to a facility closer to his family. "Joe immediately took on full responsibility for the dog," says Smith, "it was apparent that he needed more than just petting the dog. He wanted to be in full charge of him. The new facility has a pet bird, and according to staff there, it now spends most of its time sitting on Joe's shoulder."

When Joe left, Bashful became somewhat depressed, "melancholy" as Smith describes it. "He obviously missed Joe and moped around for about three days. Then he selected another patient, Peg L. He sleeps under her bed at night, just like he used to sleep under Joe's. He must sense that she is able to supply his needs." No doubt, Bashful will also be able to supply many of hers.

## Maxy

Maxy, a small poodle-mix dog, came to the Beverly Manor Convalescent Home in Bakersfield, California, as an act of fate or stroke of luck as the staff would describe it. Sharon Varner, Activity Director there, was attending a local swim meet when neighborhood children found the abandoned dog. Maxy was a stray, sickly, and badly in need of grooming, but Varner noticed she was extremely friendly.

A few visits to the veterinarian and a trip to the grooming parlor and Maxy was as good as new. Varner asked permission to bring the dog to the facility, and the administration agreed. A previous Activity Director brought her dog in, but when she left, she took the dog with her. "That dog was friendly," recalls Eileen Well, Activity Coordinator, "but not nearly as friendly as Maxy."

Maxy is extremely affectionate and very sociable; she mixes with everyone. She is small enough to cuddle on a lap and divides her day among as many different patients as possible. "Many of the patients," report Well, "call her by the name of a dog they used to own, but it doesn't matter to Maxy; she comes anyway." She has had no formal obedience training, but does everything she's told. "Our administrator has only to snap his finger and point to a room, and in she goes," says Well.

There were more surprises. One day, Maxy had pups beneath Varner's desk. "We didn't even realize she was pregnant," exclaimed Well. The pups, four tiny healthy bundles, became the focal point of the institution. The patients rallied around them. When the puppies were of proper age all four were adopted by staff members.

The litter of puppies did have one unfortunate consequence. A neighbor complained about the noise and the dogs' presence. To safeguard their program and prevent possible hassles, Smith and Varner now take Maxy home at night, alternating with each other.

But every morning the spunky little therapist is back. "She loves to come to work," says Well. "As soon as the patients see her, they begin to call her and she comes to each one in turn. She doesn't ignore anybody."

To the residents at Beverly Manor, the little stray dog is as valuable as the most revered champion. "We were very lucky to find her," says Well. "She is a gift to the hospital, a blessing."

## REFERENCES

1. Knaus, Kerrill. Personal Communication.
2. Karsh, Eileen B. "The Effect of Early Handling on the Development of Social Bonds Between Cats and People." Research presentation at the International Conference on the Human/Companion Animal Bond, October 5-7, 1981, Philadelphia, PA.
3. Editorial. "Mills College Professor Explores Aspects of Human/Companion Animal Bond." The Latham Letter, Winter 1981-82.
4. Hen0son, Nancy. "Americans and Animals: A Study in Inconsistency" (A review of the attitudinal surveys conducted by Stephen R. Kellert of Yale University). Orion Nature Quarterly, Autumn 1982.

Photo by Bob Barber.

Chapter 7

# Program Suggestions
# for Animal-Facilitated Therapy

Kerrill Knaus, the placement coordinator for Canine Companions for Independence, says: "Once a dog begins work at a facility, the possibilities of how a dog will be used are only limited by the staff's ability to creatively employ the animal in activities."[1] The purpose of this chapter is to suggest programs that can be used to maximize the effectiveness of the in-house animal therapist.

## *PHYSICAL ACTIVITY AND EXERCISE*

Most health experts agree that a brisk walk is one of the most beneficial forms of exercise possible, providing as much as 90% of the benefits of more stressful and regimented programs such as jogging. Walking has the additional benefit of requiring little preparation and no regimen. It is an ideal exercise for the elderly, but seniors, who may already feel without purpose, can easily become bored and lose motivation if their only aim is aimless walking. Walking the dog, however, is a meaningful and enjoyable activity that has value not only to the elder, but to the animal also. The pet animal can thus provide motivation that may otherwise be lacking.

Explains Knaus:

In physical therapy, dogs can be used to increase motivation. For example, Mr. Jones is supposed to walk; however, simply pacing up and down the halls is so tedious that after a few minutes he returns to his room to watch TV. Yet, if Mr. Jones is told that the dog is getting too fat because no one will take the time to exercise him, he could be inspired to greatly extend his own exercise period in order to take care of his furry buddy. An additional asset to this would be that not only would he receive companionship during his walking time, but by practicing the dog's various commands, he could greatly reduce the monotony of his activity.[2]

But the dog can even provide incentive for the patient who is unable to walk it personally. A picture of Phila, a therapy dog who belongs to one of the authors, hangs in the hall at the Roosevelt Hospital where she is frequently a visiting therapist. One elderly woman walks down to the hall every evening to look at her picture. Phila has given this woman a reason to walk and much needed activity.

The leisurely act of stroking a pet dog or cat can be beneficial and soothing to gnarled, arthritic hands, and Dorothy Walster, health educationist for the Scottish Health Education Group, has noted that the shoulder exercise involved in caring for a caged bird is healthful.[3]

## SPEECH THERAPY

We have already seen that the presence of a pet animal can prompt an otherwise non-communicative person to speak. Often the patient's lack of response is self-imposed; and the dog provides a reason to break this silent vigil.

The dog can also provide the incentive for a patient who wishes to speak but has difficulty doing so; for example, a stroke victim. Anyone who has witnessed the painful process of returning to the spoken world for one so disabled knows how tedious and frustrating the ordeal can be. Each word is a strain and an effort. Imagine the frustration of trying to communicate with another person when you can only vocalize a few words or phrases.

The dog, however, is trained to respond to a single word: its name will bring immediate recognition; a command, "sit," "stay," or "come," results in a definite behavior. The patient who has worked so hard to re-learn the word has an immediate and definite reward for his or her efforts. Never mind that it is only a single word or two; it is a breakthrough and more words will come later. For now, the patient knows that he can communicate with at least one other being at the facility and be understood: the therapy dog.

## MOTION TO MUSIC THERAPY

Most dogs are only too willing to move along with a human friend when the occasion permits. Invite the therapy dog to the music class and watch how eagerly the pet participates. The dog, Honey, in the JACOPIS study (Chapter 2) was always a willing participant.

## REMINISCENCE THERAPY

"Life review is an important aspect of working with the elderly," says Leo Bustad. "Encouraging reminiscence is an effective tool. Animals can trigger reminiscences."[4] When Bashful walked into a reminiscence class; the therapist immediately saw a way to employ the therapy animal to the situation. The result was a very successful session.

## SPIRITUAL THERAPY

When Jules Cass read an article about Therapy Dogs International, one statement, in particular, had an impact. The story mentioned that hospital chaplains in England often make their rounds accompanied by a dog. "This is something I could immediately get my chaplains working on," says Cass.[5]

The comforting presence of the dog can relieve anxiety in the patient. If the person is troubled, the soothing experience of patting the dog may calm him sufficiently to discuss his problems with the human chaplain.

## PATIENTS' SPECIFIC NEEDS

The needs of an individual patient will be as varied as the residents of any given facility. One specific example, showing how staff can deal with an individual's problem, is suggested by Kerrill Knaus:

> One facility used their dog in a situation where a gentleman was refusing to eat. After extensive questioning, staff discovered that he felt it inappropriate to be constantly given free meals when he was doing no work to contribute to the well-

being of the home. "If you don't work, you shouldn't get to eat," was his philosophy. Because of the severity of his physical limitations, he was unable to do any of the more traditional activities such as gardening or helping the nursing staff with basic chores. He was assigned to monitor all the care and feeding of the Social dog, being told that it was simply too much work for the nurses to have to care for the animal in addition to their regular work. He groomed the dog, cleaned water and food bowls, and he made himself the dog's personal advocate in situations of dissension. He worked with the Activity Director to delegate the dog's daily assignments. Within a day's time, he was back in the dining room and happily interacting with other residents and staff. He once again was a needed individual, with a sense of purpose.[6]

Two additional examples are supplied by Leo Bustad.

This anecdote," he says, "involves our work with a nursing home which has a pet therapy room containing Handsome, the Persian cat. The health care team at the home meets to decide which resident can derive the greatest benefit from living in the private therapy room. The current resident, Marie, was chosen because she had no family or friends, would not communicate, and remained curled in a fetal position with no interest in living. She also had sores on her legs from continual scratching. When other measures failed, she was moved in with Handsome. Whenever she began to scratch her legs, the cat played with her hands and distracted her. Within a month the sores were healed. She began to watch the cat and to talk with the staff about him. Gradually she invited other residents in to visit with him. Now she converses with strangers, as well as the nursing home staff about the cat and other subjects.[7]

This episode is even more dramatic. A frail, elderly man was brought to the nursing home from the local hospital. He had been discovered in a severely malnourished and confused state in a rural farmhouse, living alone in filth. Once his condition stabilized, he was brought in restraints to the nursing home since he refused to eat. The staff was unable to break this cycle until an aide found the Center's three kittens in bed with him. When the cats were removed, he became agitated. A reward system was devised whereby the cats would be returned to him if he ate. He gained 40 pounds and interacted with other residents. The cats were the bridge that brought him back to reality. The director of nursing stated that otherwise she believes he would have died.[8]

## OCCUPATIONAL THERAPY

Therapy animals can provide occupational therapists with a multitude of therapeutic possibilities. We have already discussed the therapy pet as an incentive to exercise and physical activity, and noted throughout this book how the presence of the animal functions as a social catalyst. Also, pets provide a potpourri of sights, smells, sounds, and touch to stimulate the senses. Petting, playing, watching, and interacting with the therapy pet provides hours of valuable therapeutic activity as well as leisure and entertainment. If the therapist is involved in out-patient care, the use of guide dogs, hearing dogs, and signal and service dogs could provide clients with psychological and physical assistance vital to independent living.

Additionally, the presence of a therapy animal can induce patients to re-vitalize old skills and even to learn new ones. Often the inactivity and lethargy of the elderly institutionalized resident is not so much an unwillingness to do something, but a sense of purposelessness connected with activity in a vacuum.

To creatively employ interest in the animal to these activities, the Activity Director should ask: "What does the animal need that the patients could provide?" For example, at the Recreation Center for the Handicapped in San Francisco, a group of mentally retarded adults constructed a pen for their resident companion rabbit, Bubba.

A dog who is kept outside will require adequate shelter and a secure and ample pen. A project like this could involve many residents and should be initiated as soon as the facility knows it will acquire the animal. But even an indoor dog will appreciate a private bed that could be constructed by the patients. A blanket, sewn by resident sewers, or an afghan, knit or crocheted by the needlework hobbyists, would be a welcome and warm bedding for the facility's new resident.

And what canine, large or small, doesn't appreciate a coat or two? There are entire industries that cater to the pet owner who wishes to buy these items for his animal companion. The home's residents might want to take up a collection to get this pup paraphernalia, but better—why not encourage them to make it themselves. Collars can be tooled from leather, worked in fabric, or even personalized with needlepoint. A leash could be fashioned from macrame. The key here is to see what the interests and abilities of the residents are and proceed from there. Many elderly women (and a growing number of men who have learned the health benefits of such activity) are skilled at needlework and sewing. These pursuits can provide leisurely and soothing activity for hands plagued by arthritis. Most health experts agree that inactivity generally promotes further debilitation; yet the initial discomfort and stiffness can discourage much-needed activity. Fashioning an item for the beloved pet, however, can provide enough impetus to overcome this initial hurdle.

A resident cat will enjoy a bed and also a scratching post easily made from carpet remnants. A cover for the kitty commode can be constructed from heavy cardboard. The cat would welcome the privacy and the housekeeping staff would appreciate this added bit of tidiness.

Cappy McLeod, a former nursing home activities director, suggests an interesting project that might inspire the green thumbs of the facility: harvesting catnip. While the herb is drying, craft activities can be utilized to make feline toys. McLeod, who is an artist and writer, even offers a pattern for a catnip mouse in her informative booklet *Animals in the Nursing Home: Guide for Activity Directors* (for availability, see Appendix).[9]

A resident caged bird would like a cage cover at night; this is easily made from a small amount of material and well-placed stitches. If the bird is tame enough to occasionally leave a cage, a playpen could be constructed. In the Mugford and M'Comisky study of elderly pensioners who were given parakeets, the researchers noticed that one elderly gentleman fashioned a very elaborate playpen for his pet. There is very little we landlubbers can do to enhance the environment of a tank of fish, but these little creatures too can be used to stimulate creative activity as we shall see in the next section.

## STIMULUS TO CREATIVITY

The individual interests of the patients must be considered in any therapy program; and not all patients are interested in handicrafts or needlework. But, is there an artist in the ranks that might view the therapy animal as a suitable subject for his talents? We probably don't need to remind you that famed Grandma Moses didn't even pick up a palette till she was of advanced age; so even if a patient has never before attempted such an activity, now might be the ideal time to start.

Samuel Corson found such a patient in his studies at the Castle Nursing Home. The elderly man who was withdrawn and uncommunicative had been a resident of the home for over 20 years. After he met the dog, he began drawing and painting pictures of dogs. The patient shared his artwork with the staff and even displayed his efforts on his walls. Corson remarked that some demonstrated quite a bit of skill and perception.[10] In the Australian study, researchers Salmon and Salmon discovered that the therapy dog, Honey, prompted a deaf woman to take up painting.

The presence of the therapy animal could be used as a stimulus for creative pursuits: drawing, painting, photography, poetry, a dramatization. The possibilities are only limited by the individual inclinations and abilities of the patients. But the animal is the inspiration and the impetus. For these pursuits, even a tank of fish would be a suitable and fascinating subject.

Cappy McLeod found that making animal scrapbooks was a worthwhile activity. The project was initiated by one of McLeod's charges, an 84-year-old woman, and the finished books were donated to children in area hospitals. The residents selected animal pictures from magazines, greeting cards, and wrapping paper and did all the cutting, glueing, and pasting themselves. The books were so well-received that the group immediately went back to work making more.[11]

To consolidate a group's creativity, an Activity Director might begin a friendship quilt project. The friendship quilt is a traditional craft that is enjoying a resurgence in popularity today. Each member of the group, in this case, the institution, contributes one square to the project's completion.

Now the novelty of this project is that unlike the usual concept of a sewn quilt, the squares can be as individual as the persons who create them. One person may contribute a drawing; another a photograph or a poem. Staff can work with patients to help select designs that would work in the overall format and are of uniform size. Aside from this, the possibilities are limitless. For this project, the common theme could be the resident companion animal. That solves the problem for residents who insist they have ''nothing of interest'' to create. Staff might be encouraged to contribute a square also or just be involved in assisting patients and assembling the finished project. The final work is a group effort that the entire facility can be proud of. It could be displayed in the institution's reception area or even entered in a state fair if your facility is in an area where this is a common activity. The point of the project is to provide the seniors with a mutual goal and promote camaraderie as well as to stimulate the special talents and interests each one has. The common bond and inspiration, the therapy animal, will provide the perfect subject and inspiration.

## CONTINUING EDUCATION

Many seniors might scoff if someone suggested that they spend their free hours learning new skills and exploring new interests. Yet in many ways the later years are an ideal time to learn. The elder is free, in most cases, from concerns about family and the demands of a career. And an active, questing mind is vital to sound emotional health.

But for the elderly person who is institutionalized and expects to be for the remainder of his life, the value of continuing education seems pointless. What is the purpose of pursuing a new skill or interest? Where and when could he ever hope to use it?

Once again, the role of the therapy dog expands. As anyone who has an interest in canines knows, there is a wealth of fact and lore on the subject. Books range from care and training to myth and folklore, and every one of the more than 200 breeds recognized by the American Kennel Club has at least one volume written about it. There are at least three fine all breed canine publications: *Pure-Bred Dogs American Kennel Gazette, Dog World,* and *Dog Fancy.* Additionally, many pure bred dog organizations publish magazines devoted to their select canine.

Patients, after coming to know and love their new companion, could be encouraged to learn as much about the dog as possible. How did the numerous breeds of dog develop; where did they originate? How do other cultures perceive the dog? The dog is already trained—how was this accomplished? These are just a few of the topics that could be "researched" by patients and later reported to the group, and possibly elsewhere.

## GUEST GROUPS

Cappy McLeod says three groups that would be welcome guests to the nursing home are scout troops, church groups, and 4-H clubs. McLeod says by working with troop leaders of various groups, meetings can be scheduled at least monthly. All that is needed is an activity room set up with tables and chairs, as the scout leader will plan the agenda.

The project, she says, is beneficial to the children also, since it educates them early in life that a nursing home does not have to be a negative experience. Additionally, by their involvement with elders, the youngsters have an opportunity to earn various merit badges in volunteerism and community service.

Church groups offer a second type of youth-elder involvement. McLeod describes one special group comprised of a second grade Sunday school class and eight elderly residents of a nearby nursing home. The group studied the animals of the Bible and made an exquisite appliqued wall hanging for the church. At the presentation the children and seniors walked hand in hand down the aisle to present their masterpiece to the congregation. Friends, family, and nursing home staff attended this truly memorable moment for old and young.[12]

Still a third activity could involve 4-H clubs and their dog obedience projects. Says columnist Edi Munneke, who with her husband wrote a handbook that is used for novice obedience training:

> For years, I have known about the 4-H organization that promoted activities for the rural youth of America. As more and more families left the farms to settle in urban areas, this organization has expanded to include interested city children. Where the children used to work mostly with pigs, sheep, cows, and horses, these animals were seldom owned by urban families, but most households did include a dog; so for practical reasons, the training and care of dogs has become an ever expanding activity for 4-H members.[13]

## OUTSIDE ACTIVITIES

Al Munneke, though wheelchair-bound, participated in the sport of obedience until his death at the age of 75. Perhaps there is an elder in your institution who is so inclined.

Photo by Bob Barber.

Is there a patient who has taken over the dog's exercise, enjoys testing the dog's training, even expressed an interest in further training the dog himself? Would this person enjoy entering the dog in an obedience competition?

Most dog groups sponsor what are called match shows in which future serious competitors get needed practice in showing their dog, either for breed or obedience. These match shows are fun, usually require only a nominal fee, and do not have the pressure of more serious competition. A senior who is interested enough might be encouraged to pursue this activity. In fact, it could be a field trip for any members of the institution who were able to get out. Again, this activity promotes kinship and camaraderie within the group for even if not all patients can participate, they can cheer on the ones who do. Since it is the group's dog, any victory is shared by all. And defeat? As we mentioned, these matches are fun and since the victories are not counted towards an obedience or show title, they do not carry the pressure of more serious competition. The joy of participation and the excitement of competition should more than compensate for any disappointment or defeat.

## PET SHOW

A pet show has all the ingredients of a sure-to-please event: visitors, animals, refreshments, excitement, and fun! With a little planning and some help from interested groups (scout troops, dog clubs, etc.), this event could be the high spot of the facility's social calendar.

Cappy McLeod put one together with the aid of journalist Phil Arkow, the residents of the nursing home, and the therapy dog's veterinarian. She invited all the scout troops that had participated in activities with the home, all of whom were to bring an animal, a photo, or drawing of their pet. Additionally, the children were required to write an essay about what being a responsible owner means to them. Awards were based on longest legs, shortest tail and designed so that everyone would eventually receive a blue ribbon.

The event was initially scheduled outside, but an unexpected rainfall moved the activities indoors. The project was just as festive and successful. McLeod reported no dog fights and no breach of house training. A special event, the "Rodent Race," in which rats were placed in round plastic exercise balls and cheered across the floor,

Photo by Bob Barber.

Photo by Bob Barber.

139

was particularly well-received. The only accident was a single spilled glass of punch.[14]

Eileen Fattal scheduled a dog show inviting members of the local kennel club. The event was very successful because there were a number of different breeds represented, and some of the dogs, she says "really put on a good show."

The suggestions in this chapter are but a few of the many rewarding and worthwhile activities involved with loving, learning about, and interacting with animals. Much, of course, will depend upon the individuals within a facility, their health, interests, and abilities. However, as one final thought, let your imagination be your guide, and don't impose restrictions on your patients that they do not impose on themselves. A challenge, an expectation of accomplishment can do much to regenerate interest in life and living. Not every activity will work everywhere, but you will never know unless you try.

## REFERENCES

1. Knaus, Kerrill, Personal Communication.
2. Ibid.
3. Walster, Dorothy. "Pets and the Elderly." *The Latham Letter*, Summer 1982.
4. Bustad, Leo K. and Hines, Linda M. "Placement of Animals with the Elderly: Benefits and Strategies." In *Guidelines: Animals in Nursing Homes. California Veterinarian* Supplement, 1983.
5. Cass, Jules, Personal Communication.
6. Knaus. Personal Communication.
7. Bustad. op. cit.
8. Ibid.
9. McLeod, Cappy. *Animals in the Nursing Home Guide for Activity Directors*. Colorado Springs, Colorado: McLeod, 1981.
10. Corson, S.A. and E.O. "Pet Animals as Nonverbal Communication Mediators in Psychotherapy in Institutional Settings." In *Ethology and Nonverbal Communication in Mental Health: An Interdisciplinary Biopsychosocial Exploration*. Corson, S.A. (ed). London: Pergamon Press, 1979.
11. McLeod, Cappy. op. cit.
12. Ibid.
13. Munneke, Edi. "Obedience News," *Dog World,* November 1978.
14. McLeod, Cappy. op. cit.

# Chapter 8

# Pet Visitation Programs

Journalist Phil Arkow, whose comprehensive overview of pet therapy programs is now in its 3rd edition, remarked that "when this report was first published in 1977, the author was aware of only 15 humane societies conducting pet-facilitated therapy programs; today, the number is more than 75 and climbing."[1]

Dog clubs, both breed and obedience, are no strangers to these activities. In fact, reading dog magazine reports of individuals who were successfully involved in these programs planted the seeds for Therapy Dogs International. With the growing awareness of pet therapy and its special benefits to the elderly, we will probably be seeing more and more of these programs in coming years. And as the pet visitation study by Francis et al. (Chapter 2) demonstrated, these programs are effective.

There are both advantages and disadvantages to a visitation program as compared to a live-in mascot. Visiting therapy dogs or other animals are cared and provided for by the individuals or organization sponsoring the event. The institution does not have to make any special provisions for the pets; in fact, during the session, staff members often notice a reduction in tension and lessened demands on their time; they can take a "break" while the dogs are there. And the visits have a carry-over effect. Patients become more responsive on "Dog Day"; one report told of an elderly woman who steadfastly refused to leave her room until she heard the dogs were coming. Then she was the first in line at the dayroom. Staff can utilize these visits as a point in common with the patients, something to talk about and anticipate. And, if the program is creative and exciting, it will be the highlight of the patient's month. Therapy Dogs International executive director Milt Wynn recently received a call from a lady who had just taken a new job as an activity director at a geriatric facility. To plan her programs, she asked her patients which particular events they enjoyed the most. "The dog show" was the overwhelming response, so she called Milt to schedule a repeat visit.

Visiting animals, however, cannot provide the continuing reinforcement of love and affection that the patients want. Visits can be weeks or more apart and different animals may be used for each program; thus, a personal bond between patient and pet is not easily established. However, if the same animal visits the same patient frequently the bond is established. Patients especially fond of the animals may experience a letdown when the program is over though this can be important therapeutically, particularly if the patient is withdrawn and uncommunicative in general. The enhancement of the environment, the warm, homey atmosphere generated by the presence of an in-residence mascot, and referenced so often in the studies, cannot be sustained by a visitation program.

Finally, Linda Hines, director of the People-Pet-Partnership Program, notes that a frequently cited problem with pet visitation programs

> . . . involves the waning of volunteer and resident interest when humane society animals are brought in by volunteers for weekly visits. This may be due to a lack of meaningful long-term interaction of residents with the animals as individual personalities, and to a lack of variety in the types and abilities of the animals.[2]

Hines, however, also remarked that several successful programs involved obedience-trained and show dogs.

But many institutions may, for various reasons, not be able to accommodate a live-in animal mascot. Also, a facility with no prior experience in pet therapy will admittedly be reluctant to start such a program. Pet visitation programs, therefore, can be a valuable preamble paving the way for more comprehensive animal therapy programs. Recall the facilities in Chapter 6 that decided to get a therapy dog after a visitation program was well-received. These programs may also be an adjunct to existing in-residence programs. Institutions who have successfully incorporated a companion animal on the wards might enjoy the occasional visitation, particularly if the program is creative and exciting. Certainly, the companion canine would appreciate socializing with his own species for awhile.

Most importantly, as Leo Bustad said: ''For old people, too often in the family and especially outside the family, attention and love are not common commodities. Companion animals may be a significant part, and in some case, the only source of warmth, affection, love, and devotion for the elderly.''[3] For some elders who may be delegated to an institution for the remainder of their lives, the brief encounter with visiting animal therapists may be the only contact with pets they will have.

## GUIDELINES FOR SUCCESSFUL
## PET VISITATION PROGRAMS

Just as pet visitation programs can, by their good example, be excellent precursors of more extensive pet therapy programs, they can also be detrimental if they are ill-conceived or improperly conducted. Uninformed volunteers can in their enthusiasm overlook basic precautions and safety procedures, and, though intentions are the best, actually cause more harm than good. Fortunately, the basic measures to insure a successful pet visitation program are simple and easy to follow, and to readers experienced in these programs, our guidelines will appear to be little more than responsible pet ownership and common sense. However, we believe that for pet therapy to realize its potential as a widespread and respected therapeutic tool, everyone who is even minimally connected with it must set an exemplary example. By following these guidelines, dog clubs, individuals, and humane societies will be able to implement a successful and enjoyable pet visitation program.

### (1) Animal Selection

(a) *Appearance.* All animals who are taken into public institutions must be healthy, clean, and well-groomed. They should have all current innoculations recommended for their species and should be free of external parasites. A long-haired breed who has a tendency to shed should receive an additional quick combing or brushing prior to its introduction into the facility to minimize the problem of loose hair. For dogs we recommend a soft leather collar for control, appearance, and patient safety. Certain other types of collars may be suitable for training or other situations, but we have found that the leather type makes a nice appearance and minimizes the possibility of a patient bruising a finger. Remember that some of these people may be a little wary of petting a strange animal; we want to make contact as easy and pleasant as possible for them.

(b) *Elimination.* Be sure the animal has had an opportunity to exercise its normal elimination functions prior to its entrance into the facility. Dog and cat owners should keep a pooper scoop and some plastic bags handy in case the pet needs to use the institution's grounds. This is *not* the sort of calling-card you wish to leave behind.

(c) *Socialization and training.* A hospital or geriatric facility is not the place to train or socialize a young animal. This should be accomplished before the pet is acceptable as a visiting therapist. Young puppies and kittens can be very suitable, but some socialization and training should already be completed. A pet visitation program is also not the place to try to accustom an adult animal to strangers. Again, this should already have been done before the pet interacts with patients.

To become a member of Therapy Dogs International, a dog must have some level of obedience training. This means that the dog must be under the owner's control and supervision at all times. We recommend that novices keep dogs on a leash throughout the entire visit with the possible exception of special obedience demonstrations and shows. Later, after a facility is accustomed to the particular dogs and the dogs have become accustomed to the institution, more flexibility is possible. But it's best at the beginning to take a few extra precautions.

(d) *Temperament.* An animal taken into an institution should be sociable, friendly, relaxed, and unafraid of strangers. Under *no* circumstances use an animal that has exhibited growling, snapping, biting, or other aggressive tendencies, even if you feel that the pet is far too small to do any real damage. To hardy and robust adults, a tiny "tempest in a teacup" is more amusing than dangerous, but frail, elderly individuals may be somewhat fearful of our pets. Even if no physical damage is done, the negative impression generated is damage enough. And needless to say, excessive undesirable vocalization by any animal will not be welcome in an institution.

(e) *Types of animals.* If you plan on bringing in animals other than dogs and cats you best check with the facility to be sure that the patient population would have no aversion to them. Leo Bustad recalls an anecdote from the early days of pet therapy that illustrates this so well.

The activity director in a local nursing home decided she would like some resident animals and selected gerbils. The placement was a disaster. Several residents beat on the cage and tried to let them out to stomp on them. We discovered that the residents with farm backgrounds saw them as rats—something to be exterminated.[4]

We have, however, had enormous success with a somewhat "exotic" domestic species, the African pygmy goats, and one Therapy Dogs International associate insists that the patients respond best to these delightful companions. Chapter 11 gives many examples of non-canine therapists; virtually any domestic species can be well-received given the right situation.

## (2) Programs

When you have selected suitable animals for your visits, next design a creative and entertaining program. A humane shelter using several species may want to plan a short talk about the history and lore surrounding each animal presented—perhaps its domestic history and unusual facts. A well-trained dog offers numerous opportunities, limited only by the special ability of the canines and the imagination of the trainer. An obedience demonstration is always enjoyable, and some clubs have eventually integrated the patients themselves in the program. The next chapter illustrates numerous examples of Therapy Dogs International programs used successfully at various institutions. Always allow plenty of time for the pets to socialize and interact with the patients, as for many, this will be the highlight of the visit.

## (3) Opening Institution Doors

Linda Hines, director of the highly successful People-Pet-Partnership Program, says:

First, when trying to establish a program in a nursing home, it is helpful if the success of another program can be described. The administrators are usually interested in pertinent articles about other programs and the benefits derived. A resource library containing relevant articles is very helpful in this situation. There is no substitute for a personal visit by a knowledgeable volunteer to the administrator and activities director of the center involved. He or she presents the benefits, describes possible activities, and offers specific assistance.[5]

The novice attempting to introduce his or her pets to a nursing home environment may meet with some resistance. Animal-facilitated therapy is still an infant field, and those unfamiliar with the successes it has already achieved may see only the potential problems associated with bringing an animal into the facility. We advise the newcomer whenever possible to get involved with a dog club or humane shelter which is already implementing such a program. (See Appendix I and II.) But for an organization or club that is just getting started in this worthwhile endeavor, that has suitable pets and a nicely thought-out program, here are some additional guidelines:

(a) Contact the Activity Director at the nursing home. You may make a preliminary contact with a letter and follow-up with a phone call. These directors seek out meaningful and interesting programs that will enhance the lives of their patients. If the preliminary response is favorable, arrange for an interview at which time you will discuss your proposed program more fully.

Here is a sample letter written to a fictitious nursing home director:

Dear Miss Doe:

For years, dog clubs, schools, and individuals with obedience trained dogs have traveled to nursing homes and hospitals visiting with people who miss their pets and bringing smiles to those who have fond memories of the dogs with whom they once shared their lives. The value of a friendly, obedient dog as therapy for troubled children, heart patients, and the elderly is documented repeatedly in current studies.

Compassion Canines is a charter of Therapy Dogs International, a worldwide organization whose volunteer members have one thing in common: a desire to share their affectionate, well-mannered pets with others who might benefit from them. Several of our members would like to bring their dogs to visit your patients at Compassion Community Nursing Home. Our dogs have performed successfully at many community functions and in other area institutions. I have enclosed, for your review, a letter of commendation about our program from Mrs. A. Jones, the administrative supervisor of Compassion Children's Hospital and an article that appeared in the Compassion Times that more fully describes our activities. Also enclosed is a leaflet, "What is a therapy dog?", that further discusses the scope and value of this activity.

I will be calling you in a few days to set up an interview at which time I can more fully discuss our program. Compassion Canines programs have proven to be both entertaining and therapeutic to institutionalized residents. We are confident that they will enrich the lives of the residents of Compassion Community Nursing Center.

Sincerely,

This preliminary letter serves several functions. If the activities director is unfamiliar with pet therapy programs, it provides a quick and written introduction to the work. Also, if the director for any reason would need prior approval before scheduling the program, the materials that you have provided will give him or her something in writing that can be used to convince a superior of the value of your program. Don't overstuff your introductory letter. If you have 100 articles about your group and 100 letters of commendation, select the nicest of each. When you visit, you can bring your portfolio or scrapbook as additional endorsement.

(b) *Scrapbook.* If your dog has been involved in any kind of public demonstration, thus proving its social graces, this will enhance your chances of admittance. For example, an obedience or show winner might be more welcome. Obedience titles will also show that your pet is well-behaved and has good manners. We suggest that a club or individual keep a scrapbook of their pet(s)' accomplishments, just like an individual keeps a portfolio of their professional achievements. Included could be newspaper or magazine accounts, commendatory letters about previously successful programs, snapshots, etc. You should also include in your scrapbook articles about the value of pet therapy and the beneficial effects of the human/animal bond. Clubs may wish to solicit a volunteer member to compile a club portfolio for their activities.

After some successful programs, you may wish to call in local media (newspapers, T.V. stations). Most journalists are interested in human interest stories that happen in their own home town. Ask permission from the facility first. Most institutions are only too pleased to get this type of favorable publicity. And your organization will get a plug too!

## (4) Institution Conduct

Be punctual, have your program well-planned and your pets clean and neat, and follow the institution's rules and regulations. Introduce yourself to staff on duty. After the program, when you approach a patient, *always* ask the patient if they like dogs. For example: "Hello, my name is Elaine and this is Phila. Do you like dogs?" If the patient says yes, proceed. "Would you like to shake hands?"—handler gently places paw on lap. "Would you like to pet the dog?"—handler brings dog closer to patient's reach. If you have a small, gentle dog, you may ask "Would you like (dog's name) to sit on your lap?" If a patient resists or shows any fear, just let it be. But approach again the next time. Often, the residents need only to see that they have nothing to fear.

Janice Blight, head of Prince's K-9 Cuddler's Chapter of Therapy Dogs International, has some additional pointers to share with readers new to pet visitation programs. Blight's guidelines were written for her own new charter members who requested advice on how to approach patients.

a. Blight recommends that dog owners bring along, in addition to a pooper scoop, baggies, and grooming utensils, paper towels and disinfectant for clean-up; a blanket for use with bed-bound patients; and crackers, so the patients can offer the dog a treat.
b. Always introduce yourself to the floor nurse, as she is usually a big help.
c. Give your name and the dog's name to the patients. If visiting a patient in a room, ask permission to enter. If the roommate becomes upset with the dog, retreat and come back another time.
d. For bed patients: If a small dog is asked to come on the bed, use the blanket. If you have a large dog, use the blanket for the dog's head to rest on.
e. For wheelchair residents: Watch dog's tail and paws. Look for tubes, bottles, or bandages. Patients' arms or legs can be brittle, and the weight of a leaning dog may be too much for them. Also watch the dog's paws if it sits up. A scratch could be dangerous to a diabetic. Small dogs can be held up to be petted; or you can use a converted baby stroller to get the dog at the correct height. The stroller can also be used at bedside to give your own back a rest.
f. For walker patients: Wait until the patient sits down and is sturdy before the dog is presented.
g. For walking patients: If they wish to walk the dog, keep by their side to help steer them clear of other patients.
h. Finally, use only crackers when you present treats for the patient to feed to the dog. Most patients, says Blight, eat the treat themselves!

## SHARING THE WEALTH

Finally, we would like to ask organizations with successful pet visitation programs to share the information with others who may just be beginning to get established. Document your efforts, your failures as well as your successes. If a particular approach does not work, try to determine why. If you have learned something that you think has been overlooked in the literature to date, share this information so that others can benefit from it also. We also invite any individual or club whose pet qualifies to become a member of Therapy Dogs International. Complete information is listed in Appendix I of this book. When several members of a group become Therapy Dogs International, the organization can establish a charter in their community.

Finally, you will never know what a rewarding experience this can be until you try. Camille Gagnon of Brewster, Maine, told us a detailed account of her experiences with her therapy Chow dogs Ming and Mellie. We think her story, which she calls "Petting to Remember," will be of particular interest to anyone wishing to begin a pet visitation program.

### *Petting to Remember: One Volunteer's Experience*

Becoming active in pet therapy at a local intensive care facility was not a well-planned, well-organized decision on my part. Like so many other canine activities, I just started to do it, and found that all involved enjoyed the experience. It began when I joined a local all-breed club and participated in occasional demonstrations about pure-bred dogs. The Chow Chow, as the breed is officially known, is a Chinese hunting dog that dates back at least 2000 years. It is a medium-sized dog characterized by a bushy, ample coat often red or red/orange in color and a blue tongue. Since Chows are a relatively uncommon breed, most people are not familiar with them. We presented our dogs and briefly recounted their history. Some dogs performed tricks, and obedience dogs would demonstrate the various levels of obedience work. Questions from the audience were encouraged. At the nursing home demonstrations, however, I noticed that patients were less interested in the presentation than the chance later to pet the dogs.

Working for a Visiting Nurse Association that rents offices in the City public health and intensive care nursing home enabled me to meet and become familiar with that facility's Activity Director. A friend/co-worker (owned by her seven dachshunds) and I were frequently asked to give small demonstrations for the patients at this facility. We learned from the Activity Director that although the institution was receptive to acquiring a full-time resident pet, neither staff nor patients were able to properly take responsibility for it. We thus decided to visit on a more regular basis, with the focus on petting and personal contact between patients and dogs.

We discussed this entire proposal with the Activity Director, and her chief concern was the regularity of attendance of people and (especially) dogs. She did not want to promote this program and enthuse patients if the dogs could not come as scheduled. The three of us worked out a weekly time slot that was designated Pet Day. Dachshunds and Chows were committed on a regular basis, with friends and relatives dropping in occasionally at that time also. For the size of this home, two people can handle four dogs (with the help of staff members) for optimum contact with the patients, so we settled on two to four dogs attending regularly.

On our first day the Activity Director guided us around the facility and introduced patients. We were also gently advised that patient reaction might be minimal. I admit to having doubts and wondering how this was going to work out, if at all. Many of these patients are seriously ill and many are very frail. We started wandering down the hall, introducing the dogs to the patients. Dog reaction to the patients was varied. Stroke and other brain-damaging conditions occasionally leave the victim with a degree of spasticity. One chow reacted suspiciously to such persons, one dachshund seemed wary but otherwise friendly, and one chow and one dachshund could have cared less. Other reactions to the various types of wheeled chairs, beds, tables, tubing, oxygen tank, etc., were also varied. All the dogs seemed to be interested in these devices, but not overly concerned with them. We found it important to help the dogs adjust to this new environment. A food treat, praise, a moment alone, or whatever works for a particular dog can reassure the animal and help him/her regain needed composure. Remember: this is a totally new situation for most dogs.

The following week was much the same, but after the third or fourth week, I noticed changes in several patients. Patients, who at first hardly glanced at dogs, were watching them approach. A few who had pet the dogs in the beginning were smiling more and often repeating a dog's name or saying "nice," "pretty," "good." Several asked if we had been here last week, and several asked if we would come again next week. More patients were telling us about their own dogs, and the dogs seemed to be thoroughly enjoying themselves. One elderly gentleman who had never spoken before caressed my Chow, Ming, and cried in his fur for five minutes. After this episode I realized that a person's loss of independence upon entering a nursing home, especially an intensive care nursing home, allows for less expression of emotion or individuality. The dogs also remind patients of pets previously owned and encourage bedridden or less mobile residents to look forward to a break in the antiseptic routine of hospital life. The dogs' weekly visit allows the patients to feel in a tactile and emotional way that they are still alive and still possess these emotions. All the dogs involved seemed to learn what to offer individual patients. The scheduled weekly visit also enabled the dogs to familiarize themselves with the daily routine at this particular hospital.

They learned how to navigate around wheeled chairs and beds, didn't mind squeezing in tight places and learned how to sit pressed against chairs close enough to allow a patient to reach them. The individual personalities of the different dogs appeals to different patients, too. Ming is not openly affectionate, but has a quiet dignity that appeals to many. When he sits beside a patient, it's as if royalty in person is sharing a bit of himself. Mellie, my female Chow, is one year younger than Ming and the direct opposite in character. She is vivacious and full of life. She runs right up to people, checks if there is a tidbit available, but always loves them anyway. She frequently kisses patients. Snooty, a Dachshund, coolly accepts patients' attentions, while Ramona, a young long-haired Dachshund, is enthusiastic, loving, and somewhat particular. She only kisses male patients! We have other dogs that participate too, each one's personality a little different, thus contributing to what each patient most wants and expects in a dog.

Perhaps the most important thing to point out is that all the dogs selected were reasonably well-mannered. They are our housepets in addition to being show dogs and title holders. We do not use this program to actively train or socialize our dogs; this is done before they are brought to the home. Young puppies can be welcome, but only if they cope well.

For my part, as the dogs' companion, I have found it especially important to be patient and to listen. Every week a lovely elderly lady pets Ming who sits at her feet and tells me about her black Chow now living with a nephew. Every week I am happy to hear her story and the stories of others. Sometimes it is just a word, sometimes just a sentence, and often just a smile. But the smile that lights up the faces of the patients when a dog goes to visit says it all.

## REFERENCES

1. Arkow, Phil. *"Pet Therapy": A Study of the Use of Companion Animals in Selected Therapies,* 3rd Edition. Colorado Springs: The Humane Society of the Pikes Peak Region, 1982.

2. Hines, Linda M. *The People-Pet-Partnership-Program.* Alameda, California: The Latham Foundation, 1980.

3. Bustad, Leo K. *Animals, Aging and the Aged.* Minneapolis: University of Minnesota Press, 1980.

4. Bustad, Leo K. and Hines, Linda M. "Placement of Animals With the Elderly: Benefits and Strategies." In *Guidelines: Animals in Nursing Homes. California Veterinarian* Supplement, 1983.

5. Hines, Linda, M. op. cit.

Chapter 9

# Therapy Dogs in Action

A typical Therapy Dogs International program includes several volunteers and their dogs since a variety of different breeds and size animals makes for an interesting demonstration for the patients. For example, Ursula Kempe is a long-time member of Therapy Dogs International and her superbly trained German Shepherd Dog Sam is a splendid example of a large working dog. Maisy Campbell, on the other hand, has three delightful Cairn terriers. Cairns are a Scottish breed originally bred in Scotland to hunt vermin; they are small and shaggy and have exuberant personalities. They are the perfect size to sit on a lap or be cuddled in a patient's arms.

Before the program starts, we spend a few minutes saying hello to the patients. These demonstrations are commonplace for the patients at Roosevelt Hospital in Menlo Park, New Jersey, where one of the authors is employed, so the dogs and residents are old friends. Sam, Phila, and the other large dogs make the rounds, while the Cairns spend a few minutes being cuddled. Whenever Maisy can't find one of her terrier trio, it's a given the perky little dog is sitting on a patient's lap.

To open the demonstration, we introduce the volunteers and the dogs. If an unusual breed is present, we tell the audience a little about that type of dog. For example, on one of our visits, a new member Audrey Musick and her Keeshond Dog joined us. The Keeshond is a small Dutch breed that sports a coat of plush, luxuriant fur and resembles a miniature wolf. Although the breed is recognized as the National Dog of Holland, it is relatively rare in this country. Then we show the audience what a well-trained dog can do. Therapy Dogs International canines have at least a CD degree or its equivalent, so they heel, sit, stay, lie down, and come when called easily and effortlessly. The more skilled dogs such as Sam and Ailsa, one of Maisy's terriers, demonstrate the advanced work. The contrast between the large German Shepherd and the pint-sized Cairn is a point of interest for the audience. People expect large dogs to be trained (how else could you control them?), but to show that a small dog can manage this work too surprises many.

Ailsa has a UD title and thus can perform scent discrimination tasks. Maisy rubs her scent on a dumbbell and places it on the floor with a group of unscented dumbbells. When Maisy says: "Find it, Ailsa," the little dog proceeds to scent out the correct one and return it to her owner. Ailsa has become a bit of a "ham," though, and always circles the lot, carefully sniffing each one, before she selects the proper one. She makes the audience think she is struggling to do this task, but patients who have seen her perform know better. Someone usually calls out "she'll find it." And, of course, she does.

For Sam's scent discrimination task, we ask the patients to volunteer slippers. A willing nurse gathers the bunch and places them on the floor. Ursula then adds her own slipper to the group and instructs Sam to find it. Sam is an expert at detecting a specific human's scent, and the audience is told about his work as a search and rescue dog as a point of interest. The dogs demonstrate the broad jump, the high jump, and the directed retrieve; that is, they retrieve a dumbbell and jump over the barrier selected by their owner. For their UD titles, you may remember, the dogs have also been taught to respond just to hand signals. Whenever one of the dogs is worked this way, we always point it out to the audience. Many are intrigued that the dog does not even require a verbal command to obey.

After the individual dogs have demonstrated their abilities, we work them as a group to show the audience how it's done in actual obedience competition. For our last exercise we instruct the dogs to lie down and leave the room. Patients often call the dogs and try to get them to come; but of course, they don't, demonstrating once again the value of training.

After the demonstration the patients and dogs visit. The small ones can be placed on a willing lap; the large ones are introduced by their owners. We always ask: "Do you like dogs? Would you like to pet the dog? Would you like a kiss?" Even the patients who may say no the first time watch us carefully. By the next visit they usually want to make friends too.

We sometimes have over 100 patients attending one of our demonstrations, so it is important that everyone who wants to gets a

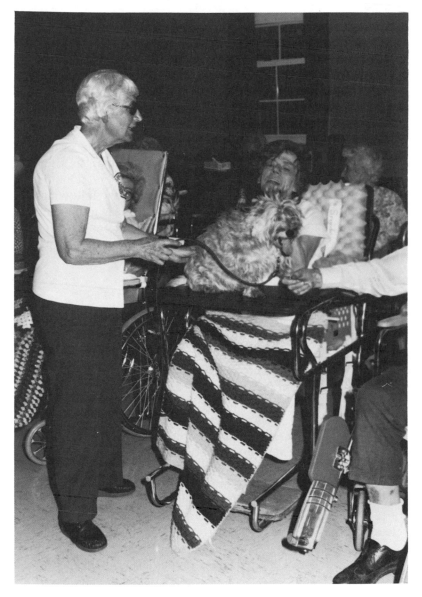

TDI Member Maisy Campbell and Cairn Terrier Therapy Dog Ailsa demonstrate bedside manners. Photo by Bob Barber.

chance to interact with the animals. If there are enough dogs, everyone will get ample time to pet and love them. But for the patients, it
seems, sometimes, that no matter how long a session they have, it
still isn't long enough.

Currently, Therapy Dogs International has more than 300 members worldwide. They have taken their pets to a variety of institutions to interact with patients and have encountered individuals with
many diverse disorders and disabilities. The value of documenting
these accounts is expressed well by Dr. Leo Bustad who says:
"These observations, even though of limited usefulness as scientific
data, can nonetheless provide insights into areas where more precise
studies can be undertaken."[1] The purpose then of the following section is twofold: (1) to provide volunteers with ideas to enliven and
vary their demonstrations, and (2) to provide additional documenta-
tion to the scope and effectiveness of pet therapy in various patient
populations.

## CHAUNCEY

During the past two years two Saginaw, Michigan, area hospitals
have been blessed with the antics of A.J. Slaughter III and his 6½
year old Doberman Pinscher, Chauncey, who happens to also be a
Utility Dog and one of the few American-bred, owned, and trained
Schutzhund III Dobes.

Chauncey and A.J. dispense therapy at the Saginaw Veterans Administration Hospital where A.J., a disabled Vietnam veteran, was
once a patient. They have given more than 60 performances to disabled veterans on the hospital's back lawn. Chauncey displays scent
discrimination tasks and hurdling and to the enjoyment of all, she
shows what a real working Doberman can do in various stages of
police and military work. Chauncey, who like her owner is a
veteran of the U.S. Marine Corps, searches buildings, performs
search and rescue tracking, and has even assisted in criminal appre-
hensions. At most of their demonstrations there is a mock arrest
made with the help of one of A.J.'s assistants. Afterwards they
show the patients that a Schutzhund-trained dog is also gentle and
very loving.

At the Saginaw Osteopathic Hospital, however, Chauncey made
her closest ties with a terminally ill patient. Although the woman
eventually died, her last months were cheered by the frequent visits

of her canine friend. Her relationship with Chauncey was a simple one: they just sat and talked.

## *ROCKY*

We first met Rocky in Chapter 4, and this fine therapy dog owned by Edi Munneke, columnist for *Dog World* magazine, continues to bring joy, not only to his owner, but to others as well. The combination of a well-trained dog and an imaginative handler makes for an exciting and varied sure-to-delight program. Volunteers looking for ways to liven up their demonstrations should get some new ideas here.

Nine-year-old Rocky and I still like to accept invitations to entertain. We take other dog friends with us whenever possible. I have small scale jumps to carry along, so we can always adapt our work to the physical surroundings. I take along a store carton containing a raw egg which I have someone place on the floor for me. Rocky brings the egg back to me without cracking the shell!

I have someone throw out a newspaper and Rocky retrieves it for me just as he does every night at home. While Rocky and I take a walk, I lose my billfold; of course, after I explain the seriousness of the situation to Rocky, he finds it for me. I have some members of the audience place $1 bills in a circle on the floor while I place a $10 bill with the $1s. I then explain to Rocky how tough times are and how I can use all the help I can get. I then instruct my dog to go find the biggest bill.

You and I know that Rocky is smelling the money, but the audience always thinks he is reading the numbers. Rocky always watches me very intently, waiting for his cue while I am chatting, but the audience thinks he understands the conversation. We fit in enough obedience exercises to make an interesting program. We always end up with a social time. Rocky spies a friendly face and puts up his paw for a shake; when the shake is over, he wants that hand put on his head for petting. If the person doesn't respond, Rocky nudges his arm until he catches on. If there are refreshments, Rocky always gets his share—how can anyone resist that wagging tail and those pleading eyes![2]

## LADY

The tremendous need of the institutionalized elderly for affection
and companionship has been observed frequently in the literature. It
is poignantly illustrated by this account from Iola Wickham, of
Liverpool, New York.

> I take our Sheltie dogs to the Plaza Nursing Home in Syra-
> cuse, New York once a month for pet therapy programs. On
> one of these occasions, when I was ready to leave, I couldn't
> find my Little Lady. Since I had three other dogs with me that I
> was watching at the time, I was a bit concerned.
>
> I thought she may have gotten on the elevator and become
> mixed up with the wheelchairs. I became alarmed and a nurse
> noticed my anxious searching about the place.
>
> "Are you looking for your little dog?" she asked.
>
> "Yes," I replied excitedly.
>
> "Take a look at that little lady in the wheelchair going down
> the hall," and she pointed in the direction.
>
> When I caught up with the dog-napper, I found a scene that
> would have been humorous, were it not so moving. With one
> hand the elderly woman was clutching Lady so tight she was
> gasping for air; with the other she was attempting to make the
> wheelchair roll rapidly down the hall to her room.
>
> Her eyes pleaded with me as much as her words. "I want to
> take her to my room," she said.
>
> It almost broke my heart to take the little dog away from
> her. I promised her to bring Lady back next week.

Wickham and another Shetland Sheepdog owner and volunteer,
Helen Simpson, of Liverpool, New York, have also had a great deal
of success taking their pets to perform for retarded children, even
though the children visited are, in general, unresponsive.

The youngsters who have an extremely short attention span watch
intently for the thirty-plus minutes while the dogs perform their obedience work. Afterwards, during the socializing time, even those
children who are somewhat fearful of the small canines overcome
their reluctance and pet the shaggy performers on the back.

"We were previously warned not to expect much reaction since
the children ordinarily didn't respond to much," reports Simpson.
"To our delight we got an excellent response from the children who

especially loved to pet the dogs. Later, the teacher informed us that the children had reacted more to the dogs than they had to any other program.''

## TRAXLER'S SIBERIANS

How can a volunteer deal with a patient, particularly a child, who has a dog-related phobia? One suggestion comes from Joyce Traxler.

The Siberian Huskies belonging to Joyce Traxler, who operates Traxler's Coley Canine Obedience Training School in Omro, Wisconsin, pursue a variety of activities that help the elderly, the mentally deficient and the less fortunate. During the Christmas season, the amiable canines don Santa suits and hats, put bells on their collars, and visit children in nearby hospitals. Often, Traxler invites the patients to take their turn at training a dog. One little boy, 5-year-old Scotty, loves dogs, but is afraid of them, so for him, Joyce brings along Peggy, a battery-operated Pekingnese toy dog that sits up, barks, and walks, and functions much like the original except that it doesn't give kisses. This simple and thoughtful technique allows the youngster to participate in and get full enjoyment from the program.

## COACO AND MORRIE

If a patient regresses, volunteer visits may temporarily be discontinued; however, the fond memory of those encounters may aid in recovery. Sara Sayle Williams, of Shaker Heights, Ohio, and her standard brown poodle Coaco pay regular visits to Frances, a multiple sclerosis patient. ''We gave her a picture of the dogs, Coaco and Morrie, one Christmas,'' says Williams.

> Although Morrie, a small silver poodle, never visited the hospital, we told Frances many stories about him. When Frances' condition worsened, we were asked to discontinue our visits. One day, however, I was called out of a meeting at the hospital. There with her mother was Frances clutching a picture of the dogs. Her words—the first she had spoken in six months — were ''How are Coaco and Morrie?'' So again I told her another tale and Frances, Coaco and I visited once again.''

## CHAMPION POODLES

For some volunteers, even their own physical disability doesn't stop them for spreading good will. Rebecca Tansil, owner of Andechez Poodles in Baltimore, Maryland, has led many of her dogs to obedience and breed championships; but she believes that involvement in animal-facilitated therapy is the "greatest contribution that dogs and their owners can make to society."

Tansil currently has three therapy dogs and works closely with "Pets on Wheels," a volunteer organization who regularly visit twenty area nursing homes. Says Tansil:

> My sister Blanche, who always accompanied me on these trips, suffered a stroke last year. After months of therapy, she once again can participate—but from a wheelchair. One of our poodles took over as her nurse when she came home from the hospital, and stays with her 24 hours a day. We get a round of laughter when we arrive with the dogs and one person is in a wheelchair with her "poodle nurse" on her lap. It's always great fun for the patients.

And good therapy for the participants!

## DIRK VAN VITKAY

A furry Keeshond, Dirk Van Vitkay, and his owner Mavis Vitmus of Columbus Heights, Minnesota, are regular visitors to many of the area's nursing homes. Talented Dirk is a special favorite with the residents, and his ability to learn new and unusual tricks provided the impetus to recovery for one particular patient. Mavis Vitums reports:

> In early 1982, Dirk and I began visiting an elderly pastor who had suffered a severe stroke and lost his power of speech. Since his entire life had been devoted to telling the story of Jesus, he felt he was no longer able to witness; he was convinced he no longer had a purpose on earth and wished to die.
> After extensive work with Dirk, I asked the pastor to help me with a new trick. Dirk had learned to limp when I pretend to shoot him in the foot. He continued to limp until the pastor

Rebecca Tansil and her champion poodle Mister Ex demonstrate the high jump. Photo courtesy of Rebecca Tansil.

beckoned him to come. Then he would sit on his hind legs, place his front feet on the pastor's lap, and lower his head in prayer. After a brief silence, Dirk would bark once and then joyfully trot off on all fours.

I taught Dirk to respond only to the pastor; and it worked. The pastor saw a way to witness without words. He and his wife selected a dog from the animal shelter and using the instructions I gave them began to teach the trick to their own dog. They are now an evangelical team traveling throughout the country.

"Dirk knows instinctively who needs him most," says Vitums, who is organizing a local chapter of Therapy Dogs International.

Currently, his special favorite is a blind and deaf lady whom we visit weekly. She stiffens, then relaxes, and throws her arms around him. She pats him from head to toe for about two minutes. Then she sits up straight, smiles and pats his head twice. I know of no way I or any other human could bring such love and joy to her. She is still smiling much later when we pass her room to leave.

### GREATER LOUISVILLE TRAINING CLUB

The Greater Louisville Training Club has a very active Therapy Dogs International unit, and the dogs come in all sizes: from tiny Yorkshire Terriers to massive Great Danes. Polly Walker reports that some facilities were less than enthusiastic when the club began the project. "They predicted all kinds of doom," she said, "especially dog fights. Now they can hardly wait for our next visit. Sometimes we are the only reason the patients will get out of bed."

The club puts on a lively show and features a circus troop complete with a colorful circus wagon. The dogs wear costumes, and one human volunteer becomes Mac the Clown and adds her original lyrics and music to the program. The poodle troupe take turns pulling each other in a toy wagon. Popcorn, a toy poodle, plays the role of Houdini, the famed escape artist, as he blithely pops out of his enclosure. Fifi, the club's first toy poodle to earn a UD title, likes to wear a tutu and climbs a barstool to say her prayers. And Beau Bleu (Blue Boy), Walker's handsome, utility-trained standard poodle, carries tiny Papillions and puppies in Walker's purse.

Photo courtesy of Pauline Walker.

Photo courtesy of Pauline Walker.

Walker suffered a serious auto accident in the fall of 1982 and her therapy dogs who had delighted others now dispensed their special brand of treatment at home. The poodles learned to wash their own feet when coming inside and easily adjusted to her metal walker and her crutches. After several months of recuperation, Walker, on crutches, resumed her volunteer visits and notes: "I truly think I gain more therapy from taking my dogs to perform than the audiences."

Walker reports one rather humorous "complaint." Upon seeing the immaculately groomed show-styled poodles, one woman announced that she did not like: "Fancy, fuzzy dogs." She liked "plain, old dogs." Beauty may be in the eyes of the beholder, but training wins out, and when the scent hurdle races began, Beau Bleu, as the only UD dog present, easily stole the show. The lady, seeing the superb stuff this canine was made of, relented and cheered him on. Unfortunately, she didn't know French. "That's they way to do it, Black Bottom," she yelled.

## BUTTONS

Another poodle who has won the hearts of many patients is Buttons, a white toy owned by Sharon Thompson of Oberlin, Ohio. Thompson and Buttons are members of the Golden Crescent Dog Fanciers Association and participate in many demonstrations in area institutions.

In addition to his basic obedience work, Buttons has mastered many tricks and is always hard at work learning new ones. The perky little dog shakes hands, rolls over, turns around, begs, speaks, and waves.

"Button's small size makes him an instant hit with many of the nursing home residents," reports Thompson, "as they can easily pet and fondle him in their laps. Many times an unsuspecting nose has received a quick kiss from little Buttons. Squeals of delight make him all the happier, and his tail wags a mile a minute."

## PATRICK

Patrick is an eight-year-old Collie who has survived several brushes with death. According to his owner, Virginia Sevebeck, of LaGrange, Ohio, her dog's life has been spared to enable him to

Photo courtesy of Pauline Walker.

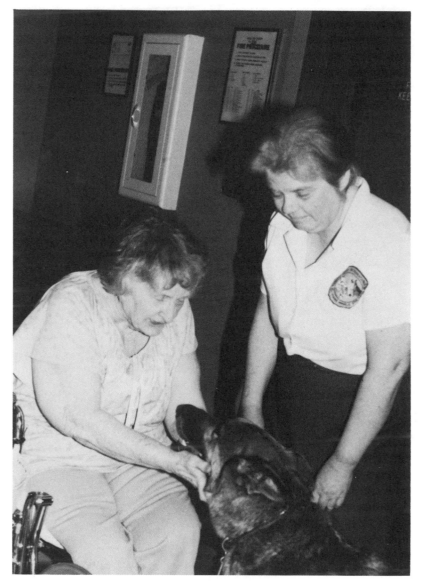

Photo by Odean Cusack.

work as a therapy dog. Patrick's resemblance to another famous Collie provided the breakthrough for one patient.

While Sevebeck and Patrick were visiting with patients at an area institution, a nurse wheeled in a young man in his mid-twenties. "He was completely paralyzed and his face had no expression," tells Sevebeck.

As I approached him, I smiled and leaned forward. Patrick touched his hand with his nose. The nurse told me he rarely attempted speech. "This is Patrick," I said, "He's my Collie and he has come to see you." I took his hand and placed it on Patrick's head. We watched his fingers slowly move over my dog's fur and a smile dawned on his face. "Lassie, Lassie," he said. The nurse was astonished. "It's unbelieveable," she said.

Months later, on a return visit to the institution, the young man was already in the waiting room anticipating his special friend, whom he still calls Lassie.

Because of the success of the visiting therapy dogs, Sevebeck reports that many institutions now permit the volunteers to visit with bed-bound patients in their sleeping rooms. The dogs, as usual, adapt readily and make contact with their new friends by sticking their heads through the bed rails.

## EBUNYZAR

Ebunyzar, owned by Hannah Hayman of Cazenovia, New York, was a massive Newfoundland and a superb representative of a heroic and service-oriented breed. These gentle black bears are adept in the water and have an innate life-saving instinct. Even as young puppies, the dogs are capable of securing a drowning person and many in the breed have been honored for such feats. Boatswain, the Newfoundland immortalized by English Romantic poet George Gordon, Lord Byron was said to possess: ". . . all the Virtues of Man without his Vices."[3]

Ebunyzar's service, however, was of another sort. Until his death in 1982, Big Eb and his handler were so in demand in area pre-kindergarten programs and geriatric institutions that they could not fill all the requests. Through her gentle giant, Hayman has helped

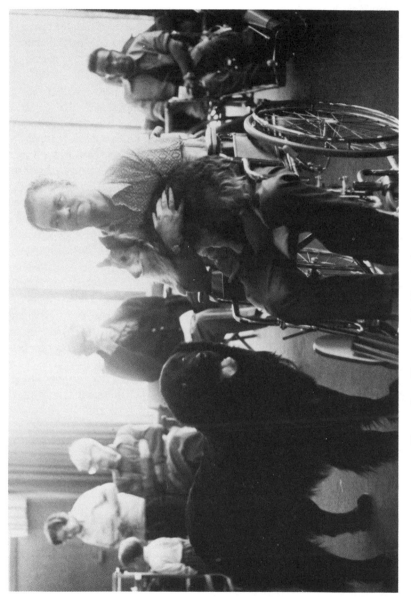

Therapy Dogs Ebunyzar and Goldie. Photo by Hannah Hayman.

children overcome their fear of dogs and mistrust of adults and surroundings.

Daniel, for example, immigrated from France and could speak no
English. Thus he was withdrawn and rarely interacted with the other
children and the teacher. His curiosity about the big dog, however,
provided a breakthrough. His first word spoken at school was
"Ebunyzar," and before the end of the school year, he was speaking English quite well.

As a toddler, Terry had been disciplined with an ill-tempered
dog; thus, he panicked at the mere sight of a canine. A program of
de-sensitization using dog books, pictures, and dog puppets began.
Later Eb was brought to the classroom. Terry was informed beforehand and provided with a secure place and assured that the dog
would not intrude on this area. At first, Terry could not even watch
other children pet and groom the dog. One day, Eb carried a basket
of cookies to each child. Terry watched and finally asked another
child to get a cookie for him. "From that day on," reports Hayman,
"Terry's self-concept improved. Though he was still self-conscious
with dogs, he no longer panicked. Also, his trust in the adults
around him grew so he was able to function better every day."[4]

At the opposite end of the age spectrum was Harriet, who at age
96 was overcome by the ravages of time and disease. During her
final years her single joy and comfort was Ebunyzar. Days would
pass when the frail woman would not eat or speak nor respond to
any stimulus, but a visit from Big Eb prompted great improvement.
His effect on the woman was so beneficial that the staff requested
the dog be brought to her bedside during her withdrawn spells. The
frequent visits continued for six years till Harriet's death at the age
of 102. Eb, the gentle giant of a therapist, died 3½ months later.

## PRINCE AND JOY LEE

Janice Blight of Shavertown, Pennsylvania, is the founder of
Prince's K-9 Cuddlers Chapter of Therapy Dogs International, and
along with the charter's namesake, Prince, a handsome black poodle, travels to area nursing homes. "Prince thinks every lap or hand
is meant for him," she says,

> and is not deterred by beds, canes, crutches, or wheelchairs if
> it means someone will just pause to love him for a short time.

Joy Lee. Photo courtesy of Janice Blight.

While Prince interacts with one patient, I watch the reactions of the others. I ask anyone who seems interested if they would like to pet or walk him; and I get very few refusals.

Many of the patients are happy just to pet and love Prince, but the same story always emerges. "I had a dog before I came into the nursing home," they say. Then they pet Prince and tell me about their own dogs. Many begin to cry. I somehow manage to leave them smiling, though.

Blight has also trained a young poodle, Joy Lee, as a companion to her mother who is troubled with arthritis and has difficulty picking up dropped household articles. "Joy picks up any articles asked for," reports Blight, "silverware, cooking utensils, bottles, dish cloths, and a hair brush. She is especially delighted when my mother requests the walking cane; and eagerly opens the door for her young-at-heart senior citizen friend. She actually learned to turn a door knob by herself when she wanted to get out of the cellar." Joy Lee, whose training began at four months of age, also visits nursing homes. "She stands 25 inches high," says Blight, "and is just the right height to place her head on a patient's bed to be petted."

## ROBBIE

Harriet Augustus of Parma Heights, Ohio, has a heartwarming story about her first visit to a nursing home with her Norwegian Elkhound Robbie, which aptly illustrates that the visiting pet therapist may have an effect on patients who do not immediately respond to them.

"There was a man, Henry, who had a stroke," says Augustus.

He was able to speak, but the staff had been unable to interest him in anything; he wouldn't even respond to questions. After the obedience demonstration, we took the dogs around for petting, but he seemed disinterested in them too. When we were leaving, however, the manager asked if we would bring the dogs in to say good night to everyone. I was going to pass by Henry's room, but the manager asked me to bring Robbie in anyway. Henry was sitting in his wheelchair, and Robbie put his head on Henry's knee. To our surprise, Henry put his hand on Robbie's head and rubbed it. We said good night and started to leave; and Henry said, plain as day: "Good night Robbie." The manager was so excited she told everyone she met that Henry spoke and said good night to Robbie.

## FLICKA AND CHARM

Toni Ann Gardiner of Jamaica, New York, is a Rehabilitation Counselor at a New York state psychiatric facility and works primarily with chronic schizophrenics from age 16 and up. With her former guide dog Charm and her present guide dog Flicka, both golden retrievers, she has had 11 years exposure to working therapy dogs. She describes some of the methods she has used to help her clients.

One patient named Paul was non-verbal when I met him. He very much wanted to pet my dog, but I told him that he would have to ask permission. He did so and was allowed to play with Charm. He would frequently come to my office, ask to play with Charm and then speak with her several minutes. He is now completely verbal.

Rosie, a disturbed, retarded young lady, would often come to my office to groom Charm. As she brushed and combed my passive Golden, we would talk about her problems. Rosie is now employed at a sheltered workshop outside the hospital and only comes here to sleep.

Millie is a current patient in her fifties who is impressed with Flicka. She comes to my office daily to pet Flicka and to talk with me. When she first began to visit my dog, she was quite silly and often violent on her ward. Now that she has the ability to physically caress and be cared about by an animal, she has settled down, is taking the high school equivalency course, and is working two mornings a week in one of our sheltered employment programs. She is much more rational and is much better able to function.

Both Flicka and Charm have been present on both geriatric wards and wards for the mentally retarded. When the patients see us coming on to the ward, many of them request patting the dog. As Flicka is very outgoing, each person thinks that he or she is very special to Flicka, and this helps to build self confidence and self-image. Many patients who were previously frightened of dogs learn that a dog can be gentle and friendly and will not harm them.

Therapy Dog Goldie owned by Iola Wickham. Photo by Iola Wickham.

To date, few research studies have dealt with the effects of pet therapies on specific populations; however, as effectively illustrated in this chapter, a wide spectrum of patients of any age group, both physically and mentally afflicted, could benefit from this treatment. Even with the limitations of a pet visitation program, breakthroughs are not only possible, but increasingly more common and widespread. Pet therapy is not effective for every patient, but recalling Mary Thompson's thoughts: for the Henrys, the Harriets, the Rosies, the Millies, the Frances, "How sad if we don't at least give it a try."[5]

## REFERENCES

1. Lee, Ronnal L.; Zeglan, Marie E; Ryan, Terry; and Hines, Linda M. *Guidelines Animals in Nursing Homes. California Veterinarian* Supplement, 1983.
2. Munneke, Edi. "Obedience News," *Dog World.* October 1982.
3. Lord Byron (George Gordon). "Inscription on the Grave of a Newfoundland Dog."
4. Hayman, Hannah L. "Dogs Serving the Community." *Off-Lead.* December 1975.
5. Thompson, Mary. Personal Communication.

Chapter 10

# Animal-Facilitated Therapy in the Community

A people/pet program need not be limited to an institution or a closed-group setting. In fact, perhaps the happiest and most beneficial relationships between pets and people are realized when the community as a whole recognizes the value of a companion animal and offers guidelines and assistance to individuals and groups who want to promote this vital dimension of living. Elders who live alone often require financial and other support services to enable them to keep a pet. And for the solitary senior, the placement of a pet in their lives could provide elements of love, affection, and companionship that are missing elsewhere.

## PAW PALS[1]

The Pets Are Wonderful Council (PAW) based in Chicago, Illinois, is a not-for-profit public service organization dedicated to communicating the joys of responsible dog and cat ownership to the American public. In addition to serving as a clearinghouse for pet information, PAW also is developing special consumer education and community relations programs designed to enhance consumer knowledge and understanding of the positive benefits of people/pet relationships.

One such program, designed to match willing young people with adults in the community who may need help in caring for their pets is PAW PALS. Youngsters who participate in the program must have completed a Boy Scout, Girl Scout, or 4-H pet care badge or project and know how to take good care of dogs and cats. Additionally, the children must enjoy caring for pets and wish to help other pet owners care for their animals.

A PAW PAL is instructed to seek out people in the community

who would like help in caring for their pets. The children then will offer to walk, groom, or feed the pet. Pet care sheets are provided so that the young person can keep careful records of exactly when and how he has cared for each animal. Fees are optional and depend upon the scout or 4-H group leader, and PAW remarks that some groups will want to offer their time as a public service.

A program such as this is an ideal way to bridge the generation gap that often arises between elders and young people because of negative experiences each group has had with the other group. Scottish education expert Dorothy Walster remarks that both populations have much to contribute to each other. Seniors have a wealth of life experience and knowledge to share with children who are just beginning to travel the road the elder has worn thin. Youngsters have enthusiasm and energy and usually spare time to commit to their hobbies. Walster also observes that these populations often share similar problems: loneliness, a need to be assertive, and the need to find a role. Youngsters are still searching for their particular role in life, while the elderly, displaced from a former role, are often seeking a new one.[2]

A PAW PAL program could be coupled with a humane society's pet placement program to offer the support and assistance the older person would need in caring for a new pet. Complete details about the program and a sample packet are available from PAW (see Appendix II).

## PETS BY PRESCRIPTION

For the elderly person who lives alone and is no longer a working and active member of the community, the world can seem a bleak place indeed. Visits from friends and family are far too few. Limited mobility, physical impairment, or poor health can be insurmountable obstacles to even short outside excursions. Without meaningful activity, there is little incentive or reason to keep spirit or morale high. Without companionship or purpose, the lonely elder can easily sink into a morass of despair and depression that is as debilitating to health as the worst disease.

An animal friend, however, can do much to provide companionship, love, affection, and a sense of being needed, so vital to the elderly. We know that interaction with pets promotes physical and emotional good health; it may even do more.

In September 1980 several national papers reported a very sad story about a 77-year-old woman in Cocoa, Florida, who was forced to give up her small pet dog Sparky. Mrs. Marsteller, a widow, lived alone, except for her small pet at the School Street senior housing project. In the summer of 1980 she was advised by housing officials to give up her pet Sparky or move. With only a meager income and nowhere else to go, she reluctantly took Sparky to the Humane Society where he was adopted by Lt. Beau West, a Brevard County sheriff's lieutenant. For awhile Mrs. Marsteller visited her old friend, but when her visits ceased the kindly lieutenant checked on her at home. He found her drifting further and further into senility. She did not recognize him, but when he told her that he was the man who adopted her dog, she asked, "How's Sparky?"

Friends and neighbors in the School Street housing project verified Lt. West's concerns. Mrs. Marsteller, they said, stopped her daily walks, refused to bathe, and almost stopped eating. Within two months after she sadly turned Sparky over to the Humane Society, she died, and friends insisted it was of a broken heart.[3]

Whatever the cause of Mrs. Marsteller's death, obviously the presence of her little dog did much to give interest and purpose to her life. And certainly there are countless others who now live alone who would welcome and benefit from a pet.

Placing cats and dogs in the private homes of lone seniors is a relatively recent project in the field of animal facilitated therapy. Selection of both the animal and the recipient must be made very carefully. Not only must the elderly person wish to have an animal, but he or she must also be able to provide for its needs. If the recipient is incapacitated in any way, special physical accommodations may be necessary. Ideally, a support service to assist the elder if he or she has any additional needs or problems should be available.

Currently, there are several programs that have embarked upon this very exciting aspect of pet therapy. One such organization is Pets by Rx sponsored by the Contra Costa Veterinary Medical Association. The purpose of the organization is to inform the general public on the therapeutic value of a pet and to coordinate related activities. The group intends to contact nursing home activity directors and help them in the selection, care, and management of the resident animal therapist. The ultimate goal is that the institution itself would become totally involved in the care of the animal and the activity coordination of the program; and that the staff would document the changes brought about in the patients by the new therapist.[4]

CATS (Children and Animals Together for Seniors) is a federally and privately funded program started by actress/singer Judith Feldman. The New York-based operation gives pets to the elderly and provides them with free pet food, medical care, equipment, and services, including children who volunteer to walk the animals. The animals are strays or unwanted pets from local shelters, and the children volunteers are all instructed in proper pet care. In one successful placement, Feldman gave an eight-year-old German Shepherd dog to a despondent 79-year-old man who had recently lost his own pet. A young neighbor walks the dog and also runs errands and visits with the elderly man. "It's nothing but hugs and happiness now," says Feldman.[5]

The San Francisco SPCA has a broad-based animal therapy program that includes placing animal mascots in institutions, training and placing hearing dogs with the deaf, and promoting pet ownership among senior citizens. The effort involved in a successful placement is described below.

## DOLLY AND MIDNIGHT[6]

The human subject was Dolly Silva, 80 years old, who suffered a disabling stroke in the summer of 1981 which affected the right side of her body. A previous automobile accident which weakened her legs as a young adult further aggravated her condition. Dolly was unsteady and often fell without warning. Since a sudden movement could result in a fall and subsequent serious injury, she required a walker to move from her chair or bed and had to learn to move slowly and cautiously.

Dolly was also frightened and alone. Social workers described her environment as "sparse." She relied upon the visits of a few good friends, but the visits were never as often or as long as she would prefer; and Dolly spend most of her day alone in a chair, watching television. But Dolly was also a determined and independent lady. Even though her lack of mobility caused her depression and boredom, she refused to give up her own apartment.

Dolly's friends solicited help from the In-Home Art and Recreation Program of Mount Zion Hospital and Medical Center which sends specially trained art therapists to elderly housebound persons. The therapist, Barbara Taorimina, discussed a wide range of possible interests with Dolly, but found only polite disinterest until she mentioned her dog. That was the magic word. Dolly's face beamed and she quickly produced albums of animal pictures, not only friends' and her own former pets, but any animals. This collection was her lifelong hobby, and therapist Taorimina concluded that what Dolly needed most of all was a pet.

The next contact was the San Francisco SPCA. Representatives from the Society interviewed Dolly, her friends and landlady, the hospital's social work and therapy personnel at length. "After meeting Dolly—hearing the stories of pets she has had, feeling the love she has to give to an animal, recognizing the patience and willingness to care for any pet, understanding her want for companionship—we all were sure that this would work!" says Richard Avanzino, the Society's president.

The next step in placement was to find Dolly a suitable animal companion and friend. Midnight, an adult female stray cat, came to the SPCA with a large growth on her neck. Although surgery was successful and veterinarians predicted a long and healthy life for the gentle feline, adoption efforts proved unsuccessful. Midnight was selected as a Pet-of-the-Week in the Society's newspaper and even taken to a fair; she was the only animal the society took there that came back to the shelter with no new owner. Perhaps it was the unsightly surgical scar that discouraged prospective owners for Midnight, although somewhat shy, was a sweet-natured gentle animal who was eager to be petted by any hands who took the time to do so.

Dolly Silva, however, was undeterred by Midnight's past medical problem. She enthusiastically accepted Midnight as her special companion. The maintenance staff of the Society designed and constructed a special table, accessible to Dolly without bending, to hold Midnight's litter box, and the cat was trained to use her custom-designed commode.

How is the placement working out? Richard Avanzino describes this poignant partnership:

> Midnight and Dolly are now a team thanks to the combined efforts of so many good people. Shy at first, Midnight is getting used to Dolly's walker. She's learned to follow Dolly to her chair if she wants her head rubbed. Dolly tempers her full excitement with patience and understanding, appreciating that special bond as it grows between them. Feeding Midnight, pampering her, gently stroking her, simply enjoying the constant presence of another living being . . . this strong individ-

Dolly and Midnight: A Successful Placement. Photo courtesy of San Francisco SPCA.

ual need no longer resent the weakness of her present condition, the patient's status of always being provided for. Leave it to Dolly to say it all: "I've always been a giver, not a taker. Midnight lets me give again."

Like other animals selected for their placements, Midnight received a thorough medical screening and was spayed. She will also receive free lifetime medical care from the Society. Dolly receives a continual supply of pet food coupons and is regularly visited by one of the Society's staff.

The ingredients of the San Francisco SPCA's successful placement programs are: careful planning, careful selection and matching of both pet and owner, anticipation and elimination of possible problems (cleaning the litter box in this example), and follow-up support. The Society estimates a cost in excess of $1,500 to make each placement, but to someone like Dolly Silva, the results are easily worth a million!

## *PEOPLE-PET-PARTNERSHIP-PROGRAM*[7]

The wide-based and highly successful People-Pet-Partnership-Program began formally in Pullman, Washington, in 1979, but elements of the program were active as early as 1974. Momentum and guiding force behind the project is Leo K. Bustad, Dean of the College of Veterinary Medicine at Washington State University and president of the Delta Society. An energetic senior himself, Bustad's enthusiastic and persuasive endorsement of pet/people relationships and their resultant therapeutic effects is largely responsible for the success and scope of the Pullman project.

The initial objectives of the project were:

1. The education of school children and others about the responsibilities of pet ownership and the potential of pets for enriching their lives.
2. The utilization of animals in therapy for the physically, mentally, and emotionally handicapped.
3. The promotion of pets and companionship programs for the elderly, the lonely, students in dormitories, persons in nursing homes, and others.
4. The establishment of a referral system to enable area residents

to obtain specially trained animals (for example, hearing dogs for the disabled).

5. The establishment of a clearinghouse to provide information on animal-facilitated therapy programs and to link resource people with persons wishing assistance in the area of utilization of pets.

6. The formation of a consultant group to work with those people-pet problems and to define areas where pets are helpful.

Currently, the People-Pet-Partnership-Program has three basic programs: Public School Partnership (PSP), Partnership in Equine Therapy and Education (PETE), and Companion Animal Partnership (CAP). For the purposes of this volume, we will only be looking at the Companion Animal Partnership; but we encourage anyone interested in the other programs to obtain a monograph of the complete People-Pet-Partnership-Program available from the Latham Foundation (see Appendix II).

## COMPANION ANIMAL PARTNERSHIP

"The success of a People-Pet-Partnership-Program depends upon the enthusiasm and commitment of volunteers," says Linda Hines, director of the Pullman program. "Their interests and expertise determine their areas of involvement and thus the scope of the program. All activities happen only because they agree to plan and undertake them."

To begin, Hines suggests scheduling an initial informational meeting and inviting representatives of local helping agencies to attend. For example, for a program that will place animals with senior citizens and in nursing homes, you may wish to contact:

a. all area nursing homes
b. city and county councils on aging
c. area humane societies
d. senior citizens center
e. mental health center
f. university or college for a specialist in aging and/or behavior, and/or health
g. local veterinarians who might be interested to work on a consulting basis or who might offer their services at a lowered rate for the program
h. area physicians and other health professionals.

Dr. Leon Bustad with Bridgette, Mrs. Bustad's Hearing dog. Photo courtesy of People-Pet-Partnership Program, Pullman, WA

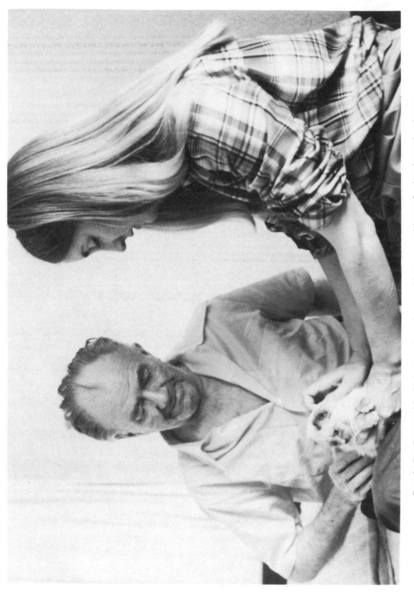

People-Pet-Partnership Volunteer introduces a kitten to resident of a local nursing home. Photo courtesy of People-Pet-Partnership Program, Pullman, WA.

Obviously, a university or veterinary affiliation such as the Pullman program has would be immensely helpful. Posters can be placed in areas of key academic interest: education, psychology, animal sciences, or therapeutic recreation. In an urban setting, notices can be placed in a local or college newspaper. Public service announcements are also a valuable means of alerting interested persons to your effort.

At the Pullman Program, Bustad and Hines have found that the greatest benefits are derived from the expertise and input of a large and diverse number of members. Program meetings, thus, are open to everyone and there is no fee for a membership. Everyone who becomes active in a program becomes a part of a council. The Pullman group currently has 66 members which include professionals, students, and laypersons.

"Keeping a diverse group of volunteers functioning," says Hines, "requires three conditions: they must be kept informed; they must participate in meaningful activities, learning and growing themselves; they must be appreciated and thanked. The organization structure, objectives and programs of the council all have evolved at Washington State University from a very open system governed by the wishes of the volunteers."

### Determining Objectives

Vital to the success and longevity of any program is determining goals that (1) meet the needs of the community and (2) can be implemented by the people/pet council. These goals can be addressed at the initial informational meeting and attendees should be encouraged to address this issue.

Let's assume that your people-pet-program is, initially, going to be primarily a program for the elderly. The objectives might be:

1. to place (if legally permissible) an animal mascot in as many areas nursing homes as could accommodate the pet.
   a. if not legally permissible to have a pet in-residence to arrange for regular and innovative pet visitation programs.
   b. to work legislatively to alter current statutes so that 1 can be accomplished.
2. to provide support for non-institutionalized elders who have a pet. This might include offering financial assistance via pet

food coupons, discount veterinary service; or it could involve a service for walking a pet or taking it to a veterinarian if the elder was indisposed or even a temporary care for the pet if the owner was hospitalized.

3. placement of pets with non-institutionalized elders who would benefit from such a companion and follow-up (as in 2).
4. obtaining and placement of specially trained pets (such as hearing and signal dogs) with elderly who would need such an animal.
5. referral service for seniors who have problems with a pet.

The People-Pet-Partnership Program has identified several areas as possible program possibilities. Those that would be particularly apt for seniors include:

a. Establishment of an animal loan service to make selected animals available to foster homes.
b. Implementation of a wallet or purse card for persons who live alone to carry with them; if they are involved in an accident, it will notify authorities that their animals need immediate care.
c. Revision of forms for patient admission to hospitals and other medical facilities asking: "Do you live alone?", "Do you have pets?"
d. Development of an emergency care plan to provide for animals displaced by personal or local disasters.
e. Transportation to veterinarian's offices of animals belonging to people of limited mobility.
f. Political action to lobby for changes in legislation to permit animals in health care facilities and in government-sponsored housing for low-income elderly.
g. Design of a window sticker to alert rescuers to types and location of companion animals in case of fire.
h. Development of a program to train animals to assist the handicapped in various ways (fetching glasses, turning on lights, "hearing" for the deaf), or establishment of a resource file to identify where such animals can be obtained.
i. Placement of a trained animal on a pilot basis with an aged person in an apartment complex for the elderly. Council members would visit regularly to help solve problems.
j. Establishment of a telephone "hot line" to answer callers' questions about pet-owner problems.

## Structure

The Pullman People-Pet-Partnership-Program involves a director, co-director/advisor, and a coordinator for each of the major programs. Duties in this program are described for each position. The Director is responsible for scheduling, planning, and conducting meetings; making public presentations about the program; maintaining membership and mailing lists; publishing the newsletter; working with coordinators to plan programs and keep them functioning; helping recruit volunteers; collecting items for reprint file and handouts; planning fund raising; and answering correspondence. Hines suggests that an ideal program have at least a halftime director, as well as secretarial support, which in the Pullman program comes from volunteers and Washington State University staff.

The co-director helps arrange speakers and educational activities, makes presentations to service and professional groups, visits animal-facilitated therapy programs in the U.S. and abroad, attends as many meetings as possible, and keeps in close contact with new developments and research in the field worldwide. Hines remarks that a widely respected, knowledgeable co-director provides credibility, status, and visibility. Not every community group will be fortunate enough to have a co-director of the international renown and stature of Leo Bustad; however, as pet therapy grows, more and more respected professionals are entering its annals. The community group is urged to check for such a professional in their midsts.

Coordinators. The ideal coordinator is a knowledgeable volunteer. His/her responsibilities include: planning program meetings and fund raisers, making public presentations, and recruiting volunteers. An additional position might be that of an instructor who would assist the coordinator by training volunteers.

Hines also mentions that a program separate from a University must incorporate and obtain a tax-exempt status, a procedure which involves electing a board of directors, writing by-laws and articles of incorporation, and completing IRS forms. Sample by-laws are included in the People-Pet-Partnership-Program monograph. (see Appendix II)

## *COMPANION ANIMAL SERVICES, INC.*[8]

Companion Animal Services, designed and directed by Robert M. Andrysco, is an innovative new program just beginning in Columbus, Ohio. A specialist in the human/animal bond, Andrysco in-

Farm Day sponsored by the People-Pet-Partnership Program in conjunction with the local 4-H clubs. Photo courtesy of People-Pet-Partnership Program, Pullman, WA.

itiated the service to effectively deal with some of the problems inherent in animal facilitated therapy.

Since 1978 [he says], various organizations have attempted to implement pet-therapy programs to serve the elderly in Columbus, Ohio. They have been able to provide services for only a small number of individuals, and they have been unable to make the transition from pet-visitation to pet-therapy. Individuals are sporadically visited without psychological evaluation and little attempt is made to identify target symptoms, tailor a therapy program to a particular individual's problems, and monitor progress.

The reasons for their failure are several:
(1) Lack of time and available resources;
(2) Lack of training and professional expertise; and
(3) Lack of success in coordinating services with other organizations.

All of these problems can be overcome by an organization, the primary functions of which are to:
(1) Supply a community service;
(2) Evaluate and modify the service as required;
(3) Coordinate the efforts of various organizations; and
(4) Educate the geriatric and health-care facilities, community service organizations, and the general public.

The programs which will be individually tailored to the needs of each institution and its residents proceeds in five phases.

## Companion Animal Services Project Protocol

### Phase I

Introduce service to administration and staff and initial organization of project (approximately 4 weeks).

1. One-day seminar to introduce service and general plan of the program to nursing home staff.
2. Weekly meetings between Companion Animal Services personnel and nursing home staff to discuss:
   a. Possible hazards of project and how to avoid and/or overcome them (e.g., sanitation problems, residents allergic to pets, legal and insurance problems, etc.)

b. Role of nursing home staff, their time involvement, which staff to be involved, explain cost/benefit ratio to administrators.
c. Role of Companion Animal Services personnel, their time involvement (Companion Animal Services personnel to assume role of volunteers in eyes of residents for evaluation purposes).
d. Role of volunteers; where will volunteers come from, how Companion Animal Services will help.
e. What Companion Animal Services wants out of the program—evaluation data to further the idea of pet therapy and how to improve quality of service, etc.
f. How to use pets in therapeutic manner, time involved, time of day to complete, length of therapeutic visits, etc.
g. Discussion of pet care, full-time versus part-time pets, types of pets available, and which ones are the best, kennel if needed, if part-time pet—how will it be brought to and from facility.
h. What staff should expect in form of responses by the residents, how to take therapeutic advantage of these responses, etc.
3. Locate veterinarian, introduce to facility, discuss his role, and arrange his visits.
4. Screen and select residents; collect demographic data on residents.
5. Introduction of evaluation material, how it will be used, how it will benefit staff, etc.
6. Insurance, legalities, consent forms, etc.

*Phase II*

Preliminary therapeutic visits (approximately 5 weeks)

1. If part-time pet, arrange transportation; if full-time pet, build kennel; discussions of pet care continue.
2. Begin data collection on residents (surveys, rating scales, videotapes, etc.)
3. Weekly discussions with staff continue to discuss residents' responses, variables being analyzed, and any other questions.
4. Pet gets final OK from veterinarian and behaviorist.

*Phase III*
Therapeutic visits with pet animal (approximately 5 weeks)

1. Pet introduced to the facility; visits with residents continue.
2. If kennel is involved, adapt pet to it.
3. Evaluation continues on all participating residents.
4. Weekly discussions continue.
5. First visit by the veterinarian; details of pet care discussed.

*Phase IV*
Program evaluation (approximately 5 weeks)

1. Second veterinarian visit, continue discussion of pet care; facility must meet requirements to maintain pet therapy program.
2. Pet animal is currently in kennel full-time.
3. Evaluation continues; Companion Animal Services personnel transfer evaluation procedures over to staff, while teaching them how Companion Animal Services will evaluate; future communication between Companion Animal Services and facility discussed.
4. Determination of how many times residents should be visited and teach staff how to determine.
(Continuing indefinitely)
5. Monthly visits by Companion Animal Services personnel to check on pet, residents' progress, discussions with staff, etc.
6. Companion Animal Services remains available for last minute consultation.
7. Monthly visits by veterinarian.
8. Monthly visits by Humane Society.
9. Monthly evaluation communication between Companion Animal Services and facility.

"The combination of community service and rigorous evaluation procedures," says Robert Andrysco,

> make Companion Animal Services unique among similar organizations throughout the country. It has been demonstrated that there is a strong need for this type of service, and that there is an intense interest on the part of potential beneficiar-

ies, contributors, volunteers, and other members of the general public.

## REFERENCES

1. PAW PALS Leader's Guide. Pets are Wonderful Council.
2. Walster, Dorothy. "The Two-Way Benefits That Companion Animals Bring to Children and the Elderly." Paper available from The Latham Foundation.
3. Editorial. *Phildelphia Daily News.* September 23, 1980.
4. Editorial. "Pets by Rx," *The Latham Letter,* Spring 1982.
5. Weinbrenner, Don. "Her Pet Operation is All About Cats," *New York Daily News.*
6. San Francisco SPCA leaflet.
7. Hines, Linda M. *The People-Pet-Partnership-Program.* Alameda, California: The Latham Foundation. 1980.
8. Andrysco, Robert M. "Companion Animal Services, Inc." Proposal prepared for the Columbus Foundation, December 1982.

Chapter 11

# Non-Canine Therapists

Although we have emphasized the use of dogs as co-therapists, they by no means have a monopoly on love and friendship. Many species of animals can be utilized depending, of course, upon the individual circumstances. In this chapter, we will look at some of the programs that employ non-canine therapists and some applications of pet therapy beyond geriatrics.

## CATS

In the Clark Brickel study discussed in Chapter 2, the in-house cat mascots provided numerous valuable benefits to the patients. In fact, cats are currently the second most popular animals used in therapy. Like canines, cats offer tactile stimulation, comfort, affection, and opportunities for one-on-one interaction. Generally, however, they require somewhat less care and virtually no training. A neutered animal of either sex will normally present few behavior problems and will be a rewarding and endearing companion.

Momma Cat was a stray who wandered onto the grounds of Barboursville State Hospital in Barboursville, West Virginia, and stayed on to become the special pet and mascot for 98 mentally retarded adults there. The patients took full responsibility for her care, and regularly accompanied her to cat shows, one of their few recreational outings, where the healthy housecat consistently won honors in the pet category. Justine Koch who directed volunteer services at the hospital related an example of the incredible bond between the cat and her keepers. The patients particularly enjoy the single cup of coffee allotted them daily. One day, shortly after they had received this treat, Koch noticed that three cups of coffee had been placed next to Momma Cat's food and water bowl which was kept in the hospital laundry. Momma Cat was awarded the 1974 Top Cat honor

*193*

from the Pet Food Institute for her unique role in this community. Sharing honors with Momma Cat that year was Tiger, a stray who was a friend to the children at the St. Joseph's School in Wisconsin. Sister Jane Tojek, an art instructor at the school, let the troubled youngsters, all wards of the state and from disrupted homes, talk and interact with the cat and reported numerous stories of Tiger's special therapeutic effects on the disturbed children.[1]

Cats can be successful prison pets. According to Joey Tabscott who worked in those facilities for over 30 years, the prisoners appear to have a universal urge to acquire affection from some living creature. Tabscott told of a particular cat, Suzy Q, who was adopted by a ward and whose presence was as enjoyed as if she had been a female movie star. One prisoner, who had previously been held in low-esteem by his fellow inmates, gained prestige and a leadership capacity because of his knowledge about cats and their care. Another prisoner, a particularly refractory case who at first rejected the cat, was later heard pouring out his soul to the small feline.[2]

Recall Leo Bustad's case of the elderly woman, bed-ridden and withdrawn, who compulsively scratched herself raw, until she was introduced to a cat (Chapter 7). Bustad's People-Pet-Partnership-Program has placed many cats with the terminally ill, so they won't die alone.[3] And Mary Thompson of the Veterans Administration Medical Center in Coatsville, Pennsylvania, reports a cat, a ward mascot, who spends all its "off-duty" time comforting a terminal patient.[4]

## A FLOPPY-EARED THERAPIST CALLED BUBBA[5]

A white rabbit named Bubba is an extraordinarily successful therapist according to The San Francisco Society for the Prevention of Cruelty to Animals. Portions of the poignant story which appears in their publication are reprinted here:

> Sitting alone, staring at nothing, Timmy's eyes light up as Bubba the bunny approaches and nuzzles his shoes. Timmy is the only verbal member of the Tigers, a group of severely mentally retarded adults enrolled at the Recreation Center. The people who work with Timmy every day encourage him to broaden his scope, to speak more clearly. It is difficult for him, a daily struggle. The resident rabbit is helping him make

Bubba, the floppy-eared therapist. Photo courtesy of San Francisco SPCA.

the effort. Bubba is something that interests Timmy enough to want to talk about.

"Bunny rabbit," he says carefully when asked what kind of an animal Bubba is. And "white" is the response to a question about Bubba's color.

But Bubba is more than a white bunny rabbit for Timmy. He is the bridge which the young man crosses to rejoin the speaking world. For a time, Timmy is able to converse with anyone willing to listen. His face is eloquent with joy as he gently strokes the rabbit and succeeds in sharing his few words with his visitor.

For another patient, Lexi, "Buh Buh" is one of the few sounds she has ever been able to utter. And for Dianne, who is severely withdrawn and locked within herself, Bubba's presence is one of the rare times that she appears to react to her surroundings. Sometimes, not always, she reaches out to pet him and smiles, and her therapists feel that she may slowly be beginning to come out of herself.

Though so easy to sense, it isn't yet possible to measure precisely how many of these happenings are due directly to Bubba's gentle presence. What is measurable are the practical skills the bunny is helping to teach. The lessons take place because, as planned, the Tigers themselves have learned to help care for Bubba, to assist in providing him with his basic needs.

Mark took three months to learn to carry Bubba's water bottle down the hall, but he knows his is not a small accomplishment. Bubba needs water to live and depends on Mark for this vital substance. Perhaps he can learn to furnish it for himself. What the Tigers learn about Bubba's care is helping them comprehend things about themselves. The new understanding could help lead them to lives of greater independence.

Bobby learned to pour pellets into Bubba's bowl by practicing pouring sand from a container for weeks. Tommy helps clean Bubba's habitat. The rabbit pen itself, with tall sides to prevent Bubba from jumping out, or someone unsupervised from reaching in, is an object of no small pride to the clients at the Center who helped construct it.

Another mission for Bubba is a visit with the Polliwogs, a group of 12 children, all under the age of three and all severely retarded. Says their program leader Karen Rassi,

Bubba, the floppy-eared therapist. Photo courtesy of San Francisco SPCA.

The children are more alert and gentle around the animals, animals like Bubba, than around anything or anyone else. It's the softness, but it's a lot more. It isn't the same with stuffed animals. As young as they are, the children are very much aware that Bubba is alive.

Bubba was rescued from the Golden Gate Park by the San Francisco SPCA and placed at the Center. Staff officials had been searching for the perfect bunny for months. Prior to his placement at the Recreation Center, Bubba spent three weeks at the SPCA's education department and visited local schools and senior citizens. Nothing bothered or upset this rabbit, not noise, not activity. He was gentle, curious, and affectionate to all he met. In short, a perfect choice.

### BIRDS AND SMALL RODENTS

Probably the most famous example of animals in prison is the story of Robert Stroud, the "Birdman of Alcatraz." Stroud's devotion to his charges was so complete that he eventually became a world expert on the diseases of birds and their treatment. His treatise, "Stroud's Digest on the Disease of Birds," is still in demand by aviculturists today.

Not all prison animals become as widely known as Stroud's birds, but they do appear to have a definite beneficial effect on the prisoners. Pete, a kestrel (or sparrow hawk), was critically injured by a hunter's bullet and nursed back to health by inmates at Massachusetts State Prison. The injuries were so severe that a leg and wing were amputated, and the bird was unable to be returned to the wild. In addition to nursing the hawk, the prisoners also made him an outdoor cage and fed him daily. Interestingly, the hawk never became social. In fact, Pete exhibited belligerence towards the hands that fed him which mattered little to inmates who seemed content just to care for the injured creature.[6]

In 1975 psychiatric social worker David Lee introduced a fish tank and a few caged budgies as ward mascots at the Lima State Hospital for the Criminally Insane. As the prisoners interacted with the animals, he noticed a capacity for caring in what he considered "the most difficult, refractory group to treat." Later, Lee introduced small caged rodents, hamsters and rabbits. His program is currently one of the most successful and widely referenced in the arena of animal-facilitated therapy. Lee has found that patients with pets are less depressed, less violent, less suicidal, and less in need of drugs than patients in wards without pets.

Currently, the Lima program consists of 175 animals and involves about 200 inmates. The species include deer, geese, ducks, goats, and chickens which live in the courtyard; and various birds, small rodents, a lizard, and a cat who are the individual pets of the inmates. No dogs are used in the program because of state regulations and, as Lee points out, a prison is not a suitable place for a dog.

"The program's philosophy," says Lee,

is simply to help depressed and suicidal patients to help themselves. Having a pet brings with it instant responsibility and companionship. The pet's total dependency tends to cause the patient to react and this reaction when monitored properly is usually positive, giving the patient a new focus for his attention. Hopefully, the unique bond between patient and pet will have overall positive results and be therapeutically beneficial.

The animals on the ward have succeeded in reducing tension among the prisoners and provided the added boon of enhancing communication between inmates and the staff. The program is also used as an incentive/reward program. Prisoners who care for the livestock in the courtyard may eventually be rewarded with a pet of their own.

Recently, Lee completed a one-year comparison study of two 28-bed honor wards in the hospital. "The only difference was that one ward had pets and the other did not," he explained. "During that year the ward without pets had twelve fights and three suicide attempts while the ward with the pets had one fight and no suicide attempts." The program has even inspired an informal humane group within the prison who discuss pet problems on the wards and circulate petitions, such as "Save the Harp Seal," for other groups. One former patient, upon release, found employment at the Atlanta Humane Society. And if that is not enough, Lee's pet therapy program is also the most economical program at the institution. Following the successful example of Lima, three other Ohio state correctional institutions have begun similar programs.[7]

## HORSES AND LIVESTOCK

Equestrian therapy for the handicapped is a French innovation, adopted by Britain, and gaining widespread acceptance on our shores. In the U.S. today, there are approximately 160 accredited institutions that allow a physically handicapped child a chance to ride and associate with horses.

According to psychiatrist Michael McCulloch these programs offer threefold psychological, social, and physical benefits. For children confined to a wheelchair, the horse, for one time in their lives, allows them to sit higher than their peers, giving their self-image a boost. A child with the aid of the animal can compete with other children in sports events. Finally, the physical condition required to ride the animal provides incentive for the child to continue his tedious regimen of weights and pulleys.[8]

An example of a formal study in equestrian therapy is given by Natalie Bieber and conducted at the handicapped unit of the Village School in North Haven, Connecticut. The children ranged in age from 6-17 years of age and their handicaps included spina bifida and cerebral palsy. Bieber instituted her program three days a week during a five-week summer session. She utilized one-day riding, either on the horse or in a pony cart, and two days in the classroom using the association with the horses as a springboard for learning.

"The children in the program had a poor self-image, and realistically so," she explains.

> Confined to their wheelchairs, they spend many hours in front of a T.V., watching the beautiful people. What do the beautiful people do? Very often they ride horses or are involved in horse-related activities. By the association with horses, I was hoping to transform my kids into the beautiful people.

Results based upon subjective evaluations by the staff at Village School concluded that all but four of the children were benefitted significantly by the program. The children were stimulated physically, socially, and intellectually, and one child, who was severely withdrawn and retarded, showed beginning signs of communication, prompted by a picture of a horse.[9]

Although farm animals may seem unlikely visitors to geriatric institutions, Melinda Magee, public relations director for the Monterey County SPCA, says the elderly with a farming or ranching background particularly enjoy piglets and lambs.[10] We and other Therapy Dogs International members have had much success with African pygmy goats. And Leo Bustad says:

> Not only the handicapped, but also many healthy older people could benefit by riding horses and affiliating with therapeutic riding clubs. I witnessed the joy of an 85-year old aunt who resumed riding a horse after not riding for 40 years. Both she and the horse are the same equivalent age; both are alert and spirited, but gentle.[11]

## PROJECT INREACH

The animals used in the previous projects have been traditional, familiar subjects, animals well within the range of ordinary experience and association. However, the final example presented in this chapter, Project Inreach, will discuss the interactions between autistic children and Atlantic bottle-nosed dolphins, certainly a most unusual species.

Atlantic bottle-nosed dolphins, of the biological order Cetacea, are large sea mammals measuring about 11-12 feet in length. Extremely social in nature, they swim in groups called pods and have been observed assisting females of their group in childbirth. They respond not only to distress calls from their own kind but, if legend is to be believed, to ours as well, gently pushing stranded sailors to a safe shore. The dolphin brain is well-developed and complex, and many cetacean researchers have suggested that the animals have far more than a rudimentary intelligence, possibly a language expressed in the clicking sounds that are also used by the animal to navigate through its expansive ocean home. This echolocation allows the dolphin to perceive not only the shape and size of an object, but its density as well.

In recent years, captive dolphins have been used in many aquaria and are star performers because of their remarkable ability to learn a complex series of maneuvers and tricks in a relatively short period of time. The animals form strong bonds with their trainers and, especially in the absence of others of their species, seem to seek out human association. In fact, the human voice, touch, and presence appears to have a healing effect on a distressed or debilitated sea mammal. Friendly and accommodating as they may be, dolphins are not domestic animals and should not be regarded as such. In a captive setting, their role is more akin to guest, or perhaps prisoner.

Project Inreach was designed by Betsy Smith, associate professor at Florida International University, and Henry Truby, president of the World Dolphin Foundation. Previously, Truby and Smith observed neurologically impaired children responding enthusiastically to free-swimming dolphins and the dolphins in turn responding to the children with uncharacteristic patience and gentleness. They asked the question: "Could dolphins prompt communication responses, previously unrealized, in children diagnosed as autistic, language-impaired and retarded?"

To find out the researchers solicited eight children and their families from the Southford Society for Autistic Children and three dolphin entertainers from the Wometco Seaquarium. In the first session, the children and their families were introduced to the dolphins and the setting. By the second and third session, the researchers initiated play behavior: ball tossing between parent, child, and dolphin and splashing water on the dolphins, for example. Several children responded by reproducing the clicking sounds of the animals and by spontaneously beginning play with no prompting from parents or staff.

By the sixth and final session, two children were actually in the pool with the dolphins. They clicked, splashed, spit out water, and in general exhibited behavior similar to that of the playful sea mammals. Although Truby and Smith had planned eight encounter sessions, they abandoned the project early fearing the risk of injury too great in their present environment. Parents of the children reported sadness after the project ended. Sessions with dolphins had been among the happiest they had ever known as a family; they reported joy and relaxation immediately following each session and an alleviation of tension that lasted for several weeks afterwards.

But the most extraordinary aspect of the project involved the individual reaction of one boy, Michael Williams, aged 18 and labeled non-verbal autistic since the age of six. Michael did not normally reproduce human sounds. In her research paper presented at the 1981 International Conference on the Human/Companion Animal Bond, Smith recounted the story of a boy and a dolphin.

> At the second encounter with the dolphins, Michael began to make clicking sounds to get the dolphin Sharkey's attention to engage in ball-throwing. Michael clicked at all sessions. Lis-

tening to the tapes, it requires close attention to distinguish between his clicks and the dolphins.

To date when Michael sees billboards or television commercials with dolphins, he responds by clicking at the image. This is abstraction to image and an indicator of learning. Six months after the project came to a halt, he began furious clicking in a local drugstore, and Mrs. Williams found him clicking at a flotation device in the shape of and painted like a dolphin.

One year after the project halted, Michael's class went to Seaquarium on a field trip. He broke away from his group, went to the project area and stood outside the locked gate clicking to get in to the dolphins.

During the fall of 1981, NBC's "Those Amazing Animals" sent a film crew to record Michael's first encounter with the dolphin Sharkey for over a year and a half. He began to click as soon as he heard Sharkey's signal and for over three hours while the film crew demanded retakes, sat on a platform and engaged in water play with Sharkey.

The last verified continuous verbal response from Michael was reported just weeks ago (September, 1981). The Williams have a book with a picture of a dolphin in the middle of the text. Since the beginning of the project, he after being shown the book once on random occasions without outside stimulation will take the book, leaf page by page till he comes to the picture of the dolphin, and will click at the picture.

Smith also reported that Michael's teacher noted the boy had an increased attention span after the dolphin encounters. He appeared happier, more relaxed, and did not smack his head and bite his nails for long periods of time.

Smith further observed cooperative behavior between Williams and another child who, although schoolmates, had never previously acknowledged each other's existence. Together, the boys picked up a bucket, carried it, and poured it over the dolphin. Interaction between them has not been observed since.

The full implication of Michael's behavior cannot be appreciated unless one is familiar with or has worked with autistic children. Autism, which has no known cause or cure, is defined as the profound inability to establish affectionate and meaningful relationships and language, summarized Smith and, in concluding her presentation remarked: "Unlike other studies in which the animal is the tool of the therapist, in this project, and only this project, the dolphins themselves are the therapists."[12]

In a follow-up project with Williams and the dolphins, Smith reports that his progress continues. At a session with the gentle cetaceans, Williams' father asked him if he cared to get onto a floating platform. Instead of shaking his head, his normal response, he answered "Yep." He continues to make this, his first human vocalization, and uses it in the proper context.[13]

In Chapter 3, we discussed current research investigating the human/animal bond. The story of the boy and the dolphins, however, as one of the most unusual studies in animal-facilitated therapy, is an indication that, in spite of the wealth of present research into this bond, its extraordinary nature and far-reaching significance is only beginning to be explored.

## REFERENCES

1. Editorial. "It's a Cat's World." *The National Humane Review*, August 1974.

2. Tapscott, Joey, "Lady of the Cages." *The National Humane Review*, January-February 1970.

3. Bustad, Leo. "Companion Animals and the Aged." Address at the 1981 International Conference on the Human/Companion Animal Bond, October 5-7, 1981, Philadelphia, PA.

4. Thompson, Mary. "Pets as Socializing Agents with Chronic Psychiatric Patients: An Initial Study." Presentation at the 1981 International Conference on the Human/Companion Animal Bond, October 5-7, 1981. Philadelphia, PA.

5. Editorial. "The Therapist with a Floppy Ear." *Our Animals*, San Francisco SPCA, Spring 1982.

6. Flaherty, Joseph A. "Jail Bird." *The National Humane Review*, July-August 1958.

7. Lee, David. Personal Communication.

8. McCulloch, Michael J. "Pet Facilitated Psychotherapy." Address at the 1981 International Conference on the Human/Companion Animal Bond, October 5-7, 1981, Philadelphia, PA.

9. Bieber, Natalie. "The Integration of a Therapeutic Equestrian Program in the Academic Environment of Children with Physical and Multiple Disabilities." Presentation at the 1981 International Conference on the Human/Companion Animal Bond, October 5-7, Philadelphia, PA.

10. Editorial. "Monterey (California) County SPCA's Pet Visitation Manual." *The Latham Letter*, Fall 1982.

11. Bustad, Leo K. *Animals, Aging and the Aged.* Minneapolis: University of Minnesota Press, 1980.

12. Smith, Betsy A. "Project Inreach: A Program to Explore the Ability of Bottlenose Dolphins to Elicit Communication Responses From Autistic Children." Research presentation at the International Conference on the Human/Companion Animal Bond, October 5-7, 1981, Philadelphia, PA.

13. Ibid. Personal Communication.

# Chapter 12

# Evaluating the Program

As we discussed in Chapter 7, evaluating the effects of pet therapy programs is one of the foremost challenges facing researchers in the discipline. In this chapter we will discuss some guidelines that institutions can use to assess the effects of their programs.

## DESIGN

### Individuals versus Populations

To assess the effect of any variable, in this case pet therapy, one must be able to evaluate the change in the population/individual that is a direct result of the introduction of this variable. Generally, the pre-treatment or non-treatment condition is designated the control and the post-treatment or treatment is designated the experimental. The effect of the variable thus is the difference between the control and the experimental. Two examples follow:

1. The population that is treated with pet therapy is compared to a similar population that is treated equally in all respects but is not treated with pet therapy. Ideally, all factors that differ between the groups (age, sex, mobility, diagnosed condition, etc.) should be assessed to determine if any of these variables could account for any significant difference in the results. These studies are difficult because (a) individuals do vary in many significant aspects and (b) unless the two populations are kept isolated, there is a possibility of carry-over from the experimental group to the control. A possible design is to measure the effects on two separate institutions; one who had access to pet therapy and one who did not. One example of this procedure is the Pet Visitation Study by Francis et al. discussed in Chapter 2.

2. An individual himself can be both the control and the experimental. That is the baseline, pre-treatment condition of the patient

can be determined and then compared to the post-treatment (after pet therapy) condition. This is a very effective design and has been used successfully by many researchers (JACOPIS, Andrysco, etc.). This design has the advantage of holding most factors constant, thus eliminating the possibility that something other than the treatment accounts for the change in the individual.

Two elements that must be considered in this design are (a) novelty and (b) attention. Introducing a pet to a facility is a new experience for most patients; it contains elements of entertainment, sensory stimulation, and excitement that may not previously have been available. Also, the evaluation procedures used (tests, questionaires, etc.) focus attention on the patient, probably more so than the individual has had in the past. This in itself could account for some of the change in the resident.

To hold these variables constant, consider testing the individuals at various points along the continuum. That is, a pre-test before the introduction of the pet, a post-test 6-8 weeks later, and an additional post-test 4-6 months after initial introduction. Additionally, one can determine if the effect is ongoing, however gradual. For example, there might be a dramatic change indicated in the first evaluation, and only a slight improvement in the second phase of evaluation. Another individual may show a mild improvement throughout the study. Another individual may have no reaction during the first phase, and strong improvement during the second. The effects will also vary depending upon the pet potential of the animal selected and the way the animal is used in therapy. The novelty impact of a tank of fish, for example, may pass in just a few days. A dog, however, that is used in formal therapy will continue to have an impact on the patients throughout its residence.

## How to Measure Effect

### Standardized Tests

There are a number of standard psychological tests that are used to measure, for example, morale, ego strength, happiness, etc. They have the advantage of validity; that is, they are deemed a true indicator of the condition measured, and they have been tested on a number of populations. The disadvantage is that an institution may not have the time, knowledge, or personnel on staff to administer such tests, especially to a large population of patients. Additionally, proper evaluation of the results of these tests requires statistical analysis and interpretation. This is easily done today by computer, but many institutions do not have the means or the expertise to do this themselves.

## Videotape

The use of videotape in evaluating therapy programs is a tool of the future. It allows the researcher to review the session in depth, as many times as required to scrutinize the behaviors and comments that took place. Often, slight changes in facial expressions, hand movements, and body language can be overlooked during the actual interaction. It is also an excellent training procedure to show novice pet therapists exactly what to look for.

The disadvantage is that the equipment itself is costly, and no precise measures are available for its application. Robert Andrysco used this method to evaluate some of his sample who interacted with the dog Obie. Although he noted a positive response in all patients, statistical analysis of the encounters was inconclusive.

## Precise Variables

In his population at Lima State Hospital, David Lee found that groups interacting with pets had fewer fights, fewer suicide attempts, and tended to require less medication (Chapter 11). In Robb's study of the wine bottle, the plant, and the puppy, the behaviors assessed included the number of smiles, leaning toward the stimulus, eyes open, etc. (Chapter 2). Verbalization is a commonly assessed factor. Andrysco, for example, studied both the quality (positive versus negative) and quantity of vocalizations (Chapter 2). Robb noted decreased inappropriate vocalization and lack of hostility when social space was intruded. The JACOPIS study evaluated, among other things, the amount of time spent alone and a decreased workload on staff (Chapter 2). Additionally, both the anecdotal accounts and the research studies note a tendency toward "potential breakthrough behavior," that is, the appearance of a new behavior or vocalization that was previously unrealized. This could be a verbalization (speaking for the first time when presented with a dog) or a motor behavior (getting out of bed to see the dog).

Some of these factors could be analyzed quite well by an institution. For example, in a group therapy activity, such as a reminiscence class, (a) how many patients respond, (b) is it the first time for any of them, (c) are the responses more coherent, more positive than previously noted, (d) of those who do not respond, are they attentive to the dog (do they watch it, lean toward it, for instance), is the group more alert (eyes open opposed to eyes closed), is there some interaction between group members (based upon reaction to the dog).

Some other general suggestions for measurement: number of patients near the dog, patients who interact with each other when interacting with the dog, response to activity that involves dog (versus response to activity that doesn't involve dog), carry-over to other projects (see Chapter 7), does patient initiate interaction or play (or does pet).

### Subjective Evaluation

As Jules Cass has remarked, most health care professionals have their own internal criteria for determining improvement of a given patient. Could the dog provide the impetus for this recovery? A simple chart design might prove invaluable. For example:

Mr. A: withdrawn, non-ambulatory, non-verbal (though is able to speak)

*Observation:* Mr. A reached out for dogs during visitation program. Leans toward therapy dog and interacts with him when he comes. However, dog often goes to other patients who call him by name.

*Potential:* Could Mr. A be motivated to speak to get the therapy dog to come to him?

*Method:* Therapist will talk to Mr. A (who will not respond) and then call dog over by name. He will stress that the dog responds to its name, and repeat the name. When dog departs, Mr. A is told once again that the dog will return if he calls it by name.

Mrs. B is oriented, ambulatory, gets on well during the day but has a nocturnal phobia. She resists bedtime and is very insistent that staff stay with her. The condition is getting progressively worse. Mrs. B has dangerously high blood pressures and this aggravation doesn't help.

*Observation:* Mrs. B likes the therapy cat and often plays with it during the day.

*Potential:* Since stroking an animal is relaxing and reduces blood pressure, could the cat stay with Mrs. B at night?

*Method:* Before bedtime, Mrs. B is asked if she would be willing to keep the cat in her room. The nurse explains that the cat gets in the way of the night shift and really won't settle down in her bed. The cat needs attention and none of the staff has time to bother with it. Would Mrs. B be willing to talk to and pet the cat for awhile each evening?

Mrs. C is disoriented, non-ambulatory, and constantly vocalizes inappropriately. Other patients complain about her; thus she is often removed from social situations that could eventually help her condition.

*Observation:* When the dogs come, Mrs. C vocalized continually during their demonstration; however, when a small dog is placed on her lap, she is silent and seems to focus on the pet.

*Potential:* If a pet dog or cat were placed on her lap Mrs. C might remain quiet during a group session. Could we expect eventual appropriate vocalization?

*Method:* Bring Mrs. C into social situation. Place small pet on her lap.

By formulating a specific goal plan for each patient, the staff can evaluate the effect of the pet on a personal basis. Observations should be recorded and, as possible, reviewed at staff meetings. If a goal is reached, a new goal should be formulated. Once Mr. A speaks, he may be on the way toward orientation. If the cat soothes Mrs. B, eventually she may be willing to discuss her night fears, thus opening an additional avenue of therapy. Once Mrs. C stops her inappropriate vocalizations, the next goal might be appropriate vocalizations.

We have given numerous examples throughout this volume of ways that animals can be used to alleviate specific problems or simply to make the environment a more pleasant place which in itself is a step toward mental health. The ultimate success, however, of each individual program will be dependent upon how enthusiastically it is implemented by the staff of the institution involved. Pet therapy has enormous potential; in terms of benefits, costs, and feasibility of implementation, it could conceivably outdistance most other treatment modalities. No single drug, no single procedure, no formal therapeutic method, alone, can make a patient happier, healthier, more sociable, more oriented, more mobile, more self-aware, more optimistic, and most importantly, rekindle the waning will to live. Pet therapy can, and has done all of these things.

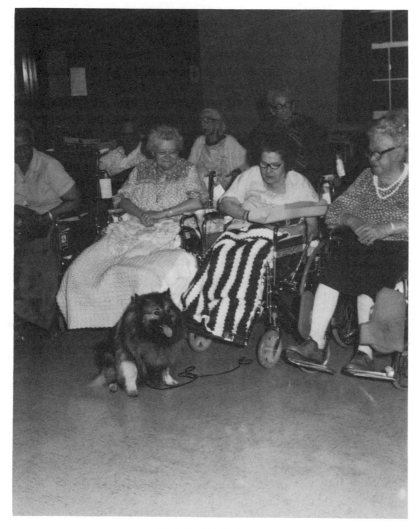

Photo by Bob Barber.

# Bibliography and Selected Readings

Andrysco, Robert. M. "Pet Facilitated Therapy In An Ohio Nursing Community." *The Latham Letter,* Spring 1982.

Ibid. "Companion Animal Services, Inc." Proposal prepared for the Columbus Foundation, Columbus, Ohio, 1982.

Arkow, Phil. "How to Start a Pet Therapy Program." The Human Society of the Pikes Peak Region. Colorado Springs, Colorado.

Arkow, Phil. "A Study of the Use of Companion Animals in Selected Therapies." Report to the American Humane Education Advisory Committee, 1977.

Arkow, Phil. "Puppy Love At The Humane Society." *Senior Beacon,* September 1980.

Askins, John. "Man's Best Friend His Best Therapy?" *San Jose Mercury News,* June 30, 1979.

Blair, Betty. "Pets Brighten Life for Sick, Lonely." *Detroit News,* September 27, 1976.

Brickel, Clark M. "The Therapeutic Roles of Cat Mascots with a Hospital-Based Geriatric Population: A Staff Survey." *Gerontologist,* 1979, *19*(4), 368-372.

Brickel, Clark M. and Brickel, G.K.A. "A Review of the Roles of Pet Animals in Psychotherapy and with the Elderly." *International Journal of Aging and Human Development* (in press).

Burke, Mike. "The Humane Society—People Who Care." *Denver Magazine,* April 1978, 34.

Bustad, Leo K. "The Peripathetic Dean." *Western Veterinarian,* 1977-78, *16*(5), 2-3.

Bustad, Leo K. "Pets For People Therapy." *Today's Animal Health,* September-October 1978, 8-10.

Bustad, Leo K. "How Animals Make People Human and Humane." *Modern Veterinary Practices,* September 1979, 707-710.

Bustad, Leo K. "Profiling Animals For Therapy." *Western Veterinarian,* 1979, *17*(1), 2.

Bustad, Leo K. "People-Pet Partnership." *Western Veterinarian,* 1979, *3,* 2-4.

Bustad, L.K. and Hines, L.M. "People-Pet-Partnership-Program." *Scientists Center Newsletter,* *3*(1), March 1981.

Bustad, Leo K. "Companion Animals and the Aged." Proceedings of *International Conference on the Human/Companion Animal Bond,* October 5-7, 1981, Philadelphia, PA (in press).

Butz, George. "Dogs For The Elderly." *Dog World,* July 1980, 131.

Cooper, J.E. "Pets in Hospitals." *British Medical Journal,* 1976, 698-700.

Corson, S.A. and Corson, E.D. "Pets as Mediators of Therapy." *Current Psychiatric Therapies,* 1978, *18,* 195-205.

Corson, S.A. and Corson, E.D. "Pet Assisted Psychotherapy." *Mims Magazine,* December 1, 1979, 33-37.

Corson, S.A. and Corson, E.D. "Pets as Socializing Catalysts in Geriatrics; An Experiment in Nonverbal Communication Therapy." *Society, Stress and Disease: Aging and Old Age.* L. Levi, Editor. Oxford: Oxford University Press, 1-47.

Corson, S.A.; Corson, E.D.; O'Leary, D.; DeHass, Gunsett, R.; Gwynn, P.; Arnold, E.; and Corson, C. "The Socializing Role of Pet Animals in Nursing Homes: An Experiment in Nonverbal Communication Therapy."

Corson, S.A. and Corson, E.D. "Companion Animals as Bonding Catalysts in Geriatric Institutions." *Interrelations Between Pets and People.* B. Fogle, Editor. Springfield, Illinois: Chas. C. Thomas, 146-174.

Corson, S.A.; Corson, W.L.; Gwynn, P.H.; and Arnold, E.L. "Pet Dogs as Nonverbal Communication Links in Hospital Psychiatry." *Comprehensive Psychiatry*, 1977, *18*, 1.

Curtis, Patricia. "Animals That Care For People." *The New York Times*, May 20, 1979.

Cusack, Odean. "Therapy Dogs International." *Pure-Bred Dogs American Kennel Gazette*, February 1982.

Ibid. "Phila the Therapy Dog Specializes in Love." *Grit*, April 4, 1982.

Ibid. "Therapists: Pets Who Heal." *Hillside Times*, February 24, 1983.

Ibid. "Why We Love Our Pets." *Orion Nature Quarterly*. Summer 1983.

Doll, Marice. "Little Pets With Big Hearts Provide Therapy of Love." *The Denver Post*, July 31, 1977.

Doll, Marice. "Young, Old Share Joy." *The Denver Post*, May 22, 1979.

Editorial. "Old Folks Need Their Pets." *The National Humane Review*, September-October 1969.

Editorial. "Pets by Prescription—A Novel Program of Minnesota Humane Society." *Colorado State Department of Public Health News*. Public Veterinary Section, November 1972.

Editorial. "Pet Therapy: A Boon For The Golden Age." *National Humane Review*, November, 1973, 10-11.

Editorial. "Canine Visits to Nursing Homes Reinforce Pet Therapy Theory." *Animal Shelter Shoptalk*. December 1973.

Editorial. "It's a Cat's World." *The National Humane Review*, August 1974.

Editorial. "Pet Placement Program Involved Senior Citizens." *Animal Shelter Shoptalk*, December 1974.

Editorial. "Canine Therapist Sparks Interest at Nursing Home." *Animal Shelter Shoptalk*, November 1975.

Editorial. "Pet Day at the Falls Nursing Home." *Animal Shelter Shoptalk*, May 1976.

Editorial. "Dogs Help Humans Regain Health." *Dog World*, October 1979, 50.

Editorial. "Dogs, Other Pets, Used to Treat Emotionally Ailing." *The Times Herald* (Norristown, PA), November 8, 1979.

Editorial. "Allowing Pets in Nursing Home Opens New Practice Opportunities." *D.V.M. Magazine*, March 1980.

Editorial. "Senior Pets For Senior Citizens." *Brief Paws—News of the Humane Society of the Willamette Valley*, Summer 1980, Vol. *15*(3).

Editorial. "No-Pet Rule A Killer?" *Philadelphia Daily News*, September 23, 1980.

Fales, Edward D., Jr. "Can Pets Help People Get Well And Stay Well?" *Today's Health*, March 1960.

Francis, Gloria and Odell, Shirley. "Long-Term Residence Loneliness: Myth or Reality?" *Journal of Gerontological Nursing*, 5(1), January-February 1979, 9-11.

Francis, Gloria; Turner, Jean T.; and Johnson, Suzanne B. "Domestic Animal Visitation as Therapy with Adult Home Residents." Unpublished paper.

Grundy, Phil. "Patient Progressing Well? He May Have a Pet." *Journal of the American Medical Association*, February 1979, *241*(5) 438.

Jernigan, Jean. "Pet Therapy Brings Happiness to the Lonely." *The National Humane Review*, November 1973.

Kearny, Mathilde. "Pet Therapy." *Massachusetts SPCA Animals.* *110*(3), May-June 1977.

Kidd, A.H. and Feldman, B.M. "Pet Ownership and Self-perception of Older People." *Psychological Reports*, 48: 867-875, 1981.

Lawson, Deborah. "Pets Vital to the Health, Happiness of the Elderly." *Montgomery County SPCA News*, Autumn 1981.

Levinson, Boris M. "Pets and Old Age." *Mental Hygiene*, 1969, *53*(3), 364-368.

Levinson, Boris M. "Nursing Home Pets: A Psychological Adventure for the Patient." *The National Humane Review*, July-August 1970.

Levinson, Boris M. "Nursing Home Pets: A Psychological Adventure For The Patient." (Part Two) *The National Humane Review*, September-October 1970.

Levinson, Boris M. "Pets and Modern Family Life." *The National Humane Review*, January 1973, 5-9.

Miller, Harry. "Pets As Lifesavers." *Dog World*, February 1979.

Millsap, Melinda. "Pets For the Elderly." *Colorado Springs Sun*, August 7, 1980.

Mugford, R.A. and M'Comisky, J.G. "Some Recent Work on the Psychotherapeutic Value of Cage Birds with Old People." *Pet Animals and Society: Proceedings of the Symposium of the British Small Animal Veterinary Association*. Anderson, R.S., Editor. London: Bailliere Tindall, 1975, 54-65.

Ory, Marcia G. and Goldberg, Evelyn L. "Pet Possession and Well-Being in Elderly Women." Unpublished paper.

Ibid. "Pet Ownership and Attachment: An Analysis of Demographic, Health and Social Interaction Correlates in the Elderly." Unpublished paper.

Price, Eleanor. "Canine Club." *Dog World*, August 1978, 61.

Quinn, Kathy. "Dogs For Therapy." *Pure-Bred Dogs American Kennel Gazette*, September 1979, 38-41.

Robb, Susanne S.; Boyd, Michele; and Pristash, Carole Lee. "A Wine Bottle, Plant and Puppy: Catalysts for Social Behavior." *Journal of Gerontological Nursing*, 6(12) December 1980.

Robb, Susanne S. and Stegman, Charles E. "Companion Animals and Elderly People: A Challenge for Evaluators of Social Support." *The Gerontologist*, April 1983.

Robb, Susanne S. "Pilot Study of Pet-Dog Therapy for Elderly People in Long-Term Care." Unpublished paper.

Ross, Geraldine. "Chum—A Turtle with a Mission." *The National Humane Review*, July 1974.

Salmon, I.M. and Salmon, P.W. "A Dog in Residence: A Companion-Animal Study Undertaken in the Caulfield Geriatric Hospital." Report from JACOPIS (Joint Advisory Committee On Pets in Society, Melbourne, Australia), 1982.

Sease, Mary S. "Pets for the Elderly." *Pure-Bred Dogs American Kennel Gazette*, May 1980, 113.

Van, Jon. "Pet Therapy for Hospitals and Prisons?" *Chicago Tribune*, January 6, 1978.

Weaver, Peter. "Pet Therapy Bringing Shut-Ins Out of Their Shells." *The Washington Post*, February 1978.

Whitaker, Helen. "Dogs for Therapy." *Dog Fancy*, December 1979.

White, Dean Casey. "Pets for Therapy." *Friskies Research Digest*, 1976, 3(4), 1-7.

White, Kay. "Dogs Make Excellent Pets." *Dog World*, May 1980, 142.

Windeler, Robert. "Dateline: Los Angeles" (column). *Daily News Magazine*, February 6, 1983.

Wolff, Ethel. "A Survey of the Use of Animals in Psychotherapy in the United States." *Women's SPCA of Pennsylvania* (A report to The American Humane Association).

Wood, Dave; "Animals Find a Home at Nursing Home." *Tribune* (Minneapolis), Sept. 1, 1980.

Yates, John. "Pets Help Us Love And Live." *Prevention*, May 1980, 85-98.

## GUIDEBOOKS FOR PET THERAPY PROGRAMS

Arkow, Phil. *"Pet Therapy": A Study of the Use of Companion Animals in Selected Therapies*. Colorado Springs, Colorado: The Humane Society of the Pikes Peak Region, 1982. (Available from the author for $10.00 at P.O. Box 187, Colorado Springs, Colorado 80901.)

Hines, Linda M. *The People-Pet-Partnership Program*. Alameda, California: The Latham Foundation, 1980. (Available for $5.00 from the Latham Foundation: see Appendix II.)

Lee, Ronnal L.; Zeglen, Marie E.; Ryan, Terry; and Hines, Linda M. *Guidelines: Animals in Nursing Homes. California Veterinarian* Supplement, 1983. (Available for $3.00 from the People-Pet-Partnership Program or the California Medical Veterinary Association, see Appendix II)

McLeod, Cappy. *Animals in the Nursing Home—Guide for Activity Directors.* Colorado Springs, Colorado: McLeod, 1981. (Available from the author for $6.50; P.O. Box 9334, Colorado Springs, Colorado 80932.)

## BOOKS ON ANIMALS AND THE ELDERLY

Anderson, R.S., Editor. *Pet Animals in Society.* New York: Macmillan 1975.

Bustad, Leo K. *Animals, Aging and the Aged.* Minneapolis: University of Minnesota Press 1980.

Corson, S.A. and E.O'L. Editors. *Ethology and Non-verbal Communication in Mental Health.* New York: Pergamon Press, 1980.

Fogle, B., Editor. *Interrelations between People and Animals.* Springfield, Illinois: Charles C. Thomas, 1981.

Levinson, Boris. *Pets and Human Development.* Springfield, Illinois: Charles C. Thomas, 1972.

"Veterinary Medical Practice: Pet Loss and Human Emotion." *Archives of the Foundation of Thanatology, 9*(2), 1981.

Proceedings of the International Conference on the Human/Companion Animal Bond, October 5-7, 1981, Philadelphia, PA (in press: for availability, contact the Latham Foundation or the Delta Society).

## BOOKS ON DOG TRAINING

Fox, Michael. *Understanding Your Dog.* New York: Coward, McCann & Geoghegan Inc., 1972.

The Monks of New Skete. How to Be Your Dog's Best Friend. Boston-Toronto: Little, Brown & Co., 1978.

Saunders, Blanche. *The Complete Novice Obedience Course.* New York: Howell Book House, 1972.

Ibid. *The Complete Open Obedience Course.* New York: Howell Book House, 1971.

Ibid. *The Complete Utility Obedience Course with Tracking.* New York: Howell Book House, 1969.

Strickland, Winnifred Gibson. *Obedience Class Instruction for Dogs: The Trainer's Manual.* New York: The Macmillan Company, 1971.

Woodhouse, Barbara. *No Bad Dogs the Woodhouse Way.* New York: Summit Books, 1978.

# Therapy Dogs International

Therapy Dogs International, a worldwide volunteer organization of friendly, well-trained canine candy stripers and their owners, evolved from my own experiences with geriatric patients and pets. I read an article in a dog magazine about a Samoyed (the wolflike Arctic breed with the bountiful lush white fur) who was taken to visit an aging patient in a nursing home. The dog was only permitted in the front sitting lobby where there were also a few other residents, but when those patients saw him, their expressions instantly changed from lackluster boredom to glowing enthusiasm. Another story told of a Puli (a rare Hungarian breed with an unusual corded coat who were originally bred for sheep herding) who comforted a man during a lengthy at-home illness. I remember thinking that if the man had to go to a nursing home he would not have been able to enjoy his dog.

Reading these stories, I recalled my experiences in England. On an assignment from the American Nurses Association, I spent two years working at an eye hospital in Sussex. Each morning there, the Chaplain would make his rounds accompanied by his Golden Retriever. The Matron (Director of Nurses) also brought her two King Charles Spaniels to work with her. It seemed every nursing home in England had a pet. Patients who showed no interest in anything else would suddenly, without provocation, reach out for the friendly paw of man's best friend. It worked in England. Why couldn't it work here too? My own dog Phila was an exceptionally gentle and affectionate German Shepherd, so I decided to take her to nursing homes, not just to visit a single patient, but to put on an obedience demonstration and visit with all the residents.

As soon as Phila had completed her basic obedience work, off we went. We began quite informally, with local institutions who were willing to let us come in and put on a show. I had trained Phila for obedience; she responds to hand and word signals, and will jump a hurdle or retrieve a glove on command. As I put her through her paces, I watched my audience and saw renewed vigor spark in tired eyes. This was something different; excitement, a break from the day-to-day routine of hospital life. For these elderly patients, many of whom had little else in their lives, it was something to look forward to. Afterwards, we socialized with the residents. For many, Phila's affectionate nuzzling and gentle paw brought back bittersweet memories. One woman put her arms around Phila's neck and wept. "She's just like a dog I once had," she told me.

The more Phila and I worked together, the more I considered forming a worldwide organization. For years, dog clubs, schools, and individuals with trained dogs have traveled to nursing homes and hospitals, visiting with people who miss their pets and bringing smiles to those who have fond memories of the dogs with whom they once shared their lives. The value of a friendly, obedient dog as therapy for troubled children, heart patients, and the elderly is documented repeatedly in current scientific studies. I knew there were many others like myself; if we could only band together and tell hospitals and nursing homes we were available.

Hesitantly, I decided to form a worldwide organization, and in May 1980 announced the beginning of Therapy Dogs International (TDI). I would invite owners to enlist man's best friend as man's best therapist. Our goal: to unite and increase the number of available therapy dogs, give them the recognition they deserve, and advertise on an international scale alerting hospitals and other institutions of the importance and sources of Therapy Dogs.

Much of the credit for the formal birth of Therapy Dogs International must go to Milt Winn, the president of the Raritan Valley German Shepherd Dog Club in Greenbrook, New Jersey. I had hoped to start something in the way of an organization, but Milt really set the concept in motion. At that time he, being newly blinded, was at the Guide Dog Foundation for the Blind in Smithtown Long Island, New York. In fact, Milt came home with his own special companion dog, Chelsea. It was Milt who thought up the name "Therapy Dogs International," and designed our fine logo. He is now our executive director.

While many pilot programs have successfully used affectionate, well-behaved animals with good dispositions but no formal schooling, to become a certified therapy dog with Therapy Dogs International, the canine applicant must have, in addition to exemplary social graces, some level of obedience training. This must be certified by a reputable dog trainer as well as the dog's owner. In addition, the dog must have a current rabies vaccination. Mixed breeds as well as pure-breds are eligible as long as the criteria are met. Members whose dogs qualify for TDI receive an identification card for themselves and a substantial yellow tag for their pet stating: ''I am a Therapy Dog.'' In California, service dogs are now accorded privileges previously reserved only for guide dogs for the blind. I expect other states to eventually follow their example. Currently, all TDI dogs are insured for property damage and liability anywhere in the U.S. through Therapy Dogs International.

Our first visit was to the King James Nursing Homes in Chatham, New Jersey during the summer of 1978. Four of us and our dogs, three German Shepherds and a Collie, put on an obedience display for the patients. Now we have more than 300 members worldwide representing many different breeds. There's even a perky Maltese Therapy Dog in far off New Zealand. As enrollment increases and the value of Therapy Dogs becomes known, I hope to be able to contact institutions in areas with member dogs and advise them of the availability of the animals to enhance the quality of life for their patients. We also have placed our therapy dogs in residence in four nursing homes, and this is just the beginning.

In a nursing home in Elizabethtown that I visited, an elderly woman who had not spoken for years reached out and called for the dogs. A member from Missouri wrote of a 90-year-old woman who steadfastly refused to leave her room. When she heard the dogs were coming, however, she was the first in line for the audience.

The dogs prompt both joy and sadness, but the tears can be as important to the patients as the smiles. Many therapists report that after a session with the animals, the patients communicate with other patients and with the hospital staff. The dogs have opened up a line of communication that was previously closed. I am particularly aware of this with Phila since she is a frequent and welcome visitor to Roosevelt Hospital in Metuchen, New Jersey where I am employed as a geriatric nurse. Many of my patients forget my name, but they remember Phila. Phila's portrait hangs in the patients' lounge on the unit where I work, and every evening one patient walks to the lounge just to see Phila's picture. Phila has given this woman an incentive to walk.

In fact, both Phila and Nessie, my yellow Labrador Retriever, are so well-received at Roosevelt Hospital they have been issued special I.D. cards, complete with their pictures, just like the facility's other employees. And Dr. Man Wah Cheung, the superintendent and medical director there, has thanked me personally for bringing the dogs to the patients.

Phila is equally welcome in church. She is the official "greeter" after Mass every Sunday morning at Christ the King Church. As soon as Mass ends, she gets up, and everybody attending, especially the children, stops to pet her. For all the holidays, she wears a ribbon on her collar the appropriate color for that holiday.

On October 4th, 1982, we attended an ecumenical day of common prayer to celebrate the 800th birthday of St. Francis of Assisi, the patron saint of animals, at St. John's Lutheran Church in Summit, New Jersey. At the end of the service, Fr. Russell Becker of the famous Franciscan Church in New York gave Phila a very special honor. He placed his hands on her head and blessed her work as a service dog. When he left his parting remark was: "She (Phila) is always welcome in my church." She is truly an ideal canine ambassador.

## APPLICATION FOR REGISTRATION OF A DOG IN THERAPY DOGS INTERNATIONAL

Complete this application, print or type. Sign it, have it countersigned by a dog obedience trainer who is considered reputable in his or her field and mail it back to THERAPY DOGS INTERNATIONAL along with a check or money order for $10.00 registration and membership fee. If your application is not accepted, the $10.00 will be returned to you.

DATE OF APPLICATION
OWNER'S NAME
PHONE
ADDRESS
ZIP CODE
DOG'S NAME
BREED

"TEACH YOUR DOG TO PUT HIS BEST PAW FORWARD"

1. Describe the level of obedience training your dog has achieved (either by classes taken or titles earned). If other, explain:

2. List dog clubs and/or dog schools you are presently affiliated with and positions held (if any).

3. List any demonstrations your dog has already participated in.

4. Does your dog get along with children?

5. Does your dog get along well with other dogs?

6. Is your dog shy or nervous around large crowds of people?

7. Do you consider your dog reliable on a "sit-stay" and "down-stay" under distracting conditions?

8. Is your dog under reliable verbal control with the leash off?

9. Is your dog "hand-shy"?

10. Does your dog have a current Rabies Vaccination? (A current Rabies vaccination is a requirement for registering your dog in T.D.I.)

11. If accepted into Therapy Dogs International, would you agree to make an effort to expose your dog to wheelchairs, crutches, and people with jerky or unusual motions in a training situation?

12. Which of the following personality traits describe your dog? Check as many as applicable.
   Adaptable
   Hyper
   Outgoing
   Friendly
   Timid
   Calm
   Shy
   Reliable

## CODE OF ETHICS

I will at all times: Present my Therapy Dog to any institution in accordance with the Rules and Regulations of that Institution (example: if the institution wishes the dog to remain on leash, I will comply) and present my Therapy Dog in good health, well groomed and display a current Rabies tag and TDI tag on my dog's collar. Note: Your Therapy Dog will be covered for liability and property damage under our insurance program while in service at an institution.

I hereby certify that I have answered truthfully the questions in this application to the best of my knowledge and ability and agree to abide by the Therapy Dogs International code of ethics.

Date                                   Signature of Dog's Owner

In my professional opinion, the dog's name which appears on this application is of sound temperament and would qualify to serve as a THERAPY DOG.

Date                                   Signature of Professional Dog
                                             Obedience Trainer
                                             (Address of Trainer)

Return to:
Elaine Smith
1536 Morris Place
Hillside, NJ 07205


## *STARTING A THERAPY DOG INTERNATIONAL CHAPTER IN YOUR COMMUNITY*

### RULES

1. You can select your own chapter name. Some examples are: Happy Paws Obedience School Chapter 3 of TDI. Rockland County Chapter 4 of TDI. Raritan Valley Kennel Club Chapter 5 of TDI, Strongheart 20/20 Guide Dogs Chapter 12 of TDI, Lee's Pet Rescue Association Chapter 14 of TDI.

2. The only commercial Chapter names allowed will be those designating a Dog Obedience Training School. Names such as Brown's Hardware, Jim's Friendly Pet Shop will not be allowed.

3. Your parent club TDI will assign the individual chapter numbers.

4. For insurance purposes all dogs must be individually registered with TDI as they are now.

5. There are no geographical boundaries for individual chapters. That is to say one or more chapters can be in the same area and work independently of each other.

6. There are no set numbers of visits that any chapter will be responsible for. If your make one visit a year or 25 visitations, just remember that every visit counts.

7. Each chapter must consist of three or more active participants. One person must be designated as a Director of the Chapter.

8. Each Chapter will be responsible for their own scheduling of events.

9. Your printed literature may be sponsored by a commercial merchant.

10. T-shirts and jackets should not carry the name of the commercial sponsor. (Example: Lee's Pet Rescue Service Chapter 14 of TDI should not carry the name of sponsor (Brown's Hardware) on T-shirts or jackets. It is permissible to put Brown's Hardware on the two color brochures.)

11. A record of your activities should be filed with TDI once every six months and a form will be provided for that purpose.

12. If you have any questions not covered by the above, please call or write: Milt Winn, Executive Director, 49 US Rte. 22 East, Green Brook, NJ 08812. (201) 968-0086.

Appendix II

# Organizations Involved in Pet Therapy

## Professional Organizations

American Humane Association, 9725 E. Hampden, Denver, CO 80231. Has a bibliography of pet therapy available.

California Veterinary Medical Association, 1024 Country Club Drive, Moraga, CA. Published *Guidelines: Animals in Nursing Homes* (order: File No. 3758, PO Box 60000, San Francisco, CA 94160).

Companion Animal Services, Inc. (For more information, contact Robert M. Andrysco, 1339-2 Presidential Drive, Columbus, Ohio 43212.)

Delta Society - N.E. 1705 Upper Drive, Pullman, WA 99163. The international society formed to investigate the human/animal bond. Leo Bustad is president. Publishes a newsletter.

The Latham Foundation, Latham Plaza Building, Clement & Schiller Sts., Alameda, CA 94501. Published a quarterly journal that contains many articles of interest on the human/animal bond and related topics. Also has a bibliography available and a series of films for rental.

North American Riding for the Handicapped Association, P.O. Box 100, Ashburn, VA 22011. For further information and a list of sources on equestrian therapy.

Pets are Wonderful Council (PAW), 500 N. Michigan Ave., Suite 200, Chicago, IL 60611 for information on PAW Pals and related programs.

## Humane Shelters Conducting Animal Therapy-Oriented Programs
(reprinted from Phil Arkow's *"Pet Therapy": A Study of the Use of Companion Animals in Selected Therapies*).

ALABAMA

*Mobile:* Mobile SPCA, P.O. Box 66223, Mobile, Alabama 36606

ARKANSAS

*Hot Springs:* Hot Springs Animal Control, 400 Kimery Lane, Hot Springs, Arkansas 71901
*Little Rock:* Animal Control Center, 3800 S. Chester, Little Rock, Arkansas 72206

CALIFORNIA

*Berkeley:* Berkeley-East Bay Humane Society, 2700 9th St., Berkeley, California 94710
*Los Angeles:* Los Angeles SPCA, 5026 Jefferson Blvd., Los Angeles, California 90016

*Monterey:* Monterey County SPCA, P.O. Box 3508, Monterey, California 93940
*Pomona:* Humane Society of Pomona Valley, 500 Humane Way, Pomona, California 91710
*Riverside:* Riverside Humane Society, 5791 Fremont St., Riverside, California 92504
*San Francisco:* San Francisco SPCA, 2500 16th St., San Francisco, California 94103
*San Gabriel:* San Gabriel Valley Humane Society, 851 E. Grand Ave., San Gabriel, California 91776
*Paradise:* Superior California Humane Society, P.O. Box 1440, Paradise, California 95969

## COLORADO

*Arvada:* Arvada Animal Control, 8101 Ralston Rd., Arvada, Colorado 80002
*Boulder:* Boulder County Humane Society, 2323 55th St., Boulder, Colorado 80301
*Colorado Springs:* Humane Society of the Pikes Peak Region, P.O. Box 187, Colorado Springs, Colorado 80901
*Denver:* Denver Dumb Friends League, 2080 S. Quebec, Denver, Colorado 80231
*Henderson:* Colorado Humane Society, 5901 E. 89th Ave., Henderson, Colorado 80640
*Longmont:* Longmont Humane Society, 14014 N. 115, Longmont, Colorado 80501

## CONNECTICUT

*Hartford:* Connecticut Humane Society, P.O. Box 6066, Hartford, Connecticut 06106

## DELAWARE

*Stanton:* Delaware SPCA, P.O. Box 6067, Stanton, Delaware 06106

## FLORIDA

*Jacksonville:* Jacksonville Humane Society, P.O. Box 5445, Jacksonville, Florida 32207
*Miami:* Humane Society of Greater Miami, 2101 NW 95th St., Miami, Florida 33147
*Orlando:* Orlando Humane Society, 664 Barry St., Orlando, Florida 32808
*West Palm Beach:* Animal Rescue League of the Palm Beaches, 2401 N. Tamarind Ave., West Palm Beach, Florida 33407

## GEORGIA

*Atlanta:* Atlanta Humane Society, 981 Howell Mill Rd. NW, Atlanta, Georgia 30318
*Ellenwood:* Humane Society & SPCA of Clayton County

## HAWAII

*Honolulu:* Hawaiian Humane Society, 2700 Waialae Ave., Honolulu, Hawaii 96826
*Kahului:* Maui Humane Society, 14 S. Hana Hwy., Kahului, Hawaii 96732

## ILLINOIS

*Chicago:* Anti-Cruelty Society, 157 W. Grand Ave., Chicago, Illinois 60610
*Lincoln:* American Humane Association, P.O. Box 785, Lincoln, Illinois 62656

## INDIANA

*Indianapolis:* Indianapolis Humane Society, 7929 Michigan Rd., Indianapolis, Indiana 48268
*Mishawaka:* St. Joseph Co. Humane Society, 2506 Liberty Drive, Mishawaka, Indiana 46544

## KENTUCKY

*Lexington:* Lexington Humane Society, 1600 Old Frankfort Pike, Lexington, Kentucky 40504

LOUISIANA

*Covington:* St. Tammany Humane Society, P.O. Box 197, Covington, Louisiana 70433

MASSACHUSETTS

*Framingham:* Massachusetts SPCA, P.O. Box 2314, Framingham, Massachusetts 01701

MICHIGAN

*Ann Arbor:* Humane Society of the Huron Valley, 3100 Cherryhill Rd., Ann Arbor, Michigan 48105
*Bloomfield:* Bloomfield Twp. Animal Welfare Dept., 4200 Telegraph, Bloomfield, Michigan 48013
*Detroit:* Michigan Humane Society, 7401 Chrysler Ave., Detroit, Michigan 48211
*Muskegon:* Humane Society of Muskegon Co., P.O. Box 767, Muskegon, Michigan 49443
*Saginaw:* Citizens for Animal Welfare Education
*Warren:* Humane Education Service, P.O. Box 65, Warren, Michigan 48090

MINNESOTA

*Buffalo:* Humane Society of Wright County
*International Falls:* Borderland Humane Society, 807 2nd St., International Falls, Minnesota 56649
*Minneapolis:* Animal Humane Society of Hennepin Co., 845 Meadow Land, Minneapolis, Minnesota 55422
*St. Cloud:* Tri-County Humane Society, P.O. Box 701, St. Cloud, Minnesota 56301
*St. Paul:* Minnesota Humane Society, 500 Rice Street, St. Paul, Minnesota 55155

MISSISSIPPI

*Columbus:* Columbus-Lowndes Humane Society, P.O. Box 85, Columbus, Mississippi 39701

MISSOURI

*Jefferson City:* Heart of Missouri Humane Society, P.O. Box 1013, Jefferson City, Missouri 65101
*St. Charles:* St. Charles Humane Society, P.O. Box 804, St. Charles, Missouri 63301

MONTANA

*Billings:* Billings Animal Shelter, P.O. Box 1178, Billings, Montana 59103
*Bozeman:* Humane Society of Gallatin Valley, 2125 N. Rouse, Bozeman, Montana 59715

NEW HAMPSHIRE

*Nashua:* Humane Society of Southern Hillsboro Co., 24 Ferry Rd., Nashua, New Hampshire 03060

NEW JERSEY

*Montclair:* Pound Animal Welfare Society, 95 Walnut St., Montclair, New Jersey 07042

NEW YORK

*New York City:* ASPCA, 441 E. 92nd Street, New York, New York 10028
————. Humane Society of New York, 306 E. 59th, New York, New York 10022
*Port Washington:* North Shore Animal League, 22 South St., Port Washington, New York 11050
*Rochester:* Humane Society of Rochester & Monroe Co., 99 Victor Road, Fairport, New York 14450

*Tonawanda:* Erie County SPCA, 205 Ensminger Road, Tonawanda, New York 14150
*Wantagh:* Bide-A-Wee Home Association, 3300 Beltagh Ave., Wantagh, New York 11793

OHIO

*Cincinnati:* Hamilton County SPCA, 3949 Colerain Ave., Cincinnati, Ohio 45223

OREGON

*Bend:* Deschutes Humane Society, P.O. Box 867, Bend, Oregon 97701
*Portland:* Oregon Humane Society, P.O. Box 11364, Portland, Oregon 97211

PENNSYLVANIA

*Allentown:* Lehigh County Humane Society, 640 Dixon St., Allentown, Pennsylvania 18103
*Eighty Four:* Washington County Humane Society, P.O. Box 66, Eighty Four, Pennsylvania 15330
*Erie:* Northwestern Pennsylvania Humane Society, P.O. Box 1065, Erie, Pennsylvania 16512
*Lahaska:* Bucks County SPCA, P.O. Box 277, Lahaska, Pennsylvania 18931
*Oil City:* Venango County Humane Society, P.O. Box 1045, Oil City, Pennsylvania 16301
*Philadelphia:* Women's SPCA of Pennsylvania, 3025 W. Clearfield, Philadelphia, Pennsylvania 19132
*Pittsburgh:* Western Pennsylvania Humane Society, 1101 Western Avenue, Pittsburgh, Pennsylvania 15233

TENNESSEE

*Chattanooga:* Chattanooga Humane Education Society, 212 N. Highland Park Ave., Chattanooga, Tennessee 37404

TEXAS

*Austin:* Humane Society of Austin & Travis County, P.O. Box 1386, Austin, Texas 78767
*Beaumont:* Humane Education Council, P.O. Box 1629, Beaumont, Texas 77704
*Dallas:* Dallas SPCA, 362 S. Industrial, Dallas, Texas 75207
*Midland:* Midland Animal Control, 1601 Orchard Lane, Midland, Texas 79702

UTAH

*Salt Lake City:* Humane Society of Utah, P.O. Box 20222, Salt Lake City, Utah 84120
————. Salt Lake County Animal Control, 511 West 3900 South, Salt Lake City, Utah 84107

VIRGINIA

*Norfolk:* Norfolk SPCA, 916 Ballentine Blvd., Norfolk, Virginia 23504

WASHINGTON

*Longview:* Cowlitz County Humane Society, P.O. Box 172, Longview, Washington 98632
*Seattle:* Seattle Animal Control, 2061 15th Ave. West, Seattle, Washington 98119
*Spokane:* Spokane Humane Society, North 6607 Havana, Spokane, Washington 99207

WISCONSIN

*Milwaukee:* Wisconsin Humane Society, 4151 N. Humboldt Ave., Milwaukee, Wisconsin 53212
*Portage:* Columbia Humane Society

WYOMING

*Cheyenne:* Laramie County Animal Control

CANADA

*Ontario: Hamilton:* Hamilton SPCA, 658 Parkdale Ave. North, Hamilton, Ontario L8H
5Z4
————: *Ottawa:* Humane Society of Ottawa-Carleton

# Organizations Which Train Special Dogs

HEARING DOGS

Hearing Dogs, American Humane, 9725 E. Hampden, Denver, CO 80231
Training Center, Colorado Humane Society, 5901 E. 89th Ave., Henderson, CO 80640
Hearing Dog Training Center, San Francisco SPCA, 2500 16th St., San Francisco, CA
94103
Hearing Dog Training Center, Los Angeles SPCA, 5026 W. Jefferson Blvd., Los Angeles,
CA 90028
Hearing Ear Dog Program, Bryant Hill Farm 26 Bryant Rd., Jefferson, MA 01522

CANINE COMPANIONS FOR THE HANDICAPPED, P.O. Box 446, Santa Rosa, CA
95403. Trains Social dogs for pet therapy in institutions, Signal dogs for the hearing
impaired, and Service dogs for the physically handicapped.

# Current Legislation

## HOUSING

In April 1983 Senator William Proxmire (D.-Wis.) introduced federal legislation that would prohibit federally subsidized housing from banning pets owned by the elderly and the disabled. In introducing this measure, Proxmire cited medical studies showing the physical and emotional benefits of pet ownership. For owners to give up their pets, he said, ". . . is more than an inconvenience; frequently it has a traumatic emotional and physical effect."

Currently, California does have such a law. It reads:

19901. Public Housing for the elderly; pets

Notwithstanding any other provision of law, no public agency which owns and operates rental housing accommodations, shall prohibit the keeping of not more than two pets by the elderly in such rental housing accommodations.

For the purposes of this section:

a) "Elderly" means any person over the age of 60.

b) "Pet" means domesticated dog, cat, bird, or aquarium.

c) "Public" means state, county, city, city and county, district, or other political subdivision of the state.

Nothing in this section shall prevent the local housing authority from requiring the removal from any housing of any pet whose conduct or condition is duly determined to constitute a threat or nuisance to the other occupants of the housing. No pet may be kept in violation of humane or health laws.

Nothing in this section shall prevent the public agency from adopting reasonable regulations relating to limitations on use of common areas by any such pets; prevent the adoption of differing terms for the tendency which are reasonably related to the presence of such pet; or relieve a tenant from any liability otherwise imposed by law for damages caused by such pet when proof of same exists.

Currently Assembly Bill No. 3149 would modify this statute that would give additional protection to the elderly who now are being charged as much as $100 extra for pet-keeping privileges.

The modifications read:

Nothing in this section authorizes a local housing authority to impose any requirement which makes the keeping of a pet by an elderly person financially prohibitive.

The local housing authority shall not be liable for personal or property damages caused by any pet in the rental housing accommodation, except upon proof of prior actual knowledge on behalf of its agents or employees of a dangerous propensity of the pet or hazardous condition created by the pet.

The adoption of any regulations pursuant to this section, or the application of any regulation adopted pursuant to this section may be appealed by an elderly resident or elderly applicant in accordance with grievance procedures of the local housing authority established to resolve tenant disputes. A copy of the grievance procedures shall be provided to an elderly tenant or elderly applicant who keeps a pet.

## PETS IN INSTITUTIONS

Minnesota has a simple statute for pets in nursing homes. It reads:

144A.30 Pets in Nursing Homes.
Nursing homes may keep pet animals on the premises subject to reasonable rules as to the care, type and maintenance of the pet.

Massachusetts recognizes four levels of health care facilities and on Level IV, the level requiring the minimum of patient care, pets are allowed under specific conditions.

Rules and Regulations for Long-term Care Facilities in Massachusetts

16.6 Pets
16.6.1 pets or other types of animals shall not be allowed in any of the following areas: patient areas in facilities that provide Level I, II, or III care; kitchens and areas used for preparation, serving or storage of food; laundries or restorative service units.
16.6.2 No commercial breeding of pets shall be allowed.
16.6.3 All pets should be adequately fed, sheltered and maintained in a sanitary manner.

New Jersey Senate Bill No. 3023 has recently been introduced. It is a lengthy bill, the statement of which reads:

This bill permits a nursing home or residential health care facility to board a reasonable number of cats or dogs whenever it is determined that the presence of such animals will serve to promote the well-being of the residents of the nursing home or residential health care facility.

## SERVICE DOG BILL

In 1980, the California State Legislature passed Senate Bill No. 2046 which extended the same rights to service dogs as were previously granted guide dogs for the blind and hearing-aid dogs for the deaf.

A summary of the bill:

Existing law prohibits the denial of equal access to housing accommodations to a totally or partially blind person, or a deaf person on the basis that such a person uses the services of a guide or signal dog.

This bill would extend such provisions to a physically handicapped person who uses the service dog, as defined.

Existing law grants a totally or partially blind person, and a deaf person, the right to be accompanied by a guide dog or signal dog in designated modes of transportation and places of public accommodation.

This bill would extend such right to a physically handicapped person accompanied by a service dog.

Existing law provides that expenses incurred by a visually handicapped person and a deaf person in connection with the care and maintenance of a guide dog and a signal dog are deductible as a medical expense under the Personal Income Tax Law.

This bill would extend such provisions to a physically handicapped person, as defined, using the services of a service dog.

# JACOPIS Assessment Procedures

As a final aide to evaluating a pet therapy program, we reproduce here the questionnaires used in the Australian study conducted for JACOPIS. Results were evaluated using formal statistical techniques; however, these questionnaires also work very well on a subjective, individual basis. The procedures measure staff reaction, as well as resident reaction, and the problems anticipated section appears to cover most eventualities. The pre-test questionnaire was administered at the beginning of the study; the monthly observation sheets provide a means to assess progress over time, and the final post-test questionnaire was administered at the end of the formal study (a time period of six months—the dog, however, is still in residence).

## PATIENT-PET INTERACTION PROGRAM
### PATIENT QUESTIONNAIRE

Patient's Name:
Age:
Sex:
Ward No.:
Assessor's Name:
Date:

This questionnaire is to be completed once a month for each patient you visit. It is important for the sake of consistency that the same staff person completes this form for the same patients each month. In other words, you are to follow-up your patients for the duration of the Patient-Pet Interaction Program.

Ask the patient the questions in Section A (Interview Schedule) as best you can; if he or she does not reply, write "no answer" beside it.

Try to record the patient's answers verbatim whenever possible.

### SCHEDULE A: INTERVIEW SCHEDULE

1. How are you feeling today? (Record Answer)

2. How are you finding (pet's name)?
   Why do you feel this way?

*233*

3. How do you think (pet's name) is taking to you?

4. Is (pet's name) causing you any trouble?　　Yes/No
   If yes, explore the following sources of trouble (check appropriate response):

| | | |
|---|---|---|
| Barking | Yes | No |
| Smell | | |
| Mess (ex. hair, waste) | | |
| Frightened of pet | | |
| Trips over pet | | |
| Pet gets in the way | | |
| Any others? | | |

5. Are there any good things about having (pet's name)?　　Yes/No
   If yes, explore the following benefits (check appropriate response):

| | | |
|---|---|---|
| Company/friendship | Yes | No |
| Love/affection | | |
| Enjoyment/fun | | |
| An interest | | |
| Something to talk about | | |
| Makes the ward more like home | | |
| Makes the ward a happier place | | |
| Any others? | | |

6. Do you think (pet's name) is a good thing or a bad thing for other people?
   Good thing/bad thing

   Why do you feel this way?

The following scales are concerned with the patient's interaction with the pet. Please answer them by either questioning the patient or from your own impression of the patient-pet relationship. Please circle the number which best describes the patient.

| | GREAT DEAL | | | AVERAGE | | NOT AT ALL | |
|---|---|---|---|---|---|---|---|
| Loves pet | 1 | 2 | 3 | 4 | 5 | 6 | 7 |
| Interested in pet | 1 | 2 | 3 | 4 | 5 | 6 | 7 |
| Encourages pet | 1 | 2 | 3 | 4 | 5 | 6 | 7 |
| Talks to Pet | 1 | 2 | 3 | 4 | 5 | 6 | 7 |
| Strokes/plays with pet | 1 | 2 | 3 | 4 | 5 | 6 | 7 |
| Grooms pet | 1 | 2 | 3 | 4 | 5 | 6 | 7 |
| Feeds pet | 1 | 2 | 3 | 4 | 5 | 6 | 7 |

|  | GREAT DEAL |  |  | AVERAGE |  | NOT AT ALL |  |
|---|---|---|---|---|---|---|---|
| Trains/disciplines pet | 1 | 2 | 3 | 4 | 5 | 6 | 7 |
| Frightened of pet | 1 | 2 | 3 | 4 | 5 | 6 | 7 |

SCHEDULE B: OBSERVATION SHEET

The following rating scales are concerned only with your impressions of the patient—do not ask the patient to answer them. Please circle the number which best describes your impression of the patient.

|  | VERY |  | AVERAGE |  | VERY |  |  |  |
|---|---|---|---|---|---|---|---|---|
| Talkative | 1 | 2 | 3 | 4 | 5 | 6 | 7 | Uncommunicative |
| Confident | 1 | 2 | 3 | 4 | 5 | 6 | 7 | Shy |
| Happy | 1 | 2 | 3 | 4 | 5 | 6 | 7 | Unhappy |
| Sociable | 1 | 2 | 3 | 4 | 5 | 6 | 7 | Unsociable |
| Sense of humor | 1 | 2 | 3 | 4 | 5 | 6 | 7 | No sense of humor |
| Laughs/smiles | 1 | 2 | 3 | 4 | 5 | 6 | 7 | Does not laugh/ smile |
| Alert | 1 | 2 | 3 | 4 | 5 | 6 | 7 | Withdrawn/remote |
| Responsive | 1 | 2 | 3 | 4 | 5 | 6 | 7 | Unresponsive |
| Easygoing | 1 | 2 | 3 | 4 | 5 | 6 | 7 | Aggressive/angry |
| Interested in others | 1 | 2 | 3 | 4 | 5 | 6 | 7 | Not interested in others |
| Mobile | 1 | 2 | 3 | 4 | 5 | 6 | 7 | Immobile |
| Enjoys life | 1 | 2 | 3 | 4 | 5 | 6 | 7 | Does not enjoy life |

OTHER OBSERVATIONS OF THE PATIENT

OBSERVATIONS OF THE DOG

PATIENT-PET INTERACTION PROGRAM
PATIENT QUESTIONNAIRE (PRE-TEST)

Patient's Name:
Age:
Sex:
Ward No.:
Assessor's Name:
Date:

These questions and observations are to be completed for each patient before the introduction of a pet.

Ask the patient the questions in Section A (Interview Schedule) as best you can;

if he or she does not reply to a question, write "no answer" beside it. If, however, the patient does not communicate at all, please turn to Section B (Observation Sheet).

This questionnaire is intended as a guide—if certain questions appear inappropriate or irrelevant when talking to the patient—feel free to omit them.

Try to record the patient's answers verbatim whenever possible.

A: INTERVIEW SCHEDULE

1. Have you ever had a pet before?    Yes/No

   Type of pet(s)              Your Age

2. On a scale of 1 to 10, how much do you like (type of pet)? (Please circle appropriate number.)

   Dislike them  1    2    3    4    5    6    7    8    9    10   Like them
   very much                                                        very much

3. Do you think it will be a good thing or a bad thing to have a pet in the ward? Good thing/bad thing

   Why do you feel this way?

4. What's the main reason you would like/dislike a pet?

5. On a scale of 1 to 10, how would you feel if we didn't get a pet for the ward? (Please circle appropriate number.)

   Very relieved  1    2    3    4    5    6    7    8    9    10   Very unhappy

6. Do you think a dog will be a good thing or a bad thing for other people? Good thing/bad thing

   Why do you feel this way?

7. Try to ascertain whether or not the patient thinks each of the following items will be a problem to them? (Check appropriate response.)

|  | Problem | No Problem | Don't Know |
|---|---|---|---|
| Accommodation |  |  |  |
| Discipline/ training |  |  |  |
| Barking |  |  |  |
| Smell |  |  |  |
| Mess (ex. hair, waste) |  |  |  |
| Frightened of pet |  |  |  |
| Damage to property |  |  |  |

|  | Problem | No Problem | Don't Know |
|---|---|---|---|
| Cruelty to pet | | | |
| Trips over pet | | | |
| Pet gets in the way | | | |
| Any others? | | | |

8. Try to ascertain whether or not the patient thinks each of the following items will be a benefit to them. (Check appropriate responses.)

|  | Yes | No | Don't Know |
|---|---|---|---|
| Company/friendship | | | |
| Love/affection | ⌐ | | |
| Enjoyment/fun | | | |
| An interest | | | |
| Something to talk about | | | |
| Makes the ward more like home | | | |
| Makes the ward a happier place | | | |
| Any others? | | | |

B: OBSERVATION SHEET

Please record your impressions of the patient on the following rating scales. Circle the number which you feel best describes him or her.

|  | VERY | | AVERAGE | | VERY | | |  |
|---|---|---|---|---|---|---|---|---|
| Talkative | 1 | 2 | 3 | 4 | 5 | 6 | 7 | Uncommunicative |
| Confident | 1 | 2 | 3 | 4 | 5 | 6 | 7 | Shy |
| Happy | 1 | 2 | 3 | 4 | 5 | 6 | 7 | Unhappy |
| Self-reliant | 1 | 2 | 3 | 4 | 5 | 6 | 7 | Dependent |
| Sociable | 1 | 2 | 3 | 4 | 5 | 6 | 7 | Unsociable |
| Sense of humor | 1 | 2 | 3 | 4 | 5 | 6 | 7 | No sense of humor |
| Laughs/smiles | 1 | 2 | 3 | 4 | 5 | 6 | 7 | Does not laugh/ smile |
| Alert | 1 | 2 | 3 | 4 | 5 | 6 | 7 | Withdrawn/remote |
| Responsive | 1 | 2 | 3 | 4 | 5 | 6 | 7 | Unresponsive |

|                                | VERY | | AVERAGE | | | VERY | |                          |
|--------------------------------|------|---|---------|---|---|------|---|--------------------------|
| Easygoing                      | 1    | 2 | 3       | 4 | 5 | 6    | 7 | Aggressive/angry         |
| Interested in others           | 1    | 2 | 3       | 4 | 5 | 6    | 7 | Not interested in others |
| Mobile                         | 1    | 2 | 3       | 4 | 5 | 6    | 7 | Immobile                 |
| Participates in activities     | 1    | 2 | 3       | 4 | 5 | 6    | 7 | Does not participate     |
| Interested in their appearance | 1    | 2 | 3       | 4 | 5 | 6    | 7 | Not interested           |
| Cares about personal hygiene   | 1    | 2 | 3       | 4 | 5 | 6    | 7 | Does not care            |
| Enjoys life                    | 1    | 2 | 3       | 4 | 5 | 6    | 7 | Does not enjoy life      |
| Wants to live                  | 1    | 2 | 3       | 4 | 5 | 6    | 7 | Wants to die             |

9. In general, how would you describe the patient's relationship with other patients?

   Very good  1      2      3      4      5      6      7 Poor

10. In general, how would you describe the patient's relationship with the staff?

   Very good  1      2      3      4      5      6      7 Poor

11. How many hours per day does the patient sleep?

12. How many hours per day does the patient spend in bed?

13. How many hours per day does the patient spend in the communal day-room?

14. How many hours per day does the patient spend alone?

## C: MEDICAL DETAILS
Medical Status:
Medication:
a) Anti-depressants/tranquilizers:    Daily dose:
                                       As per necessary dose
b) Night Sedation:                     Dose
c) Analgesics:                         Daily dose
Physical Condition:

## D: OTHER OBSERVATIONS
(Example: atmosphere of the ward; your own reactions to the pet)


### PATIENT-PET INTERACTION PROGRAM
### NURSING STAFF QUESTIONNAIRE (POST-TEST)

Name:
Ward No.:
Date:

This questionnaire is to be answered by each member of the nursing staff *after* the patient-pet interaction program.

1. On a scale of 1 to 10, how much do you like (type of pet)? (Please circle appropriate number.)

   Dislike them 1  2  3  4  5  6  7  8  9  10 Like them
   very much                                  very much

2. On a scale of 1 to 10, how much do you like (name of pet)? (Please circle appropriate number.)

   Dislike them 1  2  3  4  5  6  7  8  9  10 Like them
   very much                                  very much

3. On a scale of 1 to 10, how much do you think (name of pet) likes you? (Please circle appropriate number.)

   Dislike them 1  2  3  4  5  6  7  8  9  10 Like them
   very much                                  very much

4. What problems or disadvantages have you experienced as a result of having (pet's name) on the ward?
   In relation to yourself:
   In relation to the patients:

5. What has been the main problem in having (pet's name)?

6. What benefits or good things have you experienced as a result of having (pet's name) on the ward?
   In relation to yourself:
   In relation to the patients:

7. What has been the main benefit in having (pet's name)?

8. In general, are you pleased or sorry that you now have (pet's name)?

   Very sorry 1  2  3  4  5  6  7  8  9  10 Very pleased

9. How would you feel if (pet's name) was take away?

   Very relieved 1  2  3  4  5  6  7  8  9  10 Very unhappy

10. The following items may possibly have been a problem in having a pet on the ward. Which ones were a problem for you?

|  | Problem | No Problem |
|---|---|---|
| Accommodation |  |  |
| Feeding |  |  |
| Bathing/grooming |  |  |
| Exercise |  |  |
| Discipline/training |  |  |
| Barking |  |  |

|  | Problem | No Problem |
|---|---|---|
| Smell | | |
| Mess (ex. hair, waste) | | |
| Frightened of pet | | |
| Damage to property | | |
| Cruelty to pet | | |
| Trips over pet | | |
| Pet gets in the way | | |
| Increased work-load | | |
| Any others? | | |

11. The following items may possibly have been a benefit of having a pet on the ward. Which ones were a benefit for you? (Check appropriate response.)

|  | Yes | No |
|---|---|---|
| Company/friendship | | |
| Love/affection | | |
| Enjoyment/fun | | |
| An interest | | |
| Something to share with patients | | |
| Talking point with patients | | |
| Makes the ward more like home | | |
| Makes the ward a happier place | | |
| Decreased workload | | |
| Any others? | | |

12. Have any patients expressed positive feelings about having (pet's name)? Yes/No    How many?
    Comments:

13. Have any patients expressed negative feelings about having (pet's name)? Yes/no    How many?
    Comments:

14. Has anyone objected to (pet's name) in any way? Yes/no    How many?
    Who in particular?

    What sort of objections were raised?

15. Have any disaggreements occurred concerning (pet's name)?
    Among the patients                 yes/no
    Among the staff                    yes/no
    Between patients and staff         yes/no

    What sort of disagreements have occurred?

16. What improvements or positive changes have occurred in the patients as a result of having a pet?

17. What detrimental effects have occurred in the patients as a result of having a pet?

18. In your opinion, what effects has living in a hospital ward had on the pet?

    Other comments:

PATIENT-PET INTERACTION PROGRAM
NURSING STAFF QUESTIONNAIRE (PRE-TEST)

Name:
Ward No.:
Date:

This questionnaire is to be answered by each member of the nursing staff *before* the introduction of a pet.

1. Have you ever had a pet before?       Yes/No
   Type of pet(s)          Your Age

2. On a scale of 1 to 10, how much do you like (type of pet)? (Please circle appropriate number.)

   Dislike them  1   2   3   4   5   6   7   8   9   10  Like them
   very much                                                very much

3. On a scale of 1-10, how would you feel if you didn't get a pet on the ward? (Circle appropriate number.)

   Very relieved  1   2   3   4   5   6   7   8   9   10  Very unhappy

   Why do you feel this way?

4. What worries or concerns do you have about having a pet on the ward?
   In relation to yourself:
   In relation to the patients:

5. What benefits do you anticipate by having a pet on the ward?
   In relation to yourself?
   In relation to the patients:

6. What is the main reason you would like/dislike having a pet?

7. The following items may possibly be a problem in having a pet on the ward. Which ones do you anticipate being a problem for you? (Check appropriate response.)

|                          | Problem | No Problem |
|--------------------------|---------|------------|
| Accommodation            |         |            |
| Feeding                  |         |            |
| Bathing/grooming         |         |            |
| Exercise                 |         |            |
| Discipline/training      |         |            |
| Barking                  |         |            |
| Smell                    |         |            |
| Mess (ex. hair, waste)   |         |            |
| Frightening people       |         |            |
| Damage to property       |         |            |
| Cruelty to pet           |         |            |
| Complaints               |         |            |
| Pet gets in the way      |         |            |
| Increased workload       |         |            |
| Any others?              |         |            |

8. The following items may possibly be a benefit of having a pet on the ward. Which ones do you anticipate being a benefit for you? (Check appropriate response.)

|                                  | Yes | No | Don't Know |
|----------------------------------|-----|----|-----------|
| Company/friendship               |     |    |           |
| Love/affection                   |     |    |           |
| Enjoyment/fun                    |     |    |           |
| An interest                      |     |    |           |
| Something to share with patients |     |    |           |
| Talking point with patients      |     |    |           |

|                              | Yes | No | Don't Know |
|------------------------------|-----|----|-----------|
| Makes the ward more like home |     |    |           |
| Makes the ward a happier place |    |    |           |
| Decreased workload            |     |    |           |
| Any others?                   |     |    |           |

9. Have any patients expressed positive feelings about getting a pet?  Yes/No
   How many?
   Comments:

10. Have any patients expressed negative feelings about getting a pet?  Yes/No
    How many?
    Comments:

11. What improvements or positive changes do you think will occur in the patients as a result of having a pet?

12. What detrimental effects do you think will occur in the patients as a result of having a pet?

13. In your opinion, what effects will living in a hospital ward have on the pet?

OTHER COMMENTS ON THE PATIENT-PET PROGRAM:

PATIENT-PET INTERACTION PROGRAM
MONTHLY OBSERVATION SHEET

Patient's Name:
Age:
Sex:
Ward No.:
Staff's Name:
Date:

This observation sheet is to be completed at the end of each month for each patient. It is important for the sake of consistency that the same member of staff completes this form for the same person each time.

Please record your impressions and observations of the patient on the following rating scales by circling the number which best describes him/her.

|            | VERY | AVERAGE | VERY |   |   |   |   |                  |
|------------|------|---------|------|---|---|---|---|------------------|
| Talkative  | 1    | 2       | 3    | 4 | 5 | 6 | 7 | Uncommunicative  |
| Confident  | 1    | 2       | 3    | 4 | 5 | 6 | 7 | Shy              |

|                              | VERY | AVERAGE | VERY |   |   |   |   |                          |
|------------------------------|------|---------|------|---|---|---|---|--------------------------|
| Happy                        | 1 | 2 | 3 | 4 | 5 | 6 | 7 | Unhappy                  |
| Self-reliant                 | 1 | 2 | 3 | 4 | 5 | 6 | 7 | Dependent                |
| Sociable                     | 1 | 2 | 3 | 4 | 5 | 6 | 7 | Unsociable               |
| Sense of humor               | 1 | 2 | 3 | 4 | 5 | 6 | 7 | No sense of humor        |
| Laughs/smiles                | 1 | 2 | 3 | 4 | 5 | 6 | 7 | Does not laugh/smile     |
| Alert                        | 1 | 2 | 3 | 4 | 5 | 6 | 7 | Withdrawn/remote         |
| Responsive                   | 1 | 2 | 3 | 4 | 5 | 6 | 7 | Unresponsive             |
| Easygoing                    | 1 | 2 | 3 | 4 | 5 | 6 | 7 | Aggressive/angry         |
| Interested in others         | 1 | 2 | 3 | 4 | 5 | 6 | 7 | Not interested in others |
| Mobile                       | 1 | 2 | 3 | 4 | 5 | 6 | 7 | Immobile                 |
| Participates in Activities   | 1 | 2 | 3 | 4 | 5 | 6 | 7 | Does not participate     |
| Interested in their appearance | 1 | 2 | 3 | 4 | 5 | 6 | 7 | Not interested         |
| Cares about personal hygiene | 1 | 2 | 3 | 4 | 5 | 6 | 7 | Does not care            |
| Enjoys life                  | 1 | 2 | 3 | 4 | 5 | 6 | 7 | Does not enjoy life      |
| Wants to live                | 1 | 2 | 3 | 4 | 5 | 6 | 7 | Wants to die             |

The following rating scales are concerned with the patient's relationship to the pet. (Circle appropriate number.)

|                        | GREAT DEAL | | AVERAGE | | NOT AT ALL | | |
|------------------------|---|---|---|---|---|---|---|
| Loves pet              | 1 | 2 | 3 | 4 | 5 | 6 | 7 |
| Interested in pet      | 1 | 2 | 3 | 4 | 5 | 6 | 7 |
| Encourages pet         | 1 | 2 | 3 | 4 | 5 | 6 | 7 |
| Talks to pet           | 1 | 2 | 3 | 4 | 5 | 6 | 7 |
| Strokes/plays with pet | 1 | 2 | 3 | 4 | 5 | 6 | 7 |
| Grooms pet             | 1 | 2 | 3 | 4 | 5 | 6 | 7 |
| Feeds pet              | 1 | 2 | 3 | 4 | 5 | 6 | 7 |
| Trains/disciplines pet | 1 | 2 | 3 | 4 | 5 | 6 | 7 |
| Frightened of pet      | 1 | 2 | 3 | 4 | 5 | 6 | 7 |

1. In general, how would you describe the patient's relationship with other patients?

   Very good   1        2        3        4        5        6        7  Poor

2. In general, how would you describe the patient's relationship with the staff?

Very good  1      2      3      4      5      6      7  Poor

3. How many hours per day does the patient sleep?

4. How many hours per day does the patient spend in bed?

5. How many hours per day does the patient spend in the communal day-room?

6. How many hours per day does the patient spend alone?

C: MEDICAL DETAILS
Medical Status:
Medication:
a) Anti-depressants/tranquilizers:      Daily dose:
                                         As per necessary dose
b) Night Sedation:                       Dose
c) Analgesics:                           Daily dose
Physical Condition:

D: OTHER OBSERVATIONS
(Examples: atmosphere of the ward; your own reactions to the pet)

PARAMEDIC OBSERVATIONS:
(Examples: Group discussions, outings, interpersonal relations)

PATIENT-PET INTERACTION PROGRAM
PATIENT QUESTIONNAIRE (POST-TEST)

Patient's Name:
Age:
Sex:
Ward No.:
Staff's Name
Date:

These questions and observations are to be completed for each patient at the end of the assessment period.

Ask the patient the questions in Section A (Interview Schedule) as best you can; if he or she does not reply to a question, write "no answer" beside it. If, however, the patient does not communicate at all, please turn to Section B (Observation Sheet).

This questionnaire is intended as a guide—if certain questions appear inappropriate or irrelevant when talking to the patient—feel free to omit them.

Try to record the patient's answers verbatim whenever possible.

A: INTERVIEW SCHEDULE
1. On a scale of 1 to 10, how much do you like (type of pet)? (Please circle appropriate number.)

Dislike them  1    2    3    4    5    6    7    8    9    10  Like them
Very much                                                       very much

2. On a scale of 1 to 10, how much do you like (name of pet)? (Please circle appropriate number.)

Dislike it   1    2    3    4    5    6    7    8    9    10   Like them
very much                                                          very much

3. What's the main reason you like/dislike having (name of pet)?

4. On a scale of 1 to 10, how would you feel if (name of pet) was taken away? (Please circle appropriate number.)

Very relieved   1    2    3    4    5    6    7    8    9    10   Very Unhappy

5. On a scale of 1 to 10, how much do you think (name of pet) likes you? (Please circle appropriate number.)

Dislikes me   1    2    3    4    5    6    7    8    9    10   Likes me
very much                                                          very much

6. Do you think a pet will be a good thing or a bad thing for other people? Good thing/bad thing

Why do you feel this way?

7. Try to ascertain whether or not the patient thinks each of the following items is a problem to them? (Check appropriate response.)

|  | Problem | No Problem |
|---|---|---|
| Accommodation |  |  |
| Discipline/training |  |  |
| Barking |  |  |
| Smell |  |  |
| Mess (ex. hair, waste) |  |  |
| Frightened him/her |  |  |
| Damage to property |  |  |
| Cruelty to pet |  |  |
| Trips over pet |  |  |
| Pet gets in the way |  |  |
| Any others? |  |  |

8. Try to ascertain whether or not the patient thinks each of the following items is a benefit to them. (Check appropriate response.)

|  | Yes | No |
|---|---|---|
| Company/friendship |  |  |
| Love/affection |  |  |
| Enjoyment/fun |  |  |
| An interest |  |  |

|  | Yes | No |
|---|---|---|
| Something to talk about | | |
| Makes the ward more like home | | |
| Makes the ward a happier place | | |
| Any others? | | |

## B. OBSERVATION SHEET

Please record your impressions of the patient on the following rating scales. Circle the number which you feel best describes him or her.

| | VERY | | AVERAGE | | VERY | | | |
|---|---|---|---|---|---|---|---|---|
| Talkative | 1 | 2 | 3 | 4 | 5 | 6 | 7 | Uncommunicative |
| Confident | 1 | 2 | 3 | 4 | 5 | 6 | 7 | Shy |
| Happy | 1 | 2 | 3 | 4 | 5 | 6 | 7 | Unhappy |
| Self-reliant | 1 | 2 | 3 | 4 | 5 | 6 | 7 | Dependent |
| Sociable | 1 | 2 | 3 | 4 | 5 | 6 | 7 | Unsociable |
| Sense of humor | 1 | 2 | 3 | 4 | 5 | 6 | 7 | No sense of humor |
| Laughs/smiles | 1 | 2 | 3 | 4 | 5 | 6 | 7 | Does not laugh/ smile |
| Alert | 1 | 2 | 3 | 4 | 5 | 6 | 7 | Withdrawn/remote |
| Responsive | 1 | 2 | 3 | 4 | 5 | 6 | 7 | Unresponsive |
| Easygoing | 1 | 2 | 3 | 4 | 5 | 6 | 7 | Aggressive/angry |
| Interested in others | 1 | 2 | 3 | 4 | 5 | 6 | 7 | Not interested in others |
| Mobile | 1 | 2 | 3 | 4 | 5 | 6 | 7 | Immobile |
| Participates in activities | 1 | 2 | 3 | 4 | 5 | 6 | 7 | Does not partici- pate |
| Interested in their appearance | 1 | 2 | 3 | 4 | 5 | 6 | 7 | Not interested |
| Cares about personal hygiene | 1 | 2 | 3 | 4 | 5 | 6 | 7 | Does not care |
| Enjoys life | 1 | 2 | 3 | 4 | 5 | 6 | 7 | Does not enjoy life |
| Wants to live | 1 | 2 | 3 | 4 | 5 | 6 | 7 | Wants to die |

The following rating scales are concerned with the patient's relationship to the pet. (Circle appropriate number.)

| | GREAT DEAL | | | AVERAGE | | NOT AT ALL | |
|---|---|---|---|---|---|---|---|
| Loves pet | 1 | 2 | 3 | 4 | 5 | 6 | 7 |

|  | GREAT DEAL | | | AVERAGE | | NOT AT ALL |
|---|---|---|---|---|---|---|
| Interested in pet | 1 | 2 | 3 | 4 | 5 | 6 | 7 |
| Encourages pet | 1 | 2 | 3 | 4 | 5 | 6 | 7 |
| Talks to pet | 1 | 2 | 3 | 4 | 5 | 6 | 7 |
| Strokes/plays with pet | 1 | 2 | 3 | 4 | 5 | 6 | 7 |
| Grooms pet | 1 | 2 | 3 | 4 | 5 | 6 | 7 |
| Feeds pet | 1 | 2 | 3 | 4 | 5 | 6 | 7 |
| Trains/disciplines pet | 1 | 2 | 3 | 4 | 5 | 6 | 7 |
| Frightened of pet | 1 | 2 | 3 | 4 | 5 | 6 | 7 |

9. In general, how would you describe the patient's relationship with other patients?

   Very good  1　　　2　　　3　　　4　　　5　　　6　　　7  Poor

10. In general, how would you describe the patient's relationship with the staff?

    Very good  1　　　2　　　3　　　4　　　5　　　6　　　7  Poor

11. How many hours per day does the patient sleep?

12. How many hours per day does the patient spend in bed?

13. How many hours per day does the patient spend in the communal day-room?

14. How many hours per day does the patient spend alone?

C: MEDICAL DETAILS
Medical Status:
Medication:
a) Anti-depressants/tranquilizers:　　　Daily dose:
　　　　　　　　　　　　　　　　　　　　As per necessary dose
b) Night Sedation:　　　　　　　　　　Dose
c) Analgesics:　　　　　　　　　　　　Daily dose
Physical Condition:

D: OTHER OBSERVATIONS (e.g., atmosphere of the ward; your own reactions
to the dog)

# Index